# PRAISE FOR *STAFF MATTERS*

"Yes, staff matters. An important must-read that offers an excellent framework for thinking strategically about hiring, managing, and leading staff and creating a respectful culture that ensures their voices are heard."
— Lynn Perry Wooten, President, Simmons University

"At a time when the world of work is recreating itself, there has never been a more important time to reexamine not just what the future of work looks like but what matters most to our most important resource—our employees. *Staff Matters* not only lifts the lid on what leaders need to know; Bonnie Low-Kramen has created a road map of clarity and vision for what the world of work needs to become."
— Lucy Brazier OBE, CEO, *Executive Support Magazine*

"Drawing from her deep well of experience and candor, Bonnie Low-Kramen expertly lays out a comprehensive, research-based guide for making smart and durable workforce decisions to ensure your staff matters—now and in the future workplace."
— Johnny C. Taylor, Jr., President and CEO, Society for Human Resource Management (SHRM)

"This book contains the important back-channel information that every leader needs to know before being given even one direct report. Bonnie takes a fresh and profoundly honest look at what is really going on with the staff and how we can build a better workplace using that information."
— Deanna Mulligan, CEO, Purposeful

"*Staff Matters* is chock-full of practical advice that is normally acquired only via the School of Hard Knocks. This book is a gift for leaders, Executive Assistants, HR, and recruiters. The author goes granular on important issues that are too often ignored."

—Jack Zenger, coauthor of *The New Extraordinary Leader*

"Finally. As a Celebrity Assistant and C-suite Executive Assistant for over twenty-five years, I can confidently share that *Staff Matters* bravely states what employees wish their leaders knew but are too afraid to tell them. Bonnie has walked the talk and has now written the truth about what is really going on in the workplace. Amen."

—Angelica Canales, Executive Assistant to
Deanna Mulligan; President, NYCA

"*Staff Matters* provides examples of courageous leaders putting themselves out there for the world to see and measure, making all of us stronger, together. The book offers a practical yet heartfelt approach to moral courage, with Bonnie's research highlighting a universal and basic leadership truth: your team is the key to every success. As a twenty-six-year member of the Canadian military, I know she is right. The book is a solution-filled guide—for tactical, strategic, and institutional levels of leadership."

—Simon Kardynal, Master Warrant Officer,
CD, MA, Royal Canadian Air Force

"*Staff Matters* addresses the biggest elephant in the biggest room in business today—the fear, frustration, and chaos that reign supreme in far too many companies. Bonnie has produced a work of depth, experience, and wisdom that offers actionable hope to business leaders, HR, recruiters, and the staff. She has thoroughly and carefully broken down the elephant into small, nourishing bites that offer clarity and a road map for positive change in the workplace. I highly recommend this book to all who want to help create a more conscious and productive workplace."

—Leni Miller, President, EASearch

"As a business and communication strategist for over twenty years, I now consider *Staff Matters* the ultimate guide for my clients. The author's extraordinary knowledge and experience provide actionable and crystal-clear methods to leaders struggling to bring order to their chaotic and fragmented workplaces."

—Shelly Berman-Rubera, President and
Founder, Small Business Results

"This book is going to be epic for so many people all over the world, especially young entrepreneurs and business students. It is written as the solution to our global workplaces' biggest problems. Bonnie has done this with heart, rare authenticity, and rock-solid data. I highly recommend it."

—Jeff Hoffman, Chairman of the Board,
Global Entrepreneurship Network

"For seventeen years, I've had a backstage pass to what led Bonnie to write this book. I have witnessed what she cares about most—the people of our workplace. Bonnie loves hearing their stories, every single one. All over the world, I've watched Bonnie change lives before my eyes. This book will seriously matter for every employee and for those who hire, manage, and lead them."

—Vickie Sokol Evans, CEO, RedCape Company

# STAFF
# MATTERS

Unfiltered conversations with staff at every level.
In their words—walking in their shoes.

# STAFF
# MATTERS

## People-Focused Solutions for
## the Ultimate New Workplace

# BONNIE LOW-KRAMEN

ULTIMATE WORKPLACE
PRESS

Published by Ultimate Workplace Press
www.bonnielowkramen.com

Edited and designed by Girl Friday Productions
www.girlfridayproductions.com

Cover design: Emily Weigel
Interior design: Rachel Marek
Project management: Mari Kesselring
Developmental editor: Devon Fredericksen
Cover image credits: KwangChanakarn/Shutterstock, Angelina Bambina/ Shutterstock, anong kaewborisut/Shutterstock, Elena Zlatomrezova/ Shutterstock, Naj Ativk/Shutterstock, topvector/Shutterstock

ISBN (paperback): 978-0-9763268-4-7
ISBN (e-book): 978-0-9763268-5-4
ISBN (audiobook): 978-0-9763268-6-1

Library of Congress Control Number: 2022923004

*For the staffs of the world.*

*For our grandchildren, who will be joining them one day.*

## A Special Message to Business Students and Future Leaders

You will eventually have a staff to manage. When that happens, I want you to be as ready as you can be, equipped with information that will matter on a daily basis.

Know this: your success will depend directly on the success of your staff. No one gets there alone. No one.

Leading others requires moral courage and hard work. The best leaders rely and lean on their staffs. Every page you are about to read will support you to do exactly that. Welcome to *Staff Matters*.

# CONTENTS

*Glossary of Terms, Acronyms, and Abbreviations* . . . . . . . . . . .xv

*Foreword*. . . . . . . . . . . . . . . . . . . . . . . . . . . . . . xvii

*Preface* . . . . . . . . . . . . . . . . . . . . . . . . . . . . . . . xxi

*Introduction* . . . . . . . . . . . . . . . . . . . . . . . . . . . . xxvii

Chapter One: Empathy—In Their Shoes . . . . . . . . . . . . . . . 3

Chapter Two: Successful Succession . . . . . . . . . . . . . . . . .13

Chapter Three: Pandemic Impact . . . . . . . . . . . . . . . . . .19

Chapter Four: Ask First . . . . . . . . . . . . . . . . . . . . . . .31

Chapter Five: Giving Voice—Meet the Staff. . . . . . . . . . . . . .39

    Part 1: Leaders' Voices . . . . . . . . . . . . . . . . . . . . .43

    Part 2: Executive Assistants, Personal Assistants,

        and Administrative Support Staff Voices . . . . . . . . . .65

    Part 3: HR—Human Resource Professionals' Voices . . . . . .89

    Part 4: Recruiters' Voices . . . . . . . . . . . . . . . . . . . 101

Chapter Six: Secrets . . . . . . . . . . . . . . . . . . . . . . . . 107

Chapter Seven: Firsts. . . . . . . . . . . . . . . . . . . . . . . . 115

Chapter Eight: Hiring & Firing . . . . . . . . . . . . . . . . . . 123

Chapter Nine: Culture . . . . . . . . . . . . . . . . . . . . . . . 143

Chapter Ten: Is It Safe? . . . . . . . . . . . . . . . . . . . . . . 159

Chapter Eleven: Expectations. . . . . . . . . . . . . . . . . . . . 171

Chapter Twelve: Mentorship . . . . . . . . . . . . . . . . . . . 185

Chapter Thirteen: Money . . . . . . . . . . . . . . . . . . . . . 193

Chapter Fourteen: Respect . . . . . . . . . . . . . . . . . . . . . 219

Chapter Fifteen: Disrespect . . . . . . . . . . . . . . . . . . . . . . 231
Chapter Sixteen: Sex . . . . . . . . . . . . . . . . . . . . . . . . . . 263
Chapter Seventeen: Confidence . . . . . . . . . . . . . . . . . . . . 293
Chapter Eighteen: Leadership, Power, and Sitting in the Rain . . . 301
Chapter Nineteen: Incentives . . . . . . . . . . . . . . . . . . . . . . 311
Chapter Twenty: Workplace Hacks: Assistants' Tricks of the Trade . . 319
Chapter Twenty-One: Next . . . . . . . . . . . . . . . . . . . . . . . 325

Acknowledgments & Gratitude . . . . . . . . . . . . . . . . . . . . 331
Job Descriptions . . . . . . . . . . . . . . . . . . . . . . . . . . . . . 335
Notes . . . . . . . . . . . . . . . . . . . . . . . . . . . . . . . . . . . 345
Recommended Reading & Resources . . . . . . . . . . . . . . . . . 357
About the Author . . . . . . . . . . . . . . . . . . . . . . . . . . . . 361

# GLOSSARY OF TERMS, ACRONYMS, AND ABBREVIATIONS

AAPI—Asian American and Pacific Islander
AI—Artificial intelligence
ASAP—American Society of Administrative Professionals
BYOD—Bring your own device
CDC—Centers for Disease Control and Prevention
CEO—Chief Executive Officer
CFO—Chief Financial Officer
CHRO—Chief Human Resource Officer
COO—Chief Operating Officer
CV—Curriculum vitae (a.k.a. resume)
DEI—diversity, equity, and inclusion
EA—Executive Assistant
ELT—Executive leadership team
ERG—Employee resource group
FLSA—Fair Labor Standards Act
FIRE—Financial independence, retire early
FOMO—Fear of missing out
HR—Human resources
IAAP—International Association of Administrative Professionals

IRL—In real life
IT—Information technology
NDA—Nondisclosure agreement
NYCA—New York Celebrity Assistants
PTO—Paid time off
ROI—Return on investment
SHRM—Society for Human Resource Management
SME—Subject matter expert
VR—Virtual reality
VUCA—Volatile, uncertain, complicated, ambiguous
WAA—World Administrators Alliance
WFH—Work from home
YOLO—You only live once

# FOREWORD

In her timely and transformative book, *Staff Matters: People-Focused Solutions for the Ultimate New Workplace*, Bonnie Low-Kramen carefully identifies and emphasizes the virtues, qualities, and motivations that exemplify moral courage in the workplace.

For more than twenty years, Bonnie and I have been in conversation about the high-potential talent of those who have chosen the executive assisting profession and how outmoded workplace structures can undermine the worth of these vital individuals. During my career, I supported a world leader for ten years, which led to my role as Founder and CEO of The Duncan Group, Inc., a global recruiting and coaching firm, and the Duncan Leadership Institute, our global training entity, which focuses on the value of solutions. This experience continues to give me a rich perspective and allows me to applaud Bonnie's visionary leadership.

The core of *Staff Matters* is Bonnie's compelling research, which answers the hard questions that others tend to avoid asking. Her vigilance in uncovering complex truths helps her construct a persuasive message: be prepared to engage in courageous and important conversations!

Bonnie invites us to consider all possible solutions for professional staff challenges, and to appreciate the workplace as the perfect setting to build a culture of shared responsibility, practicing the principle of inclusion, which allows us to remove the limiting lenses through which we see the world: lenses of race, gender, wealth, poverty, and religion. The development of such a hiring strategy represents an opportunity to offer equity and social advantage to those who contribute to our economic prosperity.

Bonnie addresses human resources practices that prove precarious when challenged with unpredictable forces and how unconscious bias in hiring has massive influence on workplace culture and talent retention. *Staff Matters* confirms the need to bring leaders, business practices, and the workplace population together to address systemic societal issues at the core of "business as usual." This book moves us from the abstract to the concrete, questions the status quo, and encourages us to respect the dignity of others.

Bonnie intends to inspire the application of better judgment by all staff, and in so doing, to positively impact the outcomes of our ethical standards going forward. Her messaging is based on an astute understanding that existing motivations shift our fundamental perceptions of widely held assumptions, resulting in companies that remain trapped in marginalized, outdated beliefs and, therefore, approaches.

*Staff Matters'* data on pervasive stereotypes challenges a relentless and unrealistic disconnect between the perception and the reality: Bonnie champions equal opportunities and pay, demonstrating how the positive effects of fair treatment and compensation create pathways for advancement and increased productivity.

Bonnie wisely identifies empathy as the primary driver for essential workplace evolution. She observes how hard it is to manage effectively without demonstrating the ability to understand and support others with compassion or sensitivity.

Occupying a singular place in the world of professional support, Bonnie's perspective is reinforced by years of research and on-the-ground experience as a professional assistant. This uniquely positions her to advocate for a greater level of social and cultural harmony in the workplace. She reminds us of the profound impact that staying strongly connected to our colleagues all over the world offers to our work environment, which can unite us in a common vision.

*Staff Matters* is a book that exposes the "elephants in the room" in management breakdowns and inspires us not only to examine but to change the thinking, language, and social structure rooted in the deeply embedded inequities that characterize today's workplace. Bonnie offers a clear prescription for addressing these inequities, reminding us along the way not to let a temporary solution become a permanent mistake, and that inaction is complicity.

This book is an engaging, living monument to the diverse workplace population and a tribute to all staff. Among its core messages are that the best legacy you can leave behind are the people whose lives you have changed, that speaking the inconvenient truth is imperative for effective leadership, and that knowledge will forever overpower ignorance.

Melba J. Duncan, CEO, The Duncan
Group, New York City

# PREFACE

For twenty-five years, I worked with Oscar-winning actress Olympia Dukakis as her Personal and Executive Assistant. Olympia led the Whole Theatre in Montclair, New Jersey, and I had a front-row seat while she managed a team of more than thirty people. I worked at the theater from 1986 to 1990 and then continued my work as her assistant and publicist until 2011. Our longevity was due, in large part, to our respect and appreciation for each other and the job we each performed. My goal was to be as skilled an assistant as she was an actress. Most of what I know about managing people comes straight from this experience.

Olympia instinctively knew how to manage people and inspire excellence and loyalty. When she passed away in 2021 at age eighty-nine, her memorial service took place at the Delacorte Theater in New York City, an outdoor venue. It poured rain for the entire two-hour event, and 250 people, many of whom had traveled from far away during a pandemic, sat huddled under umbrellas. None of us could have imagined being anywhere else, and we would do it again in a heartbeat.

I am not only a former assistant myself, but I have employed an assistant since 2012. Managing people is not just a theoretical concept to me; I live it. Jennifer Wilner works with me as my virtual assistant ten hours each week. I also employ others in the areas of publicity, technology, finance, legal advice, and marketing. When I was fresh out of Rutgers University, I worked at the Pheasant Run Theatre box office in St. Charles, Illinois, and managed a staff of six.

Titles matter. You will notice throughout the book that the titles for job roles are capitalized. This is intended not only to draw the distinction among them, but to create an equalizing effect, out of respect for each role. Example: Executive Assistant.

I want to express gratitude to my father, Sol Low, who worked as the Chief Accountant at the main post office in Jersey City, New Jersey. He died in 1973, and at his funeral on a freezing January day, his assistant, Delores, was inconsolable by his grave. She told me that my father was the best manager she had ever known. She said he had treated her with respect and compassion, and she would miss him and never forget him. I will never forget her.

I have spoken in many countries, including Australia, Austria, Belgium, Canada, France, Germany, Mexico, the Netherlands, New Zealand, South Africa, United Arab Emirates, the United Kingdom, and the United States. In all of these places, I have seen that the global workplace is a fascinating buzzing beehive of fragmented activity generally suffering from a lack of effective cross-department communication. The pandemic that began in 2020 has only worsened the breakdowns in communication. However, the truth is there were plenty of serious communication issues prepandemic that were made even more glaringly apparent when staff had to work from home. The distance became far more than geographic.

Long before the pandemic, another event caused massive upheaval in the workplace: the financial meltdown on Wall Street in 2008. In a storm of layoffs, downsizing, and reorganization, workplace structures were thrown into the air like a deck of cards, and the cards have been slow to settle for the staff. Seven years earlier, in 2001, 9/11 happened. The upheaval in the way companies managed staff caused disruption of the highest order. Disaster preparedness took on new meaning, as did cybersecurity. Leaders were forced to invest millions of dollars to design new and better ways to protect their staff and data. Since then, we have seen capable former support staffers promoted to middle management. Job descriptions, titles, and compensation have been slow to change, causing significant long-term angst among staff who are fighting hard to be resilient.

On top of all this, in 2017 we saw the beginning of the #MeToo and #TimesUp movements, which took sexual harassment out of the shadows and splashed it onto the front-page news. As a result, the harassers are being held accountable with more frequency. There have been major shake-ups in government leadership and at some of the world's largest, most powerful companies.

In a world wrestling with how to recalibrate in a postpandemic environment, there has never been a more complicated time for the workplace. For everyone from leaders to staff to HR to recruiters, these complications are slowing us down, and sometimes stopping us dead in our tracks, as we figure out how to navigate them. Mental and physical health are now higher priorities at many companies.

My goal is to make sense of these complications and put the missing pieces together to find a better way to work. I envision a better workplace and a better world not only for ourselves, but also for our children, grandchildren, and those who will come after. I am optimistic about what I see, but we have lots of room for improvement, and much that is within our power to fix. I hope you share this optimism.

If so, you have come to the right book.

Right now, millions of human beings are trying to make sense of the "new normal." It is filled with high technology and legitimate concerns about hybrid work-from-home situations, the safety of staff who are coming into the office, cybersecurity, hacking, and the mainstream infiltration of robots and artificial intelligence. Many of us are working virtually and remotely, and our connections with one another are happening through webcams and videoconferencing software. Robots are taking on tasks like scheduling, and sometimes it is hard to tell whether you are communicating with a human or a bot, which can be disconcerting, no matter how old you are.

The fact that many people possess two and sometimes three mobile phones and multiple email addresses makes communication even more fragmented and challenging. Our mental attention is divided. Just take a look at people in a restaurant and notice how many are on their devices rather than speaking to their tablemates. Disrespectful? Yes, to some—but not to all. The capacity of the human brain is being tested every day.

Speaking of disrespect, chapter 15 exposes the darkest sides of our workplace, which include bullying, sexual harassment, discrimination, and racism. An ultimate workplace is not possible until we build strong bridges of understanding among our diverse staff. Support systems like diversity, equity, and inclusion (DEI) programs and employee resource groups (ERGs) are some of the ways to accomplish this.

The age range in our workplace has never been as broad as it is right now. This has resulted in a collision of the generations with some interesting results, both positive and negative. As baby boomers retire and others leave in the Great Resignation, the workplace must accommodate this mass exodus. What do we do in this unstable and dangerous situation? At best, it is another messy complication and a serious challenge to business continuity.

And we have the issue of sex, in all the meanings of that word. According to the U.S. Department of Labor, our workplace is 47 percent female. My work is training Executive and Personal Assistants, who are 93–97 percent female and as diverse ethnically as the world itself. These demographics are impacting how the humans in our workplace are interacting and working together—or not working together. This subject is a particular obsession with me, which you will read about in chapter 16.

Spoiler alert: Gender differences and gender identities matter a great deal in the workplace, and the differences need to be acknowledged and respected. The genders experience the workplace very differently, which means executives cannot successfully manage them in the same way. These issues are explored in chapter 16.

We have the wage gap (which is bad enough for White women but even more problematic for women of color), workplace bullying, sexual harassment, and the mommy penalty. Workplace discussions about gender include issues regarding LGBTQIA+ staff and the proper use of pronouns. Transgender staff also face discrimination, microaggressions, and overt hostility. Clearly, these behaviors do not promote a healthy or productive work environment for anyone, regardless of gender.

The bottom line is that clarifying issues about gender and sex will benefit not only women but humans of all genders. Addressing these challenges will help everyone and improve our world. We can do better.

The complex issues affecting the people of our workplace are at the heart of the matter. Literally the heart. As in the human beings with beating hearts populating our companies. My quest is to pull the curtain back on what is really going on in this complicated and highly demanding new environment. I could not have written this book without the support of the hundreds of colleagues and friends who gave me their honest takes on their experiences. I thank them all from the bottom of my heart. Much of it is not pretty, but the truth is better than silence and ignorance. That's why you're here.

I intend to shine a bright light into previously dark corners in order to gain deeper understanding, and this understanding will help us fix what is broken and create an ultimate new workplace. Some of the places I will take you have not seen the light in a very long time.

That is all the more reason to go there. Ready?

# INTRODUCTION

This book is based on over 1,500 one-on-one conversations I have had with Executive Assistants, Celebrity Assistants, Personal Assistants, Private Service Professionals, CEOs and leaders at all levels, HR professionals, recruiters, trainers, authors, leadership experts, business school professors, journalists, and psychologists from all over the world. They spoke to me and I listened. I asked questions, listened some more, and took notes. These conversations were not superficial small talk. Quite the contrary.

The conversations about what is really happening in the global workplace were often raw, honest, messy, and revelatory. What I have heard reveals universal truths and global trends. I have moved from confusion to clarity. What I've learned is that humans in our workplaces all yearn for the exact same things—no matter where they are or the size of their organization or their level within it.

Much of my research was done with assistants who attended my Be the Ultimate Assistant workshop. I designed this two-day workshop to address the professional development training needs of assistants who were supporting leaders at the highest levels. Each workshop is limited to a maximum of thirty students, and, since 2011, I have spoken by phone or videoconference with every student several weeks in advance of the workshop. During those confidential conversations, I asked nuts-and-bolts questions such as:

- What challenges are you bumping into with your executives, peers, and the company?
- Is the job you were hired to do the job you are actually doing?
- How many hours each week are you working?
- Are you being compensated fairly for the work you are doing?

I will tell you what I learned from these conversations.

This book is about the humans who populate our global workplace, the "architects" who are the company CEOs, executives, managers, and supervisors at all levels and the "builders" who are the staff, the implementers, the executors, the employees, the team. The human resources professionals and recruiters are builders, too.

This book is intended to build strong bridges between these groups.

Every one of these constituents is a stakeholder in today's workplace. Each serves a unique need and a specific purpose in their organization. Each one is a SME, a subject matter expert. Each person was chosen—hired for clear and considered reasons—and every one of them deserves to be respected, acknowledged, and rewarded for their individual contributions.

The bottom line is that there is no one you can name, from the richest person on Earth to the poorest, who got to where they are alone. It takes architects and it takes builders, in partnership and collaboration with one another, to build bridges.

Imagine if these architects and builders designed the bridges that led to an ultimate workplace. A workplace that addressed the many issues we face, such as workplace bullying, compensation confusion, hiring practices, and racial and gender discrimination. There is no denying that the current landscape is messy. What if a workplace encouraged staff to overcome the fear of being the messenger, and to talk with leaders and one another about solutions and ways to make things better?

If you find this notion interesting, you will find many paths leading to an ultimate workplace in these pages. Like me, you have probably read many books about leadership and the workplace. My office is filled with them.

What makes my book different? Perspective.

## Two "aha" moments that changed everything

Imagine a fuzzy picture that suddenly comes into sharp focus and takes your breath away. Two "aha" moments in 2012 gave me surprising insights into workplace relationships and changed the direction of my work. Those moments have everything to do with my understanding of the workplace.

In October 2012, I was invited to speak at the Hays Conference for Executive and Personal Assistants in London. This was my first international speaking engagement. I was told that I was the first American to speak at a conference for professional assistants in the United Kingdom, and I would be speaking to about 250 of them. It was a big deal for me.

"How many of you feel well managed?" asked the larger-than-life Susie Barron-Stubley, a renowned pioneer in the professional assistant field. As I stood at the back of the ballroom taking it all in, I watched only about twenty-five hands raise and only a few with any real power or enthusiasm. "Aha" moment number one: an alarmingly low number of assistants felt well managed by their executives.

Wait, what was going on here? How big a problem was this? Was it global? Over the next months, as I struggled to understand this state of affairs, I began asking Susie's question at my own workshops and conferences. The response was the same.

When I returned to the United States, I began researching why so few staff feel well managed. I asked very experienced assistants about this, and wow, did I get an earful. I heard about executives who had no idea what to do with assistants or how to leverage them and their skills. I heard traumatic stories about bullying and abusive behaviors, micromanaging, and passive-aggressive actions. I heard about job descriptions that were woefully generic and bore no resemblance to the role the assistants were hired to perform. I heard about low salaries and static salary bands/levels that had not been adjusted in years. I heard about unethical behaviors and rules that were unfairly applied.

Why aren't managers taking better care of their staff? Why is it not happening? How do leaders not know how important it is? Or could it be that they know but do not care?

One business school professor explained to me that shareholder and stakeholder capitalism have competing and conflicting interests. To "take care of your people" can be expensive in the short term, even though it is a profitable and winning strategy in the long term.

I started thinking about how, where, and when managers learn how to manage people. The obvious places were MBA programs, business schools, and the military. To my surprise, business school curriculums have very few classes with titles such as "How to Manage Your Staff."

As I traveled, I made it a point to ask executives if they had ever taken a class or had any training in managing people. The majority said no, and that they had learned on the job.

My research led directly to "aha" moment number two. I read leadership expert and author Jack Zenger's December 2012 article in *Harvard Business Review* titled "We Wait Too Long to Train Our Leaders."[1]

Mr. Zenger and his team had polled 17,000 leaders around the world and calculated the average age when those leaders had received their very first people management training.

That age was forty-two.

Gasp. My heart was pounding. This was it. This explained so much about why assistants feel poorly managed: their managers have simply not learned those skills. Most managers have been out of college more than twenty years before they get trained to manage people. No wonder there are problems! Jack Zenger and his team repeated the same poll in 2021. The new average age increased to forty-six. The problem has only gotten worse.

Managing others is a learned skill, like becoming an expert financial planner, doctor, or lawyer. It is not logical that just because someone is a skilled financial planner, they are an equally skilled manager of humans. The following saying is absolutely true: You don't know what you don't know.

My "aha" moments led me to realize that we can do better. Much better. By failing to train our leaders to be good managers from the start—or at least much sooner than what is currently the norm—we have left the fate of the men and women in the workforce to chance. We are hoping that our managers have had good role models in their families or at their companies to emulate. We hope that they were raised by people who taught them respect and empathy.

But what if they were not? In the United States, we should be doing this so much better. We should be leading the way, demonstrating the best systems for managing people. Leaving it to luck is not good enough, is it? After all, hope is not a strategy. My research continued.

In 2013, I went to hear Jack Zenger speak in New York City. I asked him why the subject of managing people was not in the curriculum of most business schools. He said that the wheels of change in academia move slowly and that he did not see curriculum changing any time soon.

"Bonnie, I agree with you that it should change," he said.

"So why isn't it changing?" I asked.

"Because it is hard to teach. What you are talking about are emotional intelligence and soft skills. Professors at business schools are not hired to teach that material."

"What is the immediate solution?"

Jack replied without hesitation. "Tell the assistants of the world that they need to manage their managers."

I took Jack's advice seriously, and since 2013, I have trained my students and audiences to "manage up." It is easier said than done, but managing up means being a leader (regardless of your position) who speaks up about what you see and hear and takes proactive steps to solve problems. When students and audiences hear my stories and see the data, my assistants have "aha" moments of their own. Assistants are doing their best to manage up to leaders who have not been taught what assistants are supposed to do. This is not a small challenge; and in a rapidly changing world, it matters more than ever that leaders understand what makes their people tick.

I decided to write a book that I hope will be required reading at business schools. It will give students a detailed preview of what is really happening with the people of our modern workplace and how to handle it. A new approach is needed in the new workplace. Being a leader right now, in a postpandemic world, is harder than ever.

As this book began coming into focus in 2012, one of the colleagues who served as my truthteller and bellwether for up-to-the-minute information was New York City CEO and prominent recruiter Melba J. Duncan. I am honored and deeply grateful that Melba wrote the foreword.

Several years and thirteen countries later, the answers are essentially the same. Whether they work from home, go to the office, or work in a hybrid way, the majority of staff still do not feel well managed. That is what I want to change. I hope you do, too.

I am fascinated with the workplace that is still dealing with prepandemic fallout of the status quo. Despite living in an uber-advanced time with a plethora of ways to connect, there is still a shocking lack of communication, education, and training as it relates to the business partnerships between managers and staff.

It is clear that many workplace problems are due to a lack of education and professional development training, as well as breakdowns in communication between the key constituencies: the leaders, the staff, and the HR team. There are too many silos and not enough systems in place to break them down. The silos are only made more apparent with staff working from home isolated from the rest of the team. Staff members often suffer in silence out of fear of losing their jobs and fear of difficult confrontations. Without skilled intervention, these relationships can become abusive, deteriorating, and destructive to people and organizations. Most often, staffers quit their jobs because it is easier than confronting the offending party.

In general, the vast majority of workers (managers included) in our workplace have never been taught how to effectively address challenging issues with others. Without effective training, confrontation is a stress-provoking and impossible task. It is easier to quit.

The costly revolving door of staff turnover will keep spinning unless we break the cycle.

## Full disclosure to my readers

- There may be material in this book that you view as "obvious." I err on the side of including such material because I am struck by how much of it is viewed as "new news" to Leaders, Assistants, HR professionals, and Recruiters. In a presentation we gave to thirty executives and their assistants, Monique Helstrom, former Chief of Simon Sinek, shared that one of the best ways she and Simon enhanced their communication was to commit to a ten-minute, one-to-one meeting each morning to check in. Simple, right?

This was a light-bulb revelation to many executives and assistants in the room. Obvious to some and a completely new idea to others.

- The structure of this book is designed to pull the curtain back on the burning issues in our workplace, told from the staff's point of view. Each of the twenty-one chapters shares information meant to illuminate subject matter and topics that are not easily discussed and yet can make all the difference if addressed. My goal is to pave that road to make these conversations easier.

- I will sometimes generalize. When I do, I am well aware that some of what I am writing may not apply to you or your company. I am writing what I see to be true. For example, I write that the onboarding and offboarding systems at most companies are seriously flawed and need an overhaul. I am delighted if that does not apply to your company and hope you will benefit from knowing what is happening elsewhere.

- Writing about gender can be tricky, messy, and complex, but I am doing it anyway because it is important. For example, I know there are people who believe there is no wage gap between men and women. There is. I also see a serious double standard between some of the norms for women and men. I know we have LGBTQIA+ staff in our workplace who deserve to be acknowledged and respected for who they are and what they bring to the workplace. Will there be exceptions to what I write on these subjects? Of course, but I can tolerate the complexity if you can.

- Pronouns—I want to acknowledge, respect, and honor the people of our workplace who identify as LGBTQIA+. However, for the purposes of clarity, I will be using "she/her" and "he/him" to refer to women and men. I am a cisgender female and my pronouns are she and her. Chapter 16 on sex will include more information about the use of pronouns in the workplace.

- Vocabulary choices: I intentionally do not use the word "boss." The word comes from the Dutch word "baas," which means "master," as in master and slave. I hope you will consider not using "boss," too, and find other words to use instead, such as "leader," "executive," "manager," "business partner," or "supervisor," to name a few.

- No one has paid me to mention their name, their company, or their resources. I am writing about them so my readers will learn and benefit.

Thank you for joining me on this journey. Let us begin.

Bonnie Low-Kramen

# STAFF
## MATTERS

"You never really understand a person until you consider things from his point of view ... until you climb into his skin and walk around in it." —Atticus Finch

**Harper Lee, *To Kill a Mockingbird***

# CHAPTER ONE

# Empathy—In Their Shoes

## What is empathy?

Empathy is the ability to understand what other people feel, see things from their point of view, and imagine yourself in their place. That understanding helps us to better decide how to respond to a situation.

At its core, this book is about empathy for all the humans in our workplace. My hope is that by the end of the book, all the stakeholders of our workplace will have a better appreciation for the worries, fears, goals, and dreams of the people around them. In the end, the shareholders will benefit, too.

Let's take a walk in the shoes of others and, in so doing, gain a relatable understanding about what life is like for them every single day.

One truth I know from over forty years in the workplace and talking with hundreds of people is that a real getting-to-know-you conversation that finds a simple area of commonality can be one of the fastest ways to break down walls between two very different people. (Hint: It might be your shared passion for pizza or coffee or country music.)

Seek to understand rather than to be understood. That is empathy.

## The givens: Respect and professionalism

I typically have tremendous diversity in my workshops. Diversity of age, gender, ethnicity, industry, education, economic status, and country of origin. The common denominator is that my students are all driven to be the best and want to learn how to work at the top of their game. Our workshop room becomes a microcosm of the broader workplace.

What I set up as a given is that everyone belongs there and that our diversity is to be embraced and celebrated. Every person in the workshop room and in our workplaces is there for a reason. The expectation is that every person is to be treated with respect and professionalism and that integrity to this principle should be a common denominator in every workplace.

## Starting at the top: Company owners, CEOs and all executives, supervisors, and managers

Leaders of a company, and of people, bear tremendous responsibility. This responsibility causes stress and sleepless nights. Leaders have deep and profound concerns about accountability to board members, customers, shareholders, and employees, not to mention the pressures of trying to have a personal life with family and friends. The pressures increase as they work to be profitable and yet must spend money to be innovative and stay ahead of the competition. They have the ever-present given that the buck stops with them. If something goes wrong, it's ultimately their fault.

Being the person at the top is both exhilarating and exhausting, which explains why so many people do not want to be the person "in charge." It is hard. Really, really hard.

Every person on a leader's team needs to understand the stresses the leader is under and the very real ways that staff supports the vision and mission. The most successful leaders use their voice and their platform to share transparently about what keeps them up at night and how the team can help make the ship sail more smoothly. Vulnerability and the truth work.

Empathy is the key to the hit TV show *Undercover Boss*, in which CEOs go undercover in their own companies to discover what it is really like working there. The show confirms what I have learned from my own work around the world—staffers truly want their leaders to see the work they do.

In August 2019, an important meeting of the Business Roundtable convened in Washington, D.C. The members of the group are the CEOs of America's leading companies. At that meeting, 181 American CEOs signed their names to a "Statement on the Purpose of a Corporation."[2] It said:

> We commit to:
>
> - Delivering value to our customers. We will further the tradition of American companies leading the way in meeting or exceeding customer expectations.
> - Investing in our employees. This starts with compensating them fairly and providing important benefits. It also includes supporting them through training and education that help develop new skills for a rapidly changing world. We foster diversity and inclusion, dignity and respect.
> - Dealing fairly and ethically with our suppliers. We are dedicated to serving as good partners to the other companies, large and small, that help us meet our missions.
> - Supporting the communities in which we work. We respect the people in our communities and protect the environment by embracing sustainable practices across our businesses.
> - Generating long-term value for shareholders, who provide the capital that allows companies to invest, grow, and innovate. We are committed to transparency and effective engagement with shareholders.
>
> Each of our stakeholders is essential. We commit to deliver value to all of them, for the future success of our companies, our communities, and our country.

This is a statement of empathy and commitment to the human stakeholders of our workplace. If CEOs are determined to sign their names to this stated purpose, we also need to give voice to the employees whose jobs are to manifest it in order to understand how the commitment to the staff is not happening.

## In their shoes: Diversity, equity, belonging, and inclusion

One of my favorite leadership books is *Lean In* by Sheryl Sandberg, which is about what it really means to be a woman in the workplace. Sandberg tells the story of when she began at Facebook and realized there were no parking spaces designated for pregnant women. She noted it was probably because the leadership team was exclusively composed of men. This story is as good a case as any I've heard about the value of having diverse teams. It gives us a much better chance to have empathy for others.

As a writer and a speaker, I seek opportunities to expose the "elephants in the room," the hard truths about our workplace that may be uncomfortable to discuss. For example, in February 2021, I cowrote an article with Aaisha Joseph titled "Shining a Light on Black Assistants: It's Not Black & White" to kick off Black History Month. I interviewed several Black assistants who shared honestly about their day-to-day experiences. I was surprised to learn how many professional assistants—both men and women—are concerned for their physical safety on a daily basis, no matter where they live.[3]

On my weekly livestreamed show called *Heads Together*, I interviewed Black assistants to discuss their workplace realities. Spencer Casseus of New York City told our audience that when he was considering whether to apply for a job at a particular company, he visited the website to look at the photos. If he did not see any people of color, he decided he would not be welcome there and would not apply.

Some members of our audience said they had never heard stories of daily life directly from a Black person. One of the most surprising things that Spencer said was that his interview with me represented the first time he had ever discussed discrimination with a White person. In 2021, Spencer was forty-five years old.

Other non-White colleagues shared how they frequently get mistaken for cleaners or waitstaff because of the color of their skin.

Clearly, more empathy was needed to bridge gaps of understanding. Ike Saunders of Chicago came onto the show to discuss what it is like to be an openly gay man in the workplace. As an activist in the gay community, he also explained why we all need to be informed about preferred pronouns when interacting with colleagues, friends, and family alike, rather than make incorrect assumptions. He discussed the role pronouns play in honoring and respecting others' identities, as well as ways to communicate and correct pronoun use for those who don't yet understand why and when to use "they/them" rather than "he/him" or "she/her." Our audience valued hearing this information directly from someone who walks in these shoes.

Given the increased attention to the Asian American and Pacific Islander communities (AAPI), I invited Tiffany Nguyen onto the show to discuss her own experience breaking stereotypes in the Houston workplace. Tiffany's family is from Vietnam, and she talked about the assumptions others have made about her, such as that she "must be great at math."

At a conference, I participated in a roundtable conversation about racial bias and discrimination. I asked my ethnically diverse tablemates how stressful the issue of racism was for them on a daily basis. A fiftyish Black woman said, "Very stressful. But you will never know it because otherwise I become known as the angry Black woman." A Japanese woman looked at me and said, "Not at all. I don't think about it," as her eyes filled up and a single tear rolled down her cheek.

In the Be the Ultimate Assistant workshop, we have an exercise called "The Two-Minute Lesson," in which each student teaches something to the rest of the class. In London, one of the most unforgettable lessons was from Joy Hannon. Joy told us she wears hearing aids in both ears, which dictates where she sits and how she moves in the world. She taught the rest of us how to best support our colleagues who have physical limitations. Joy explained that even when we can't see a person's physical challenge, we should not assume they don't have one. Joy taught us empathy.

Another student is neurodivergent and on the autism spectrum. She shared that she processes sensory information differently and is hypersensitive to bright lights, loud noises, and strong scents. Her coworkers understand that to perform her job, she sometimes needs to wear sunglasses and headphones indoors or move around to offset the added stimulation within the environment. Further, eye contact can be uncomfortable (sometimes even physically painful) for her due to the quick, subtle movements of natural facial expressions. To compensate for this, she looks at a person's ears or mouth, or she focuses on a place over a person's shoulder. Although she may find it difficult to recognize others' feelings and body language accurately, she makes up for it with a wealth of compassion and an impeccable memory. Since disclosing her diagnosis with her executive, their work together has completely transformed business operations within their division to be more efficient and inclusive. She serves as cochair to her company's disability employee resource group (ERG). Their mission is to celebrate the spectrum of ways they work, learn, and express themselves by providing a safe space for employees with disabilities, as well as their allies.

Being in a wheelchair for five weeks taught me a lot of empathy for those with mobility challenges as part of their everyday life. I got to experience ableism up close and personal and, frankly, it felt terrible. I broke my leg in 2014, and my recovery coincided with a trip from New Jersey to Los Angeles to teach Be the Ultimate Assistant. Navigating airports, cars, hilly streets, hotel showers, and restaurants taught me unforgettable lessons about how the world views people in wheelchairs. I was invisible to most and a bother to others. Plus, it was exhausting to always be thinking ahead, anticipating every move to make sure my wheelchair could be accommodated. While this experience was temporary, the impact has been long-term. I have deep empathy for anyone in a wheelchair for any length of time.

Another memorable two-minute lesson came from Roger Cushwa, an estate manager and former Marine. He taught us the strategy of sitting with your back against a wall in a restaurant or public place to have the best vantage to see possible trouble. He taught us a few things he learned in the military about situational awareness.

There is so much empathy to be had and so much to learn as a result. We need to intentionally create opportunities to have these conversations.

## Stanford Graduate School of Business—"touchy-feely" course

It did not surprise me when I read about the tremendously popular elective class taught at Stanford officially called "Interpersonal Dynamics." A team of professors has been teaching this class to MBA students since 1974. The goal of the class is to give students a way to understand the "core motivations and feelings of others whenever there is conflict or tension."[4] The class promotes the benefits of being in touch with your own feelings and having a heightened awareness about the feelings of others. Former students report that the emotional intelligence strategies they learned in this class give them "a competitive edge in business." The course promotes self-awareness and explores what it means to take on emotional discomfort with curiosity and vulnerability.

This kind of content is important for business students at every level—undergraduate and graduate students—to learn and practice. As long as our workplace is populated by human beings, leaders must make it their business to know what makes people tick and how to handle difficult conversations. After all, humans have emotions and feelings that, when pushed under the rug rather than embraced, can manifest in dangerous and counterproductive behaviors. Stanford sees the value in exploring these emotions using the students themselves as living, breathing examples. Brilliant.

## Have empathy for what you cannot see.
## Why? Because you just never know . . .

Our workplace is filled with complicated, talented humans who are handling all kinds of health and personal issues that may be invisible to the rest of us but impact their work lives in a variety of ways. These people are managing the best they can. Please consider the following real-life examples and then think about people you know:

1. The colleague who is prone to sudden and unpredictable migraine headaches. When she gets one, she needs to go into a dark room and close her eyes.

2. The colleague who lost a lot of weight recently. When asked about it, he said he is seeing a doctor because he cannot swallow. When he goes out for a business lunch, he pretends to eat and takes the entrée home with him. It takes him hours to eat anything.

3. The colleague who gained a lot of weight recently. When the group conversation turned to what everyone is doing to get exercise, she shared matter-of-factly that she is on steroids as part of her breast cancer treatment and she is looking forward to working out again when the treatments are over.

4. The colleague who seems to be the picture of health, yet shared that she has developed a Baker's cyst behind her knee that is painful and prevents movement. It may take many months to go away.

5. The colleague who is usually extroverted and is now sad, depressed, and short-tempered. They are handling a drug-addicted child who attempted suicide.

It's time for fewer quick judgments and more empathy.

Questions to ask to build bridges of empathy:

- Where did you grow up?
- What do you do in your spare time?
- How did you get into your career?
- What do you love about your work?

# STAFF MATTERS QUESTIONS

1. Whose shoes have you walked in recently?
2. How can it be valuable to have a conversation with someone who, on the surface, seems very different from you?
3. Who do you know who is handling a health issue that is not visible to others? Are you?

Succession planning is a process for identifying and developing a deep and invested bench. These are the future leaders and staff who can replace current leaders and staff when they resign, retire, or die. It is also a process that supports emergency leaves of absence and vacation coverage.

Succession planning is about stable business continuity. It increases the availability of experienced and capable employees who are prepared to step into these roles, sometimes with very little notice.

# CHAPTER TWO

# Successful Succession

There is a "youthquake" happening in the workplace. Millennials, born between 1981 and 1996, are the largest group in the United States workforce. In 2021, they numbered 72 million. Gen Xers are the next most populous, at 65.8 million.[5]

## Generations

Greatest Generation: Born 1901–1927
Traditionalists/Silent Generation: Born 1928–1945
Baby Boomers: Born 1946–1964
Generation X: Born 1965–1980
Millennials: Born 1981–1996
Generation Z: Born 1997–2010
Generation Alpha: Born 2011–2025

By the end of the 2020s, baby boomers will be retiring in great numbers. The time is now to prepare for the mass exodus that will inevitably happen. Preparation means being strategic about capturing the valuable institutional knowledge that these staffers hold before they leave. Paying close attention to and preparing for this potential brain drain can serve an organization well. This means succession planning for all staff, not only the leaders. It is important to make succession planning a high priority in a volatile workplace so the pipeline of talent is always ready to take over when necessary. Given the uncertain world we live in, starting succession planning years ahead of departure is a smart idea.

In most companies, there are a few staffers known as the company "Google." These are the people who function as "communications central," who remember the history of the organization, and who seem to know everything. What will happen when those people retire or leave? How do we download their institutional knowledge and skills before they go?

An ultimate workplace is one that is prepared for turnover, from the CEO on down. An employee's most important legacy can be the materials they leave behind in an orderly and clear fashion. This prevents the knowledge they hold from walking out the door when the staffer does.

These materials can include:

- A procedures manual in electronic form and hard copy
- An organized and easily understood filing and labeling system
- Video files explaining where things are and how things work
- Photos and folders clearly labeled, filed, and easily searchable
- Passwords that are shared with at least one other person. No person should be the only one with the passwords. That is true in business and in one's personal life. If one person possesses all the passwords, that single point of failure could have dire and expensive consequences.

## A word about the office of the CEO

I meet many Executive Assistants (EAs) who support the CEOs of their companies. Sometimes they are the only assistant in the CEO's office. Too often, that assistant is so indispensable that they do not take vacation and work while sick or burned-out. When the EA is unavoidably taken away by illness or accident or a death in the family, it can throw the system into chaos because there is no backup plan.

When smooth operations hinge so completely on one person, the CEO's office is too vulnerable. In this situation, burnout is a real risk factor. This is a very common issue for assistants globally. It is simply not sustainable or smart to function in this way.

A CEO and the company would be better served with at least two assistants in the office. They can back each other up during emergencies and vacations, and the CEO is never without coverage. This system helps with succession planning as well.

## I ran a one-person office for my principal and got double pneumonia

I know the dangers of being a one-person support system to the CEO all too well because I lived it for twenty-five years as the Personal Assistant to Olympia Dukakis and Louis Zorich. I did not have anyone backing me up. Their lives were so busy that there were whole years when I did not take a vacation. Looking back, I wish I had handled this differently. Working these long hours took a real toll on my health and my relationships with family and friends.

When you run a one-person office, you pay a high price physically and mentally for taking a vacation. You pay a high price before you leave and after you get back. The truth is that most assistants do some work while they are on vacation, and their leaders count on them to do so.

One year, I planned my family vacation by car to Williamsburg, Virginia. In the weeks before leaving, I worked extralong hours in order to fully prepare the office for my absence. This meant I completed all scheduling and finalized all materials for Olympia and Louis for the time I would be gone and in the days immediately after my return. I was exhausted.

It was a physical struggle to pack for myself, and I felt feverish. I thought it was fatigue and that I would feel better once I slept. I did not dare take my temperature. I still did not feel well when we loaded up the car, but I did not say anything. A short time after checking into the hotel, I couldn't deny it anymore. I was hot and sick. I said to my husband and son, "Can you take me to the hospital?"

They looked at me and did not question it. I had a 103-degree fever, and the X-ray showed double pneumonia. I missed several days of vacation while I rested inside our hotel room.

When I returned to work, I found a mountain of unopened mail and dozens of papers on my desk that told the story of what had occurred during my one-week absence. It was difficult to unbury myself; overall, I paid a heavy price for not figuring out a backup system.

When I resigned from my work as a Personal Assistant in 2011, I recruited and interviewed my potential successors. I gave four months' notice and trained my replacement for one month.

If I could turn back time, I would insist on collaborating with Olympia and Louis on devising a backup plan that allowed me to take time off in a less chaotic way. Looking back, I know that Olympia and Louis did not truly understand the heavy price I was paying and that it was up to me to tell them. As I speak with staff all over the world, their stories remind me that we can all do better.

## The big picture about succession planning for all departments

The pandemic wreaked havoc on the staffs of companies all over the world. Leaders in stable workplaces are taking a fresh look at crosstraining of staff and setting up a "shadowing" program for employees to sit in with members of other departments to develop a stronger pipeline of talent from within. This strategy is a smart one, especially when leaders invite active involvement and input from the staff themselves.

One way to stabilize and protect our companies against the next crisis is to always keep an eye on succession planning and running the what-ifs. What if that person were not here tomorrow? Who would take their place? How fast could we solve the problem? What information would we need?

The big question is: Are we ready?

# STAFF MATTERS QUESTIONS

1. In your company, what is the value of succession planning, not only for the leaders, but for the rest of the staff as well?
2. How is your infrastructure ready for the next crisis?
3. Imagine if a key member of your team was suddenly unavailable for the next week. Would systems fall apart or run smoothly?
4. Who should oversee succession planning?
5. What is one thing you can do today to improve succession planning?

"Life isn't about waiting for the storm to pass. It's about learning how to dance in the rain."

**Vivian Greene**

"Life is what happens to you when you are busy making other plans."

**John Lennon**

"In the midst of chaos, there is also opportunity."

**Sun Tzu, *The Art of War***

# CHAPTER THREE

# Pandemic Impact

The pandemic altered the day-to-day work of 74% of employees.

29% of full-time employees have reassigned job responsibilities.

53% work remotely from home.

**Business Management Daily, May 2021**
**survey of 681 U.S. employers**

No one prepared us for this.

The Covid-19 pandemic crisis was like nothing most people had experienced before. While there was some warning, the crisis caused millions of staffers to abruptly pack up their desks and open new offices in their homes, many with just a few hours advance notice. This shift happened in a matter of days. My students remember that they were mentally preparing to be out of the office for two weeks—not two years. It was a global pivot of staggering proportions.

Employers who would not have previously considered having their staff work from home now had no choice in the matter. To say this caused a massive rupture in the global workplace and in our personal lives and psyches is not an overstatement.

The pandemic hit the United States in early March 2020, and as of this writing, the workplace and the world are still adjusting and reconfiguring on a regular basis. "Pivoting" became a buzzword in 2020. Schools stopped in-person learning, which sent families into chaos. Buying laptops for kids and upgrading Wi-Fi connections were urgent, do-it-right-now concerns. CEOs stepped up and offered no-questions-asked budgets to buy necessary equipment for home offices. Restaurants, hotels, hair salons, and movie theaters shut down. Airplanes and train travel practically came to a screeching halt. And so did hiring.

With just a few days' notice, leaders made swift decisions about sending their people home to work, and most thought it would be temporary. No one predicted that it would be months and then years. The uncertainty and volatility caused leaders to hold weekly virtual town hall meetings and what would be referred to as "listening tours" for valuable input from staff.

The hospitality industry was hit especially hard and company leaders began stepping up in a big way. Chris Nassetta, CEO of Hilton Hotels, reduced his salary to zero. He read about how the frontline workers did not want to risk infecting their families by going home. He decided to be part of the solution by partnering with the CEO of American Express, Stephen Squeri, to share the cost of providing one million hotel rooms to frontline workers for free.[6]

Nassetta also made the decision to keep his employees' health insurance intact during the shutdown. This commitment to the staff during the pandemic paid off. Hilton is consistently named in lists of the best places to work.

It is fair to say that this crisis impacted nearly every person in every country on the planet. In the United States, the crisis hit women particularly hard. By April 2021, five million women had left the workplace, taking us back to 1988 levels of female employment in the United States. A year later, in February 2022, there were still two million fewer women in the workforce compared to prepandemic data.[7]

## Purpose

The pandemic shone a fresh spotlight on our individual purpose. We had no choice but to take a hard look at the enormity and severity of the global problem. As people we knew got sick and sometimes died, we had to consider our own mortality as a real possibility. Employees throughout the world were seeking answers to the same questions: *Why am I here? Why am I doing what I am doing? Do I feel fulfilled?*

As we sought purpose, volunteerism rose. Supermarket staff hand-delivered food orders to elderly and at-risk people. As the months went by, the need for purpose in work grew, and company leaders, like Nassetta, continued engaging with staff to make manifest their unique missions. In many cases, this type of engagement has had a positive impact on staff retention.

The pandemic has had a tsunami-like economic impact on some households, causing evictions and bankruptcies. Whether the women who left the workforce will return remains to be seen, as company leaders work to create plans that support child and elder care.[8]

## Mental health

Stress. Anxiety. Trauma. Loneliness. Drug Abuse. Suicide.

The mental health concerns as a result of the pandemic are major. Loneliness caused by isolation has emerged as another pandemic. Suicides, drug abuse, and alcoholism are on the increase.[9]

In June 2020, during the Q and A in a webinar, one Executive Assistant to a CEO in Chicago started to cry. She shared that the decision had been made that week to shutter the doors and to not renew the lease for the office space. The company would be 100 percent remote. She told us that she used to sit ten feet from the CEO and was privy to everything going on in the company. Working from home, she found that she missed this interaction and she missed him. The assistant realized she was grieving a way of working that she would not have again, as long as she stayed with that company. She and the CEO would need new ways to connect via videoconferencing and messaging apps.

What I see in my work is that the human beings of our workplace have had a tough time with the radical and sudden changes caused by the pandemic. I am deeply concerned about the mental health impact on all of us because the crisis has been prolonged over months and years, and the effects have been unpredictable and controversial. Unexpected conflicts over mask policies and vaccination rules have tested the strongest of business relationships. Handling all of this in a remote work environment is a challenge for anyone.

The fact that we all possess different coping mechanisms for adversity and crisis poses a big challenge for leaders who are stressed out themselves.

## Impact on women

The pandemic's impact on women has been enormous, given that they are the primary caregivers of children and they also perform most of the work to keep the home running. Misty Heggeness of the U.S. Census Bureau said, "Bringing everyone back into the house exposed the wound of gender inequality."[10]

Office workers who work from home and have children are negotiating with their employers for flexibility. Many staff refer to it as "sleeping at work," meaning that it is common for them to do their work while children are napping, in the morning before they wake up, or late in the evening after they go to sleep.

Today, many companies are supporting their staff with money for childcare and home health assistance. Company leaders see that staff are struggling financially and many are resigning because of the strain. To stem the wave of resignations and subsequent instability, companies are setting up programs to respond to the need for schedule flexibility and home care support. Companies like Salesforce have created a work-from-anywhere culture that means exactly that. Staff are not required to commute to the office unless they choose to do so.

Covid-19 issues have tested the most seasoned leaders. No course in college prepares you for your entire workforce having to work from home with just a few days' advance notice. Leaders and HR professionals have been tested, since they are the people who usually have to answer the hard questions about new policies.

The pandemic forced most everyone in the workplace to rethink the way they operate. The phrase "we always do it this way" became irrelevant overnight. As a result, leaders are now more open to new ideas and outside-of-the-box thinking.

In 2023, volatile organizational changes are still underway at a dizzying pace. The staff is dizzy too, and, as a result, many have decided to head for the exit, causing a disruption in hiring and increases in salaries. The debate continues about the benefits of staff working from home versus being present in a physical office, at least some of the time. Companies are experimenting with a four-day workweek.

The new organizational structures are still falling into place. Important decisions are being made about returning to the office, with caveats about the "what ifs" of the next variants of the virus and/or the next crisis that will present itself to leaders and the staff who support them.

## Why do staff want to work from home?

There are many reasons why staff are resisting a return to the office. Here are some of them:

- Improved work-life balance
- Health concerns about Covid in the workplace
- Increased productivity at home
- Fewer distractions at home
- Micromanagers can't hover
- No commute—less wear and tear on the body and the car
- Increased ability to save money
- Greater ability to be there for the kids, parents, and pets
- Less discrimination or racism when working from home
- Less ageism
- Less bullying or sexual harassment
- Less fear of workplace violence
- Greater ability to work more than one job

A majority of people who have been working from home during the pandemic either do not want to go back into the office at all or prefer a hybrid schedule. My students generally felt that their productivity improved at home and that they were able to focus better with fewer distractions. Fewer Black workers want to return to the office, with a majority preferring a hybrid or full-time remote working model; one reason for this is they hope to experience less discrimination by working from home.[11]

There is emerging concern over a proximity bias, placing those staff who come into the office at an advantage over those who are working from home. Several CEOs I interviewed referred to this as a "dual class society" and expressed concern about how to maintain a strong culture in this fragmented environment. Another real issue is the invisibility factor for those staff who resist turning their cameras on for video calls and may not be eager to speak. If staff cannot be seen or heard, then it is easy to see how this can have a negative and dehumanizing impact over time. I encourage staff to be alert to this risk factor in the new workplace.

Nicholas Bloom is a professor at Stanford University and a work-from-home expert. His advice is a warning to leaders and HR: "Unless employers establish a clear and level playing field, the years ahead could remain filled with chaos. This has been a massive revolution and we have a long way to go." Bloom recommends a consistent work-from-home policy that applies to all staff, such as one to three days at home and the rest of the week in the office, to achieve the best of both worlds.

What is certain is that the workplace is changed forever, and leaders do not have all the answers about how the workplace will evolve. Their best move is to stay closely connected to their people through town hall virtual meetings, flash surveys, and one-on-one conversations via videoconference or phone. As humans, we still need to hear other people's voices, especially our leaders'. In my work, I hear logical reasons why assistants want to continue working from home. They point to saving time and money on the commute, dealing with fewer interruptions, having an improved ability to focus, and managing a better work-life balance (also referred to as work-life integration), since this structure allows them to have more time with family and friends, get in a load of laundry, or prep meals. Some are even working more than one full-time job from home in order to supplement their income. Others prefer working from home because they don't feel physically or psychologically safe in the workplace. Some fear violence.[12]

My students share jaw-dropping stories of workplace bullying and sexual harassment. These students are mightily relieved to stay home, where they feel safe from harassment, bullying, violence, and illness. I urge leaders to address these issues as part of the planning for reopening offices and expecting workers to return. If staff are reluctant or refuse to come to the office, or simply resign, it is vital to understand the truth about why they might dread coming back into the office.

## A workforce responds to the crisis

Just as our American workforce responded after the 9/11 attacks on New York City and Washington, D.C., and the financial meltdown of 2008, so did it respond to the Covid-19 crisis. That meant across-the-board pay cuts, temporary furloughs, layoffs, and restructurings. This crisis also meant HR departments were stretched to the max reacting to daily changes in the situation. Staff were coming to them for answers that were simply not available because we were all in uncharted territory. At this writing, we still are.

One shift is that the administrative staff are being tapped and leveraged to collaborate and coordinate with HR departments on activities such as the following:

- Onboarding (virtual and in person)
- Re-onboarding for people who were hired during the pandemic
- Interviewing
- Revising job descriptions that have changed dramatically since 2020
- Disaster planning for the next crises
- Succession planning (cross-training and working to keep the pipeline of talent flowing)
- Cybersecurity

- Training
- Offboarding (systems for what needs to happen when staff leaves the company)

In the aftermath of the pandemic, both HR and administrative staff will be undergoing a structural transformation from 2021 and beyond.

## But WFH for how long? Forever is a long time.

Company leaders who would never have considered having their staff work from home were forced into making this an option. Many have been surprised by how well it is working. Some experts predict that most companies will employ a hybrid way of working indefinitely.

In my work, I hear a lot of conversation about the desire to work from home and/or work from anywhere—indefinitely. This desire is requiring unprecedented discussions and negotiations. The numerous considerations include:

1. Stability and access to Wi-Fi connections
2. Time zone differences for attendance at meetings
3. Webcam policies to enable the staff to see one another
4. Evaluation of what activities are best to conduct in person vs. online
5. Geographic location (If an employee chooses to move to another city with a higher or lower cost of living, how does this impact compensation?)
6. Discussion of whether companies should start hiring people from other countries
7. Evaluation of the merits of the four-day workweek and whether it can actually function in a workaholic culture

Above all else, I see a need for clarity of expectations and a full understanding of the new needs of staffers, leaders, and companies as we all figure out the protocols.

For those staffers who want to make a strong business case to work from home, it is vital to have empathy for leaders and to be able to articulate why leaders should say "yes" to the new arrangement. What are the trade-offs and what are the benefits? Anticipate and address what leaders are afraid of. Understand that this is new territory for leaders and staff alike, and working from home could be viewed as an experiment to be evaluated after an agreed-upon period of time.

Because no one wants to be trapped into a decision that may not work out, here is a powerful question: "Can we give it a try and if it does not work, we will regroup and rethink it by X date?"[13]

## Ask first

Make it standard protocol that leaders and HR ask their people first about policies that impact them. The staff has opinions and solid input. This commitment to open communication will be the difference between success and failure. The staff has demonstrated that they will quit and find other jobs if they do not get the flexibility they need. We have seen the rise of the YOLO mentality—you only live once.

The serious life-or-death consequences of the pandemic have caused staff to question their purpose and priorities. Their work needs to serve those core values that have become of primary importance to them. One of these core values is family. For example, one of my students who absolutely loved her job decided to resign and move from New York City to California to be near her family. Prepandemic, she had thought the move would be something she would make happen in five to ten years, but the crisis accelerated her timetable. She thought, "I have no time to waste," and she was willing to do whatever it took to be with her family, even if that meant getting a new job. When she told her employer, he accommodated her plan. Instead of resigning, she now performs her job remotely and gets to live where she needs to be.

## The future of work in a postpandemic world

It's VUCA out there—volatile, uncertain, complicated, and ambiguous. The disruption in the workplace and to the labor market has been unprecedented. The pandemic touched every country in the world. A

McKinsey Global Institute report from February 2021 states that up to 25 percent of the world's workers may potentially need to switch occupations, and that will require retraining and upskilling.[14]

A Gallup poll of millennials from May 2020 found that a whopping 90 percent of them valued support for professional development opportunities as their way of measuring job satisfaction, but only 40 percent reported they were receiving that support. The companies rated highest as places to work invest in staff training.

The Great Resignation and the "turnover tsunami" refer to the massive numbers of staff who have quit in search of higher-paying jobs with more flexibility. The talent shortage drives salaries upward in some sectors as companies seek high-value employees. To attract and retain them, leaders need to be transparent about company culture and set clear expectations about working in it.

## Virtual meetings are here to stay

"Zoom fatigue" is a thing. Since the beginning of 2020, staff has struggled to learn about lighting, backgrounds, and flattering camera angles. Meetings have taken on a new life as we pay closer attention to how we show up—at least from the waist up.

Video meetings are not easily managed for everyone. For some people, they require more energy and more preparation. For this reason, some companies include information in meeting invitations about whether being on-camera is required. Video calls can be exhausting, so many companies are creating "no video meetings on Fridays" rules or placing a three-hour limit on the total amount of time staff can be on video calls on any given day.

If employees were challenged by communication prepandemic, the virtual world is presenting new challenges—now everyone has a close-up and often the meetings are recorded for future reference. Therefore, it matters how we behave in meetings and how we interact with the attendees. One strategy to accelerate rapport on virtual calls is to ask follow-up questions of your colleagues. Ask a relevant question during or following the call like, "So John, when you said XYZ, can you help me understand how you think that will play out later in the year?" This shows that you were listening closely and contributes to John feeling heard, respected, and appreciated.

## The new workplace and the need for new roles

In acknowledgment of the mental and emotional strain in the workplace, some organizations have created the role of Chief Resilience Officer. Resilience is an important quality to have, especially in the new workplace. Resilience requires mental strength and is sometimes referred to as "bouncebackability." It helps us survive, adapt, and rebound in the face of disruptions and adversities.

Interest in upskilling and retraining staff is the driving force behind the creation of a Director of Training role. The need to be ready for the "next crisis" is causing the creation of Homeland Security Directors inside companies. In my work with assistants, I am urging them to actively prepare for the next crisis, be it a natural disaster, a manmade disaster, or a public health emergency like Covid. The time to do this is in the calm *after* the last storm.

## A final word

The workplace was already broken prepandemic. Given the enormity of the workplace disruption since 2020, leaders and staff have never had a better time to rethink processes and ways of doing business.

# STAFF MATTERS QUESTIONS

1. How has the pandemic impacted your organization?
2. Does your organization feel stable or unstable? Why?
3. What are three ways to improve how your team is working in the aftermath of the pandemic?

## Rule of thumb for leaders: Ask first

If you are about to make a decision that directly impacts members of your staff, ask them about it first, not *after* the fact. Asking is not only respectful, but it can lead to important and helpful information that may result in an altered and better decision.

Asking is often not about permission, but about respect. It is not a "nice to do," but rather the common courtesy and smart business practice that makes a big difference.

# CHAPTER FOUR

# Ask First

I want to emphasize the importance of leaders asking *first*, before they make decisions that directly impact staff. It is critical, and this chapter explains why. Given how much of a problem the lack of asking causes, it is one of those subjects that deserves to be taught in business schools.

It is not that every decision need be democratic; leaders have to do what they have to do. But if leaders hired employees for what they know and truly value and respect them, then it is vital to ask their opinion on upcoming decisions, especially ones that directly affect the staff.

The problem is that staff are not being asked *before* new procedures are implemented and become the new reality. This is not only short-sighted but can be seen as disrespectful, causing deep frustration and resentment that preoccupies staff and eats precious time, energy, productivity, and money. I see the defeated looks on staffers' faces when they say, "Nobody asked me." When disregarded, they often wonder why they are even there in the first place.

For all these reasons, it makes a whole lot of sense to not skip this step.

## Real-life examples

The following stories reveal the problems and the solutions related to
the benefits of asking first.

### Open floor plans

One of the liveliest (and loudest) discussions happened at the Executive
Secretary Live conference in Auckland, New Zealand, in 2017. An assistant shared that thousands of dollars had been spent to redesign her
company's office space into an open plan in which no one had an office
with walls, not even the CEO. No one asked her or any of the other
assistants before the decision was made. The goal of open floor plans is
to bring teams together in collaboration and harmony, but they often
have the opposite effect. An open plan sounds great in theory, but assistants all over the world report they are a disaster in practice.

The assistant said, "The assistants hate the open plan. I'm the assistant to the CEO, and I deal with highly sensitive documents and
conversations. My computer screen cannot be open for all to see. I also
have phone conversations that cannot be overheard, so sometimes I
have to leave the building in order to have them. Besides confidentiality, it is very hard to concentrate and focus in an open plan. Plus,
we have many introverts on the staff, and what this has done is force
people to buy the best noise-canceling headphones they can find just
to focus and concentrate."

She continued, "When the leaders heard the negative reaction
and saw the problem with their own eyes, they held meetings with the
staff. Finally. And then a compromise plan was designed, which was a
hybrid of both ideas—private offices combined with an open plan. The
assistants could have told them that, had they asked us. Of course, that
meant spending thousands of dollars more to renovate what had just
been done. Everyone could have been saved time, stress, and money
had those meetings happened first."

Note to leaders: This story from New Zealand about open floor
plans is one I have heard all over the world. I find it ironic that the
assistants knew the logic of a hybrid office layout long before the
pandemic crisis. The lesson here is to consult with the people who

will be directly impacted by your decisions during the planning process. Staff often see important things that their leaders don't. Does
it slow down the process? Potentially. Will it change the outcome of
the decision? Maybe not. Will it matter that you asked? One hundred
percent.

Note to staff: If you get wind of a decision that is about to be
made that you know is not a good one, or if you see a red flag, please
speak to your leaders even if they don't ask. Leaders don't know
what they don't know and you may save the company a lot of money.
Plus, you are already on the payroll, and you have an obligation to
speak up about something that could benefit the company. While
"offering opinions" may not be officially in your job description, and
while some staff are even told to "stay in their lane," if you have
something important to contribute, do it anyway. When I talk with
CEOs about this issue, I ask them, "If a staffer thinks there is something you need to know, do you want them to tell you?" They answer, "Absolutely. Yes."

Another story concerns a top Executive Assistant to a CEO in New
York City. During the pandemic, it was decided that the CEO's private
office would be renovated. The assistant was not asked for input on
the design until late in the construction process, when she repeatedly
asked for a hard hat tour. On the tour, the assistant was alarmed to
see that the architect had not included a coat closet; as a result, it had
to be designed and installed prior to the move-in, costing both money
and extra time. The CEO was relieved that her assistant had caught
the problem before construction was complete. It would have been
even better to involve the assistant sooner, asking, "What do you see?
What's missing?"

*Contracts*

Olympia Dukakis's agents and managers all knew I would be one of
the people reviewing contracts before Olympia would sign them.
They knew I looked for points in contracts that they would not have
any way of knowing were important. I read contracts with different
eyes than others did because I knew Olympia's preferences. These
included details such as: a specific hotel to stay in because it was in a

walkable part of town, a favorite yoga studio nearby, extra first-class plane tickets to enable someone to join her on the film shoot, her preferred make-up artist, and special foods available on set. I knew the choice of a hotel could make or break the working experience for Olympia. I also knew that making the correct choices up front saved time and money, such as avoiding having to move her to a different location.

*Paperless offices*

I stood in an office in New York City that enforced a rigid rule against leaving any paper on desks. Considering the pristine optics it provides, this idea sounds great in theory. And yes, it is certainly better for the environment. While gaining popularity in the work-from-home and hybrid environments, a totally paperless office is not an ideal system for most. The staff in this NYC office found the rule overly harsh and stressful. Who among us has not had a technology failure such as a computer crashing, a mobile phone dying in a puddle, a server going down, or an account getting hacked? That's life.

Assistants the world over know that going completely paperless is not a reasonable plan when power is not available, such as on an airplane. Anyone who travels knows that even if an airplane seat has an outlet, there is only a fifty-fifty chance it works.

One assistant to a CEO shared how the printer suddenly disappeared from her office. Someone in management had decided to leave only one printer for the company and to locate it two floors down from the C-suite. No one asked the assistant how doing this would impact her work. It was a poor decision for many reasons, and within hours, she had the printer back.

The bottom line is that if you are considering going paperless, ask the people directly impacted by the decision. I should note that even during the pandemic, plenty of leaders still preferred to print out key documents, collaborating with their assistants on the best way to keep the communication flowing. There is a big difference between what technology makes possible and what the people of our workplace are actually using.

*Text messaging*

One of my students is an assistant in Chicago, where she supports four busy executives. On a Friday, she received a text message from the HR director telling her that starting Monday, she would also be supporting a fifth executive whom she had never met. My student told me she already had a more than full plate supporting four executives and that a fifth felt like an overwhelming setup for failure.

A major step had been missed when the assistant was not asked first. To be told important information like this via text message is also disrespectful. The assistant spoke to HR on Monday and it was decided she would try supporting five executives for a month. The workload was so great that the assistant found another job and left the company.

> **UNIVERSAL TRUTH:** Text messaging should not be used for subjects that require a potentially complicated and multi-faceted discussion. If there is any chance the reader may not understand what is being communicated or infer a negative tone from the message, choose another way to communicate— face-to-face, by phone, or on a video call.

*Outsourcing HR*

Company leaders have made a decision to outsource certain functions of the organization in the name of saving money. Some companies are even outsourcing HR to people outside the country of the home organization. That is certainly their prerogative. However, outsourcing HR is causing the following problems for staff:

- Delays in getting important answers because of the time difference.
- Differing answers on important issues, depending on who is answering a question.
- Difficulty managing highly emotional issues such as bullying and sexual harassment, which are hard enough to

discuss in person. The result is that these touchy issues may not get addressed at all and staff might choose to quit.

One tech company based in Europe outsourced HR for seven years, and in that time laid off 1,000 team members. Because of the subsequent problems of doing this, the decision was made to bring HR back in-house and 800 staffers were rehired.

## And finally

Asking staff first about decisions may slow down the process of moving ahead. However, I would argue the pros far outweigh the cons. I suspect if you thought back to your own work history, you would remember when a decision was made that directly impacted you and you were not asked about it first. How did it make you feel?

This idea about asking first is highly relevant in one's personal life as well, which I found out when my son Adam was thirteen. I was given the gift of tickets to one of my favorite musical artists, who would be performing at Madison Square Garden. Wanting to be a good mom, I designated one of the tickets for my son. However, I didn't ask him first; I assumed he would be as delighted as I was. The concert was not a happy experience for him. At intermission, he said that he would have preferred "a root canal." Sigh.

Lesson learned. I vowed that would never happen again. The whole experience might have been very different had I asked Adam first and involved him in the plan, but now I will never know.

## STAFF MATTERS QUESTIONS

1. How important do you think it is to ask first?
2. What decisions have you made without asking key people first? Has this happened to you in your career?
3. What is an upcoming decision that would be best to ask others about first?

## STAKEHOLDER CONSTITUENCIES OF OUR WORKPLACE

Part 1: Leaders/Executives

Part 2: Support Staff

Part 3: Human Resource Professionals

Part 4: Recruiters

# CHAPTER FIVE

# Giving Voice—Meet the Staff

*Leaders • Assistants/Support • Human Resources • Recruiters*

A company has a name but its people give it a meaning. Every employee—from the CEO on down—is hired for a reason. Each member of a staff is a subject matter expert (SME) in at least one area, which means they are valuable to the whole of a company. The most successful organizations are the ones where the SMEs are in a state of constant communication and collaboration.

This chapter has four parts. I want us all to take an open-minded, empathetic, and healthy walk in the shoes of leaders, assistants, HR professionals, and recruiters. In doing this, we will hear straight from them, the people who are running our world's companies, and break down their silos in the process. Each one is an everyday staffer who is trying to do great work and make a living for themselves and their families. At their human core, each yearns for respect and understanding from others.

I know about these people from my 1,500 conversations.

I maintain that the road to an ultimate workplace is through improved and increased communication among the constituencies. The road is messy. So what? So is the status quo.

The constituencies of the workplace are not only the leaders, but the assistants/support staff, human resource professionals, and recruiters. They are the human stakeholders, and that word is very fitting. They all have much at stake professionally and personally.

When asked about their work, they also have a lot to say about how the workplace could improve. The benefit of paying close attention to these responses is the bridge we can build together.

I asked the staff these questions: *What if you were the CEO? What would you do?* I will share their very illuminating answers. I am 100 percent convinced that taking the time to reflect on these responses will give leaders a path to their ultimate new workplace.

What I have noticed is that the most engaged teams have open leaders—people receptive to new ideas, even from unexpected places. They let it be known that they have an attitude of curiosity. These leaders have open eyes, open ears, and open hearts. They are not this way only because it is the right thing to do, but because it is smart business.

For this chapter, I went on a search for the finest minds and the most forward-thinking people, leaders whose beliefs can help us build ultimate new workplaces.

## Fear of mistakes—make it safe

No matter what seat you occupy on a staff, you fear making mistakes. Who among us has not made a mistake? No one. Therefore, as we move through our careers, don't allow your staff or teammates to hide in the shadows of their occasional errors. As counterintuitive as it may seem, making it safe to fail is a cornerstone of innovation, productivity, and staff retention.

# Meet the Staff

"People are in greater need of your praise when they try and fail, than when they try and succeed."

**Bob Moawad, coach and author**

# PART 1

# Leaders' Voices

"The function of leadership is to produce more leaders, not more followers."

**Ralph Nader, activist**

"To get people to respect what you know, admit to them what it is you don't know."

**Dr. Mark Hillman**

It is hard being in charge. Excruciatingly hard. The kind of hard that wakes you up in the middle of the night in a cold sweat because you are not sure about making payroll, or worrying about which bill you pay when you cannot pay them all, or wondering what words you will use to fire someone.

I became a small business owner with an assistant of my own more than twenty years into my career. I was unprepared for the weight of responsibility for even the partial livelihood of another person.

## Case study: My story of leadership and managing others

After trying and failing to get work as a professional actress, I decided to take a job working in a dinner theater box office. I was twenty-three years old and made $4.25 an hour. My manager had been at the theater for sixteen years, and my thought was that I would be able to learn a great deal from her. I was very happy learning the running of a theater from the other side of the stage.

Less than a month into the job, my manager announced that she was resigning and that I would become the manager. (I got a raise to $4.50/hour.) In a heartbeat, I had become responsible for leading a team of six people whom I barely knew. I had to schedule them, manage time reports, and give feedback. I had to report to an executive I had never met. I was a young outsider who was now in charge of people twice and even triple my age. I even had to fire one of them, and I knew nothing about doing that.

I realized quickly that someone calling you a "manager" does not make you one, let alone a good one. I was not a good manager. How could I be, with no experience and so little training? I stayed for two years and learned by experience. I was forced to learn the hard way. It should not have been this way. However, this experience and the lessons I learned have informed my current work in a profound way.

The truth is that leading is hard work, and not all leaders are willing to put in the kind of day after day effort required to be responsible for the lives of others. That would explain why so few people want to be leaders, and many who do become leaders should not be. It also explains why Amazon says there are over 60,000 results for books on "leadership." Simply put, not everyone is cut out to be a leader. It's a tough gig.

In a book about building an ultimate new workplace, I am interested in pushing back against mediocrity. I see that sometimes company leaders settle for "good enough" because the road to the ultimate workplace feels too hard and messy. Is it easier and faster to fire someone via text message or on a group Zoom call where nine hundred staffers are fired all at once? Of course. Is it smart? No. Leaders need to consider the fallout from poor word of mouth and negative online reviews. News like this travels like wildfire. Faster is not always better.

As I have traveled and met the people in charge, many admit that, contrary to popular belief, they do not have all the answers. That's why they need their teams; they seek to hire people who complement their own skills and who may be smarter than them on certain subjects. It takes courage of character and high emotional intelligence for leaders to seek out staff who are smarter than themselves.

People who have never been in charge find it easy to be critical of those who are. My goal is to shine a light on leaders and hopefully provide the whopping dose of empathy that comes from knowing their personal stories and experiences. Understanding their perspective will help move us toward our ultimate new workplace.

## Nelson Mandela; his assistant of nineteen years, Zelda la Grange; and my visit to Robben Island off Cape Town, South Africa

When we discuss leadership and overcoming extreme adversity to achieve accomplishments that change the world, it is impossible to not include Nelson Mandela, the Black lawyer and activist who was imprisoned in South Africa for twenty-seven years for speaking out against apartheid. At least six of those years were spent in and out of solitary confinement.

In 1990, Mandela was released from prison at the age of seventy-one. In 1994, he became the first democratically elected Black President of South Africa, marking the end of rigid segregation known as apartheid. He served as President until 1999, and he passed away in 2013. His Personal Assistant from 1994 to 2013 was Zelda la Grange, who I consider a friend and a respected colleague. Her book about her experience is called *Good Morning, Mr. Mandela*. I highly recommend it.

Zelda speaks of "Madiba's" kindness, generosity, and respect for everyone; she moves me every time she talks of her incredible journey. (You can hear her yourself on YouTube.)

In February 2017, I spoke at a conference in Johannesburg and visited the Apartheid Museum, which was unforgettable in its pain and power. Then I visited Cape Town, where there was something so familiar about the area near the water, and I was told that it had been modeled on San Francisco's Fisherman's Wharf. And in the same way you can take a boat from the wharf to Alcatraz Island, home of the famous prison, so can you take a boat from Cape Town to Robben Island Prison, where Mandela spent the first eighteen years of his imprisonment. We saw his tiny cell and the areas where he spent his hard days. The tours are given by former inmates.

In his time there, Mandela was subjected to demeaning and demoralizing treatment by the White guards, and he was forced to endure hard labor, severe cold, and food deprivation. Through it all, he showed only respect for the guards and sought to know them and teach them. Over time, Robben became known as "Mandela University." Those guards shared their stories about Mandela's behavior with others.

While in prison, Mandela managed to write five hundred pages of notes and anti-apartheid essays. With help from other inmates, he buried the pages in the prison garden. He managed to write not one, but two copies of these pages, in case one was discovered. In fact, one of the copies was found and promptly burned. A released inmate smuggled out the other copy, which became *The Prison Letters of Nelson Mandela*.

Mandela entered Robben as the enemy and a person to be intensely feared and hated. When Mandela was finally released after a staggering twenty-seven years, he was respected and even loved by everyone he had encountered on Robben, even those who had treated him viciously. Mandela forgave them.

When he exited prison, Mandela was no longer feared by as many White people. Mandela's respect for his oppressors and his refusal to succumb to anger led directly to his being democratically elected as the President of South Africa in 1994, along with the end of apartheid. It is an astonishing story that I had heard about from Zelda and read about in her book as well as Mr. Mandela's book *Long Walk to Freedom*. That trip to Robben made an indelible impression about leadership and what inspires others to follow you.[15]

### Leaders speak: What's the secret sauce to leading?

**GEORGENE HUANG,** *CEO and Cofounder of Fairygodboss*
"Resilience and flexibility. As a leader, especially in a fast-changing environment, my job changes every year or so and I've had to adapt very rapidly to every new situation and new role in order to stay successful. And at the end of the day, what you're trying to do doesn't always work

and you need to learn to let go of things when they don't. When my cofounder and I first started our company, Fairygodboss, we got a lot of nos, but we knew there were other women who could benefit from a resource like the one we were building, so we just kept going and kept adapting until we started hearing the word 'yes.'"

**DOUGLAS CONANT,** *former CEO of Campbell Soup Company, author of* The Blueprint
"The blueprint for leadership is to be tough-minded on standards and tender-hearted with people. Honor all your stakeholders and build trust. And when things go wrong, leaders have to behave their way out of them. Engage people's hearts and show them a higher purpose."

**CATHLEEN SCHREINER GATES,** *CEO of SimpleNexus*
"Stay silent longer. This advice applies to very senior leaders who are leading teams. By having the senior folks staying silent longer, the teams are able to work through issues without having the senior leader in the room drive the process too much and stifle the more creative inputs. Teams will naturally defer to their leaders and if you stay silent longer—the team develops, evolves, matures, and takes on more responsibilities and becomes a more high performing team."

**CHRIS BRODHEAD,** *owner of Famous Founder*
"In my own experience nothing has destroyed my motivation more than a bad manager. So I try to always be overly kind and appreciative. Lavish the team with praise while acknowledging specific things they are doing well. I like to include a message of praise and appreciation with every online payment I send my team. I often receive a message back that says, 'the money is nice but the message is better.'"

## How important is trust?

**RICHARD EDELMAN,** *CEO of Edelman (from the Transformative CEO Summit, Feb. 25, 2021)*[16]
"Leaders must build trust. We are suffering from information bankruptcy and our most important goal is to provide the highest quality

information and agreed-upon facts. Trust happens when four elements are in place. 1. Proven Ability 2. Dependability 3. Integrity 4. Purpose."

**STEPHEN M.R. COVEY,** *author of* The Speed of Trust
"Trust is foundational to collaboration."

**WHITNEY WOLFE HERD,** *CEO of the dating app Bumble (one of her employees is credited with and praised for coming up with the name of the company)*
"I want them [my team] to feel like mini-CEOs in their own way."[17]

## Decision-making

**DEREK COBURN,** *Cofounder of CADRE in Washington, D.C.*
"For determining whether a particular action is good or not, we ask ourselves: If everyone started doing this, would it be a good thing or a bad thing?"

**JOE UCUZOGLU,** *CEO of Deloitte US (Great Place to Work podcast interview with Michael Bush, Jan. 29, 2020)*
"How leaders behave in a crisis matters. We must demonstrate humility and be authentic about who we are."

**KEVIN W. SHARER,** *former CEO of Amgen, coauthor of* The CEO Test
"The team. Don't break the law. Don't run out of cash. But there is no substitute for the best team. Without the team, it isn't going to work."[18]

## VIP access

To be close to a leader means having access. For staff, access can mean sitting in on leadership meetings or being privy to some/all email correspondence. It can also mean attending leadership conferences with the leader. In 2016, I spoke at the Barron's Advisor Teams Summit in Las Vegas. Invitations to this event included both leaders and their Executive Assistants, which makes it one of the only conferences of its kind. Given the response, I know that this kind of gathering should become more common; the messages of empathy are unmissable.

## Where do leaders learn to lead? It's complicated.

The majority of the world's leaders attended college and many of them attended business school. Hubert Joly, former CEO of Best Buy and author of the book *The Heart of Business*, attended HEC School of Management, a private, top-rated business school in France. He said, "So much of what I learned in business school is either wrong, dated, or at best, incomplete." Joly teaches at Harvard Business School and, in his book, he writes that the new age of business requires a new approach to leadership. The new model requires leaders who can create an environment that unleashes the human "magic" of the employees.

According to Alan Murray of *Fortune's CEO Daily*, Joly told his directors on day one of his taking over at Best Buy, "The purpose of a company is not to make money but to make a positive contribution in people's lives." Joly's approach worked.

Dr. Anita Ying, MD, MBA, professor of endocrinology at the MD Anderson Cancer Center, commented, "Schools don't teach how to work effectively with support staff. My assistants have taught me how to help them succeed in their roles, which is critical for a strong partnership and team success."

Kent Postma, a Vice President of the MD Anderson Cancer Center, added, "I used to be a micromanager until I learned that I just needed to get out of the way and allow people to do their jobs."

Retired four-star general and former U.S. Secretary of State Colin Powell put it this way: "The day the soldiers stop bringing you their problems is the day you stopped leading them. They have either lost confidence that you can help them or concluded that you do not care. Either case is a failure of leadership."

I hear from leaders who are actually afraid of their team and choose to avoid the issues because it is easier than taking them on. I am hopeful that with training, we can eliminate those fears and open up productive and candid conversations between leaders and staff.

## Business leaders respond to the new world

In our changing world, many prominent business leaders are choosing to speak out on social and political issues, despite the risks. Here is how several leaders are taking their stands with intention, care, and a view to the future.

### MARC BENIOFF, *Cofounder and Chairman of Salesforce*

In May 2020, Marc Benioff was Alan Murray's guest on *Fortune's Leadership Next* podcast.[19]

Here is some of what he said: "My job is listening to my employees and my decisions are driven by them. That meant taking action early in the pandemic to help to get Personal Protective Equipment (PPE) to the frontline workers who needed it. It meant setting a policy of no layoffs for ninety days, and I urged other CEOs to do the same if they possibly could."

About speaking out and taking strong stands on issues of social justice such as pay equity, racism, LGBTQIA+ discrimination, health care, voting rights, the environment, and homelessness, to name just a few, Benioff said, "CEOs have a role in setting the tone. That is our role in the company, and I see more activism among business leaders than ever before, like Brian Moynihan, CEO of Bank of America, and Ed Bastian, CEO of Delta. I thank them for that. The most successful CEOs aggressively act on issues. We need to act."

Benioff also commented on the education of future leaders: "Business schools will need to modify the curriculum if they want to build great leaders."

### JOHN DONAHOE, *CEO of Nike*

When John Donahoe became CEO of Nike in January 2020, he wrote a letter about Nike's diversity and inclusion efforts to their 75,400 employees worldwide.[20]

Donahoe said, in part, "While we strive to help shape a better society, our most important priority is to get our own house in order. We know Black Lives Matter. We must educate ourselves more deeply on the issues faced by Black communities and understand the enormous suffering and senseless tragedy racial bigotry creates."

To that end, Juneteenth (June 19th) became a paid holiday for Nike employees and the company's ERG group the Black Employee Network meets virtually to discuss relevant issues.

**CATHLEEN SCHREINER GATES,** *CEO of SimpleNexus*
"During the pandemic, we had leaders drive to people's homes and hand-deliver holiday gifts. Leaders took pictures and posted them on Slack channels. We created a Slack channel called SNAH (SimpleNexus at Home), which is a place to converse about the unique challenges—but mostly about the fun, creative, and interesting experiences—of the changes in the work life brought on by the pandemic. We shared holiday decorating, children, pets, weather experiences, home office décor, etc. It is everyone's way to connect and maintain some sanity. It is a fun, light view into people's lives that offers a very different and welcome kind of intimacy and connectedness. It is an activity that is important and not at all trivial."

**MIKE KAUFMANN,** *former CEO of Cardinal Health*
"It's not really an option to say nothing. If you don't make comments, at least a certain amount of your employees think you don't care or think you're not listening."

**HUBERT JOLY,** *former CEO of Best Buy, Senior Lecturer at Harvard Business School, author of* The Heart of Business
As the former CEO of Best Buy, Hubert Joly is globally admired for designing a business framework in which employees "stand at the center." In so doing, the company not only became profitable, but was also recognized as one of *Fortune*'s Best Places to Work. In his book, Joly writes, "Doing great work starts when people feel treated like individuals, not human capital, in a work environment where they can thrive. The architecture I am advocating has employees at the heart of business, creating and nurturing caring and authentic relationships, both within the company and also with all of the company's stakeholders."

When Joly started as CEO in 2012, he had no experience with retail, so he spent four days in a store speaking with the "blue shirts" and having the same experience as a customer. At team meetings, he also asked employees to tell personal stories about someone they knew who inspired them as a way to encourage empathy and humanize the Best Buy teams and customers. Understanding that the company is known for technology products, he insisted on making technology personal by focusing on the people selling and buying the products. These strategies gave Joly information that he could not obtain any other way and also built strong rapport with the staff.

## Business schools respond to the pandemic

As leadership expert Jack Zenger pointed out, the wheels of change in academia have historically moved slowly. How then can the curriculum at business schools pivot to respond to the massive changes in the workplace and the workforce, ultimately producing leaders who can succeed in the new postpandemic environment?

Universities taking a proactive approach include the following:[21]

### THE UNIVERSITY OF VIRGINIA'S DARDEN SCHOOL OF BUSINESS
According to the *Business Insider* newsletter, Darden was one of the first business schools to offer a test waiver in response to the pandemic. Students responded positively to the compassion and flexibility. In 2020, they launched a new course called "Managing in a Pandemic: The Challenge of COVID-19." The course description says, "we empower agile, creative, and critical thinkers to be catalysts for business and social transformation globally."

### THE YALE SCHOOL OF MANAGEMENT
When the pandemic hit, Yale was about to launch a new required course for all first-year MBA students called "The Executive." The focus was on real-life case studies. The pandemic caused the faculty to quickly put together a whole new case study in which students take on the management questions that this unprecedented pandemic event has raised.

### THE STANFORD GRADUATE SCHOOL OF BUSINESS
Stanford offers several new nonrequired classes and guest speakers to

inform, guide, and provide hands-on experience to future leaders in the new workplace. The covered topics include racial injustice and inequality and how business leaders are working to make positive change. These classes are "Leadership for Society: Race and Power" and "Antiracism and Allyship Journey." Another course is called "Reflections on History in the Making," which provides students an opportunity to share their own experiences on the pandemic's impact.

## Leaders talk about leading

**CATHLEEN SCHREINER GATES,** *CEO of SimpleNexus*
I wanted to know about Cathleen's approach to leadership. I asked, "As a female CEO, do you lead men differently from women?"

"Yes, absolutely. And anyone who says 'no' is not very self-aware or is relatively inexperienced. This is a general statement and there are always caveats, but here are a few key thoughts:

1.  You treat everyone fairly, but that doesn't mean you manage them the same way. Just as you manage the growth of your children somewhat tailored to what motivates them, what worries them, etc. Everyone is different. But they are all taught the same values. It is the same with leaders.
2.  I do not set out to manage men differently than women, but it is an outcome that has become a trend. Generally speaking, men have tended to be less inclined to be vulnerable and acknowledge that they are completely at a loss as to what to do—especially when reporting to a woman. These are real dynamics that can be managed. Once you diagnose that this is an issue, you teach them without them realizing they are learning and, over time, trust builds and they become more open.
3.  Women often don't have the tools to advocate for themselves. Many haven't been socialized to be comfortable with success and confidence. I spend time helping women identify what their unique strengths are and teaching them communication and advocacy skills."

Schreiner Gates shares her experience with male managers: "I think that most men want to learn how to be better managers, period. Managing women is an area that few leadership coaches call out, yet it deserves to be. Right now, it is more about programs for women to help them understand how to navigate their careers and to raise their consciousness. We are way behind in helping men broaden their skills in managing in a diverse and inclusionary world."

## Case study: New CEO who admits not knowing how to lead

### ANONYMOUS

"I first became a manager at the age of twenty-seven. I was promoted and thrown into managing others because I was a strong event producer, the company was growing, and it was the logical next step for a top performer such as myself. Only there was absolutely nothing logical about it. I had zero experience in managing people or leading a team. I was young and immature. I received no training, no mentorship, no guidance or advice. I was only given performance expectations for my team and told to do whatever I needed to do to get the work done. The results were disastrous.

"Leadership at the company would regularly and openly speak poorly of employees, call them names behind their backs, threaten to fire people, and joke about what to do with 'problem employees.' This was the culture and the leadership example I had to learn from. The problem was not the employees; the problem was the leadership. There was zero ownership, zero accountability, zero integrity, zero investment in professional development, training, or mentorship. The sad irony is that the company is in the business of professional development.

"If I learned anything from that experience, it was what not to do as a leader. It took me many years to realize that and many more years to begin learning what real leadership looks like. It starts with ownership, accountability, and integrity.

"When the pandemic hit (and honestly, even before the pandemic), I was overly consumed by my business. I was head down, laser-focused, and maybe even obsessed with my own career growth. Prepandemic, I did not network with others in my industry (events). I did not attend industry panels, educational sessions, or thought leader discussions. I had no network in my field and therefore no one to exchange best practices or lessons learned with. I never looked up, over, or around to see how others were navigating events before and during the pandemic.

"I was all-consumed with my own business and, frankly, I was in my own way—tripping over myself. I was walking around blind. It was not until I reached a physical and mental health breaking point that I removed myself from the business. I spent months away from it. In that time, I realized my mistake. A good leader is steering the ship wide-eyed, with binoculars, looking out at the horizon, and communicating with other vessels on what they are experiencing, feeling, and seeing in the waters to navigate best. I was steering the ship backward. The book *Extreme Ownership* by Willink and Babin helped me to understand that there are no bad teams, only bad managers. I was one of them."

## What makes a great manager?

**DANIELLE DE WULF,** *Administrative Project Coordinator, Janssen Pharmaceutical Companies of Johnson & Johnson, Belgium*
"The best manager I ever worked with is the one who gave me a briefing of the expected results and then added 'I give you carte blanche to make decisions since I trust you.' I felt so honored that I went the extra mile to prove that I was worth his trust and that he could count on my loyalty and competence."

## What worries staff about leaders?

**KEMETIA FOLEY,** *thirty-year Executive Assistant, Washington, D.C.*
"Apathy. Leaders can be so immersed in their own career survival, they may not be aware of insidious apathy among their directors or staff. Or even worse, their own apathy has left their staff directionless and feeling ambivalent about what their purpose is within the organization."

**LEADERSHIP COACH,** *New York City*
"An unrestrained ego. Leaders who allow their own needs to supersede the staff's are exhausting and demoralizing. This kind of ego makes it seem like the leader has blinders on; sometimes he surrounds himself with yes people to protect the ego."

## Case study: Keeping it personal

**DOUGLAS L. MEYER,** *Chief Financial Planner, Wells Fargo Advisors*
"In my thirty-year career, I have had many people on my teams. I realized early on how my teams were extensions of me and that everyone needed to row in the same direction if we were to be successful. None of the schools I attended prepared me for managing people.

"About my team—I empower them to take responsibility and I try not to micromanage. They know I have their backs when mistakes are made. They know I care about them as people and I compensate well. I take care of them and they take care of me.

"Many years ago, I began a practice of calling my friends, my team, and my clients on their birthdays. And a few years ago, I began calling my clients who are widows and widowers on Thanksgiving. I like talking to people on the phone and they appreciate being thought of on these days. Yes, some are surprised to get the call, but then they look forward to it. It has turned out to be great for business, but that is not why I do it."

[Note from Bonnie: I am Doug's college friend and his client, and I love his birthday calls.]

"In our current workplace, I worry about the less and less human contact. I see it as a bad thing because it makes it hard to mentor and more of a challenge to maintain connections. My best advice for leaders is to treat everybody like you want to be treated."

## Case study: Importance of context from a CEO in Chicago

"As CEO, I wanted to change the paid time off (PTO) policy to an unlimited PTO policy. Nearly everyone on the team was excited and supportive of this policy change, except for two team members. One felt disappointed that she would not be paid for PTO days not taken if/when she was to leave the company. Another was worried that unlimited PTO was too vague; he preferred a transparent black-and-white policy that he could easily understand and abide by.

"Before officially making the switch to unlimited PTO, I provided the team with a policy proposal sheet that clearly laid out the proposed new policy and its 'why.' The team had several days to review and digest it before we met to discuss it openly. We opened the policy proposal sheet for discussion during our next team meeting, and everyone respectfully shared their perspective.

"I had a very personal example of why unlimited PTO is so essential. It was so personal a story that it brought tears to my eyes as I shared it. The example was about how my mom could not be with my grandmother on her deathbed because she was out of PTO days and could not afford to take time off unpaid. Most of the team had never considered this scenario. It wasn't just about trips to Europe and extralong holiday weekends. It was about flexibility when we might need it the most. By the end of the meeting, everyone was on board, and we unanimously agreed to commit to this policy. We moved onward and upward as a team."

## Case study: People sitting in the wrong seats on the bus

**CATHLEEN SCHREINER GATES,** *CEO of SimpleNexus*
"I once took over an information technology (IT) team on Wall Street that was considered the lowest performing team in the unit. I was told they were a team of misfits and 'unmanageable.' However, it was clear that the prior leader took personal credit for everything that had been done well and blamed the team members for everything that went wrong. Prior to this I had always worked with high-performing teams, but I was asked to effect a turnaround with this team. There were two people in particular—one junior and one very senior—who were the ones identified to be moved out of the organization.

"I learned that the prior leader had not listened to the team members and had a number of people doing tasks that their skills and experience were not well suited for. The people were in the wrong seats on the bus.

"I took the two lowest performers and made them a research team focused on teaching the rest of us about technologies hitting the market that would disrupt the way we do things. They were creators, not soldiers, and they had tons of great ideas but had not been allowed to execute them. I took the chains off. I put them in a direct reporting relationship to me and charged them with reinventing the group. The group benefited and they became top performers. A win-win."

## How do leaders chase people away?

"People leave managers, not companies."
**Marcus Buckingham**

The business news is filled with examples of companies in which there have been flurries of resignations. The problem is very often the leader or the manager. The bottom line is that people don't leave companies where they feel respected and valued.

## Case study: Executive Assistant, Belgium

"I've been a stellar Executive Assistant for over twenty-five years. I had been working in Brussels, supporting a manager who was a bully. He yelled and was highly critical and verbally abusive with the staff. I couldn't wait to find another job. Finally I did. When I gave my notice, his response was, 'Well, it's about time. Aren't you going to apologize for your poor performance?' I said, 'The only thing I am sorry about is that you are such a terrible manager.' I have no regrets for saying that. I heard he got fired a short time later and I went on to my dream job."

## Advice for leaders from the team

In 2018, I asked assistants to answer this question: What would you do if you were CEO for one day? Here is a sampling of the answers.[22]

**SONYA PONDS,** *Executive Assistant, Washington, D.C.*
"A seasoned CEO has an understanding that she/he is the champion of the mission and vision of the company and its personnel. So, if I were privileged enough to be CEO for the day, I would implement divisional Be the SME (Subject Matter Expert) Days. A proactive workplace is an entity where management champions their employees and nurtures possibility. Why? Challenged employees articulate and demonstrate how being their best selves is impactful for their career progression and the company's bottom line. Frankly, everyone has the ability to be the go-to team player, but what is missing often is just the opportunity!"

**MINERVA SÁNCHEZ,** *Guelph, Ontario*
"Two of the biggest mental health challenges in our workplace are compassion fatigue and mental burnout. Compassion fatigue is the diminished ability to empathize with others. I would love to be able to provide training to all our frontline staff on trauma, burnout, and how to care for those impacted. These services would be made available to all the individuals we serve. Doing this would help demonstrate to the staff how much their work is valued by the organization, while at the same time providing them with an improved ability to continue to serve those who are in need of our mental health, addictions, and developmental services."

**KARA WILSON,** *Toronto, Canada*
"Change how administrative professionals' salaries are determined. Well over 80 percent of administrative duties are being performed by women who already receive a lower hourly rate then our male counterparts. Our salaries should be based on experience, working knowledge, and transferable skills—not gender or education. Nor should they be determined by third-party consultants who use the lowest market rate as a benchmark for corporations to undermine the salaries of their administrative support staff. Let us prove with fair compensation in our hands that we have value and aren't easily replaced."

**ANGELA ANSPACH,** *Indianapolis, Indiana*
"I would get up from my big comfy chair, out from behind my big executive desk, and walk the floors where the day-to-day associates are busy making the company successful. There would be nothing more humbling than being the CEO and introducing myself to associates and engaging in conversation about them, personally and professionally. I would be the CEO who cares about every staffer. The morale and productivity in the office would soar like a rocket."

**JES SLOAN,** *Boston, Massachusetts*
"I'd allow our employees time to read, research, focus, and think by declaring one day a week a 'no meetings' day, companywide. Our execs (our CEO among them) spend all the traditional working hours in meetings, with no time to process what they're hearing, reflect on what is working, and focus on improvement. There is no time to do the 'work' that they discuss all day, so folks work longer hours and have less time to refuel mind, body, and soul. The ROI on one meeting-free day/week would be tremendous to business growth, personal growth, and overall morale. I'm happy to report that in 2022, 'No meeting Wednesdays' were instituted, morphing into 'No meeting Fridays,' and employees at every level of the org chart have been reporting success."

**KEMETIA FOLEY,** *Washington, D.C.*
"I would take time to privately listen to the concerns and fears of at least three to five persons from each level of the organization chart. If I recognized a pattern, I'd know it was something that required further research."

## What leaders say about what keeps them up at night

- Keeping our people safe—physical health and mental health
- Upskilling our people so we stay competitive
- Improving employee retention by staying connected to what they really need
- Improving cybersecurity and stopping hackers who are getting smarter

- Managing a hybrid workforce and staying connected
- Finding ways to strengthen the Wi-Fi connectivity where remote workers are so there are no breakdowns in communication
- Understanding artificial intelligence and how we integrate new technologies
- Preparing for the next crisis: Will we be ready when the next epidemic or challenge hits?

## And then there's this—a revelation from my research: Guilt

"I feel guilty having an assistant." In my interviews with powerful and superbusy leaders, I was surprised by how many of them shared that they felt "guilt" about working with an assistant. One leader said, "My wife challenges me by asking why I am not doing XYZ and why I am having my assistant do such and such task." Another commented, "To tell you the truth, I don't know what I should ask her to do so I often do things myself." Still another said, "I'm a little frightened to ask her to do things for me, so I end up spending time doing things that she really could do."

My response to these comments about feeling guilty is this: time is money and leaders need to be spending time doing the things that they were hired to do. But that idea bumps up against the reality that there is very little training to help leaders understand what an assistant can do and how to fully utilize one. Therein lies the conflict.

> "If you don't have an assistant, you are one."
> **Cameron Herold, leadership expert**

Leaders—there are 168 hours in a week. My suggestion is to use your salary to calculate your hourly rate and then evaluate the administrative tasks you are doing that are better done by an assistant. You are not being paid to do those tasks, right?

That exercise usually goes a long way in alleviating the guilt. I sure hope the guilt gets reduced and, I promise you, so does your assistant!

**Back where this section on leaders began:
It's tough being in charge.**

---

"A true leader has the confidence to stand alone,
the courage to make tough decisions, and the
compassion to listen to the needs of others."
**Douglas MacArthur, U.S. military leader**

---

When we are not the one in charge it is very easy to judge what we would and would not do. The road to an ultimate new workplace is filled with missteps and course corrections. As I said, not everyone is cut out for leadership.

The bottom line for leaders is a simple question: How would you feel about working for you?

"One of the main things I've learned in my career is that you never know who is watching. I've been surprised again and again, and it has resulted in promotions and amazing opportunities. Just commit to excellence every single day and help everyone along the way, with no other motive besides doing the right thing."

**Natalie Massey, former Executive Assistant, NASA, Washington, D.C.**

# PART 2

# Executive Assistants, Personal Assistants, and Administrative Support Staff Voices

As of this writing, there were 16.6 million administrative professionals in the United States and 500 million in the world.

> "The job as it was thirty years ago no longer exists. But the role isn't vanishing; it's evolving."
> **American Society of Administrative Professionals, 2022 Survey**[23]

The assistant role is one of the most unusual in the workplace because the very nature of the work is defined by its inextricable connection to the person the assistant supports. Very few other roles in a workplace are so dependent for their very existence on another person. And because the people being supported are as different as the stars in the sky, it makes complete sense that there is so much confusion about what assistants do and how they do it.

## Let's back up a little

Karen Nussbaum was an activist in Boston in 1973, when she founded 9to5, a labor movement for those who had become the single largest sector of the U.S. workforce—office workers. At the time, these workers happened to be 100 percent female. In 2021, the group was 93–97 percent female. The organization 9to5 was dedicated to improving working conditions and ensuring the rights of women and families in the United States.

With the support of actress Jane Fonda, *9 to 5* became a feature film comedy based on the movement. It came out in 1980, starring Fonda, Lily Tomlin, and Dolly Parton, and was the highest grossing comedy of the year.

The 9to5 movement created the Raises Not Roses campaign to raise awareness of the assistant role, especially during what used to be National Secretaries Week. The event is now called Administrative Professionals Week (APW) and is observed during the last full week of April.[24]

## Breaking stereotypes: The evolving role of the assistant

Please note that "Administrative Professional" is the umbrella term for all assistant roles.

The role of Executive Assistants has changed drastically since the post-World War II images of efficient secretaries who typed sixty words per minute on a manual typewriter, filed papers, answered the phone, and made a great cup of coffee. (Oh, and she cleared the dishes, too.)

Historically, secretaries/assistants/administrative staff have not been considered a "must-have" group of staffers. They were easily replaced ("the typing pool") and not highly paid, and the work was perceived as not particularly difficult to perform. Because of this perception, assistants were not offered professional development training or considered for promotion beyond the administrative staff. It was an easy point of entry into a company, usually at the receptionist level. In the current workplace, assistant roles are still considered an easy point of entry into companies.

My own mother, Ruth Low, worked as a secretary into the 1980s. As you can see from this photo, Mom took great pride in her work.

Watching my mother, I saw the dynamics of office life; secretaries were often disrespected and intimidated by managers. She did not cry often, but I remember her breaking down after work one day because her manager yelled at her again in front of other people over an error on a document. She felt humiliated, and I will never forget the look on her face. I know that look very well now. Mom found another job not long after that.

## Changing perception: "The Case for Executive Assistants" by Melba J. Duncan for *Harvard Business Review*, 2011[25]

Technology and the global 24/7 nature of business has driven the rapid advancement of the Executive Assistant role. In May 2011, Melba J. Duncan penned what is now considered an iconic article for *Harvard Business Review* called "The Case for Executive Assistants." Duncan writes:

> "At very senior levels, the return on investment from a skilled assistant can be substantial. Consider a senior executive whose total compensation package is $1 million annually, who works with an assistant who earns $80,000. For the organization to break even, the assistant

must make the executive 8 percent more productive than he or she would be working solo—for instance, the assistant needs to save the executive roughly five hours in a 60-hour workweek. In reality, good assistants save their bosses much more than that. They ensure that meetings begin on time with prep material delivered in advance. They optimize travel schedules and enable remote decision making, keeping projects on track. And they filter the distractions that can turn a manager into a reactive type who spends all day answering e-mail instead of a leader who proactively sets the organization's agenda. As Robert Pozen writes in this issue: A top-notch assistant 'is crucial to being productive.'"

The piece concludes, "Executive–assistant relationships are business partnerships: Strong ones are win-wins between smart people. In fact, they're win-win-wins because ultimately the companies reap the benefits."

Melba's article is still considered a touchstone for understanding the high-value qualities and skills of an Executive Assistant working today. Her words paint a vastly different picture from the stereotypes of the past. Assistants often give this article to their leaders and HR as a way of improving the understanding of what is possible for the role.

There is still confusion over what exactly assistants do for many reasons. Those reasons are:

- **Titles.** While the title "secretary" has been phased out in most companies, there are over a hundred other titles for this administrative role. These include: Administrative Assistant, Executive Assistant, Administrative Business Partner, and Administrative Project Manager. Globally, the title "Executive Assistant" is still the most commonly used.
- **Job Descriptions.** Many companies have obsolete and generic job descriptions for this role that don't address the true responsibilities of the assistant.
- **Haphazard and nonexistent career paths for assistants.** The role has historically not been viewed as a pipeline into

other roles within a company. Rather, the perception has been that it is a dead-end job, not the professional career it actually is.

- **Leaders and lack of education.** Business schools, in general, don't teach the value of support staff or how to delegate to them to save time and, therefore, money.
- **Uniqueness.** There are few other roles in business that are, by definition, intended to support another person. It follows that since all people are different, with unique preferences and workstyles, every partnership between leaders and assistants is unique as well.

In the training I do around the world, I see that when leaders and HR professionals are clear about the potential of assistants to fully leverage their time and resources, highly skilled Executive Business Partners can be hired to fill those positions.

In 2022, the average salary of an experienced C-suite Executive Business Partner in a major market such as New York City or San Francisco ranges from $125,000 to $150,000, plus bonus and benefits. These six-figure salaries speak to the increased levels of responsibility held by administrative professionals.

## More about executive business partnerships

Henry Ford said, "Chop your own wood and it warms you twice." While that may be true, I would argue with Mr. Ford that chopping his own wood was probably not the best use of his time. That is why he had a staff. In our workplace, it is more important than ever to work in partnership and collaboration with the staff, the people who are already on the payroll and are uniquely qualified to sit in the seats they occupy.

**ANN HIATT,** *former Executive Assistant to Jeff Bezos, leadership strategist, and author of* Bet on Yourself
For three years, Ann Hiatt worked as the Executive Assistant to Jeff Bezos, CEO of Amazon. She formerly worked for Marissa Mayer at

Yahoo and Eric Schmidt at Google and now is a business strategist for CEOs all over the world. Her advice for assistants who want to function as Executive Business Partners is rooted in these experiences.

Hiatt's advice for assistants: "Leaders crave team members who are smart, strategic and have a bias for action. Anyone wanting to successfully partner with a strong leader needs to be equally bold, ambitious, and willing to take on big projects—often outside the confines of their traditional job description. This is where you not only learn but get noticed and build a reputation as a leader yourself. Share your talents, growth goals, and vision for impact out loud! Create a win-win scenario where you are able to grow your desired skill set by taking on challenges that simultaneously serve the greater needs of your organization."

On hiring strategy: "Jeff Bezos had a simple, yet high bar for building world class teams. He only ever hired people he had to hold back, not push forward."

On working through crisis and adversity: "No one is expecting perfect performance. Take control and put yourself in the driver's seat of your own life."

**JENNIFER WILNER,** *my Executive Business Partner*
My assistant since 2012 has been Jennifer Wilner. On her birthday in 2022, I wrote a social media post on my LinkedIn profile which received 7,382 views, rather than the several hundred views that most of my posts receive. I share this story to make the point that it matters to show sincere and consistent public and private appreciation to your assistants and to all staff. This acknowledgment is not only important to your assistant. It is important for the larger community.


## Case study: Danielle De Wulf, Administrative Project Coordinator, Janssen Pharmaceutical Companies of Johnson & Johnson, Belgium

Johnson & Johnson has company leaders worldwide committed to driving innovation for patients and to recognizing the valuable contributions of employees. I had the pleasure of working with seven

Executive Assistants at a Be the Ultimate Assistant workshop held at their Brussels location in November 2019. I was very impressed by the company's commitment to excellence, team collaboration, and career satisfaction. As a result, they have high employee retention, productivity, and a crystal-clear sense of purpose. I wanted to know how that happened.

Administrative Project Coordinator for thirty years, Danielle De Wulf explains an ongoing commitment to and support for professional development as a cornerstone for the administrative staff. This happens through programs that focus on four levels of development:

1. Health
2. Talents and Skills
3. Values
4. Relationships with colleagues

The "Healthiest Careers Center" program supports this thinking, and employees can explore other careers or areas in the company.

Feedback is important for the staff's development. There are five performance conversations each year. This fact alone sets the organization apart from so many others. These evaluations give the staff opportunities for dialogue around interests and ways to expand their roles.

For example, years ago during one such meeting, De Wulf recalls being asked to deliver an internal presentation, which was something she had never done before. It was a "stretch goal" which turned out so well that speaking and teaching became part of De Wulf's job description.

De Wulf sums it up in a pie metaphor. She sees work as a pie and a work in progress. Each chocolate crumble in her pie represents one of the many tasks she does. Ideally, the entire pie would represent work that you love and are excited about doing every day. However, in the real world, she sees the pie as having three parts. The biggest piece is "yeah" work you really like and are great at doing, so you get your kick and energy from this part of your job. The "bwah" piece represents the work you don't enjoy doing and/or are not good at. The "wow" work represents stepping out of your comfort zone and learning new and interesting skills.

When exploring new horizons and practicing new competencies, you move from "wow" to "yeah" work. And then you are ready to take on new challenges. This lifelong learning attitude is essential to keeping you on top of your game and increasing your market value.

With this pie metaphor in mind, you can make an inventory of likes and dislikes in your job, share this information with your peers, and see whether you can swap pieces of your pie with your colleagues. You do not always have to change jobs to increase job satisfaction. In the end, everyone will be doing more work that they enjoy.

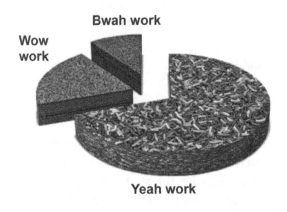

*Graphic Credit: Danielle De Wulf*

## What leaders think about assistants

**DOUGLAS CONANT,** *former CEO of Campbell Soup Company, author of* The Blueprint

"Executive Assistants are exquisite problem solvers and the unsung heroes of our workplace. For too long, they were prisoners of a system that did not serve them well, and I believe that is changing. They touch every area of an organization and are able to help leaders leverage their time in powerful ways that directly impact the bottom line. That was true for me. You get what you pay for. I have always viewed my compensation as a package deal with my EA because they empower me to do my job. They do things that I don't know how to do. Frankly, an EA's salary is a cheap date in the whole scheme of a company budget, especially considering the high value of their role."[26]

**CATHLEEN SCHREINER GATES,** *CEO of SimpleNexus*
"I have worked with EAs for the past thirty years. They were all absolutely essential to the company's success and that is what was key. I always had the word 'liaison' in their titles and this ruffled some feathers because it was not traditional. However, the role was to ensure that those who needed access to me could get it. And if they were blocked from getting resources, that they had an advocate in my office. My teams were mostly scattered around the country managing our clients in their respective geographies and, therefore, could not 'walk the halls' of HQ trying to get something done. In addition, I found that the 'Executive Liaisons' loved being so critical to the business."

**CHRIS BRODHEAD,** *Owner, Famous Founder*
"I work with a number of virtual assistants. They have various specific tasks I have designed for them and the entire business would fall apart without them. The impact to my bottom-line profits is immense. One of my favorite ways to interview staff is by taking them out to a restaurant to see how they treat the waitstaff."

## Case study: Julie Kavanaugh, Executive Director of Administration, Vectrus Corporation

Julie Kavanaugh has thirty-five years' experience as an Executive Assistant and Chief of Staff. At Vectrus, she was hired in 2020 to manage a team of seven administrative staff and promoted in 2021. She then expanded the team to sixteen people based in six U.S. cities. To get the best results from her team, Kavanaugh met one-on-one not only with the assistants, but with the leaders they support. In doing this, she gained firsthand knowledge of all the players, their preferences, and their concerns.

Each month, Kavanaugh holds a virtual team meeting led by an assistant. At each meeting, one of the assistants is asked the following questions:

- What have I learned this week?
- What was I most proud of?

- What made me laugh?
- How did I push myself?
- What surprised me?
- How did I move one step closer to my goals?

These questions promote a commitment to excellence and build team rapport. Kavanaugh often brings guest speakers to this meeting, beginning with the CEO of the company. She has set clear expectations that she believes in lifelong learning and ongoing professional development as a way of making the team as strong, confident, and skilled as possible.

Kavanaugh initiated a virtual monthly mentoring meeting that is for the assistants only and that she does not attend. The assistants take turns leading that meeting, which is a team-building and leadership experience.

On International Women's Day, Kavanaugh sent a note of appreciation to her team, which, at the time, happened to all be women. "May your day be filled with happiness, joy, and good health. Celebrate the phenomenal women you are. Thank you for all your unyielding efforts."

In conversations with members of her team, I have heard the following sentences from most of them: "We've never worked with someone like Julie. For the first time in my career, I feel free to be myself in my job."

Kavanaugh's actions show respect for her team and build confidence among its individual members. In a matter of months, her team became high performing and proactive, proving their ROI every day.

## The secret sauce: Internal assistants' networks

When it comes to building an ultimate new workplace in which the administrative staff is valued and strongly supported, one of the keys to success is support for an internal assistant network. Sometimes these groups fall under the umbrella of employee resource groups (ERGs). Ideally, they are given a budget and one or more executive sponsors. Multiple sponsors are important for the continuity of these groups in the event that one of the sponsors leaves the company. The goal is for members to come together on a regular basis, in person or virtually, for networking, team building, and information/best practice peer-to-peer learning and sharing. The groups are often led by a committee of experienced and upper-level executive assistants.

It is common for members to meet monthly or quarterly and for there to be special events through the year, especially around Administrative Professionals Week in April and the December holidays. These events can vary from country to country.

In the 2000s, there has been a marked increase in the number of these internal assistant network groups around the world. The workplace has become increasingly complicated, driving the need for information sharing among the staff. Assistants teaching one another is a low-cost way to have peer-to-peer training, specific to them.

A recent trend is to have a representative from this group attend executive leadership team (ELT) meetings as a smart way to keep the information flowing smoothly and accurately between the staff and leadership/management.

## Case study: Assistant is named acting CEO of the company

**DEBBIE FURLANO,** *Executive Administrator to the CEO, Rabine Group, Schaumburg, Illinois*
"I had been supporting CEO Gary Rabine as his Executive Assistant for five years in June 2016. I remember sitting in a hospital with my own family member after an eighteen-hour surgery. As I sat there, I started getting calls from company staff that I was to be acting President/CEO of Gary's company. Me? What?!

"Gary was spending time with his wife Cheryl after her brain surgery, and it was going to be touch and go for a couple of months. We hadn't had any discussions about me taking over for him so these phone calls were a surprise. I kept the email that went out at 12:30 a.m. to the executive team. It read:

> I will be giving Debbie the responsibility to represent me in the decisions of President/CEO. I will

> trust her to make most decisions and she will get
> me involved as needed. Debbie has shown herself
> to be totally capable of making great decisions and
> holding me as well as many others accountable.
> She is very good at being accountable. Gary

"Due to our close working arrangement, Gary knew I would always step in and help where needed, so that is why I got the email when everyone else got the email. It still caught me by surprise.

"Some of the executives were upset and also surprised, wondering why 'Debbie, the assistant' was put in charge over any of the C-suite executives or general managers. Gary was undeterred and, as a result, so was I. During that six-month period that I was the acting CEO, Gary came in once each week for an hour or two. We had to make a number of tough decisions about management and culture changes that were difficult but necessary. During those months, we created new processes when finding gaps in accountability as well. Gary backed all of my decisions during that period, and I learned how many hours a CEO really puts in. I am thankful that, as his Executive Administrator, I was able to share his burden and free up his time during this life-altering time for him. Cheryl passed away in 2020.

"In my role, I am lucky enough to be behind the curtain and able to voice my opinion, empowered to make decisions, review financials, and be a part of the senior leadership team. I also learned all the skills necessary to run my own business if I would ever choose to take that step. For me, being involved in the background and being allowed to influence decisions for a number of businesses and multiple other projects is more rewarding and fulfilling than the prestige of saying I was acting President/CEO.

"The title helped me get things done, but it was most important for me to be appreciated and fairly compensated for my contributions, which is why we are still working together today."

Note from Bonnie: Gary interviewed me for his *Ditch Digger CEO* podcast. In it, Gary says that Debbie's involvement in his businesses and in his life results in his company being two to three times more profitable. A pretty great ROI by anyone's measure, I would say.[27]

## Case study: Assistants leveraging opportunities

**NATALIE MASSEY,** *former Executive Assistant at NASA, Washington, D.C.*
Natalie Massey worked as an Executive Assistant at NASA. With twenty-five years on the job, she was one of the most senior civilians at the organization. Here is her story.

"At the age of seventeen in my senior year in high school, I applied for and received a NASA work-study program entry-level position. Although my first choice was the Library of Congress, due to my desire at that time to be a writer, NASA called first and I accepted the offer. Coincidently, two weeks later, the Library of Congress called; however, I had already committed to NASA and did not want to rescind the opportunity.

"I vividly recall the very first day of work. My father, with his steady yet comforting voice, sat me down and said, 'Remember not every Black person is your friend and not every White person is your enemy.' That statement has carried me throughout my entire career at NASA. It was a message that helped me to adapt in a professional setting, a government agency. It also strengthened my ability to engage with colleagues from all walks of life, even those who do not look like me, or talk like me. It taught me to not prejudge and to learn and work with everyone for the betterment of the job.

"I am often reminded of how hard I worked, and still do, and how eager I was to do a great job. I liked getting dressed up every day for work. I was a sponge and learned everything I could. When the work-study program was set to conclude and I was embarking on graduation, I was surprised when my supervisor offered an opportunity to work at the agency on a term basis while attending college. And if I committed to working there at least a year postgraduation, NASA would pay for my entire college education! I jumped at this opportunity.

"NASA has a mentor/buddy system that provides a great pipeline for talent. I know I was exposed at an early stage to great leadership. I have been promoted several times, mainly through referrals, and each time I worked to exceed my executive's expectations.

"After the George Floyd murder in May 2020, my supervisor came to me to ask for guidance on what NASA's plan would be to move forward with diversity and inclusion initiatives. I was honored to be asked about my thoughts and, of course, offered my recommendations, which included listening sessions with staff.

"When I think about the career of working as an Executive Assistant, I believe your job is an extension and expression of your personal values and goals. One of our mottos at NASA is 'Failure is not an option.' When teams work in true collaboration, there is a spirit of genuine compromise. Our collective goal becomes 'Let's get to a yes.'"

## Case study: Assistant saves her CEO's life

**LINDA MCFARLAND,** *former Executive Assistant,*
*San Francisco Bay Area*

One of the most powerful save-the-day stories I have ever heard comes from Linda McFarland, an Executive Assistant from the Silicon Valley. This event happened when Linda had already been working as an EA for twenty-five years, and this story proves that experience really matters.

"It was the holiday season, and our office held a luncheon on a Friday afternoon just before Christmas. I had been supporting the CEO for about six months. During lunch, I sat at the same table as the CEO. We were sharing our holiday plans, and my executive said he was driving up to Tahoe to ski for the weekend with some friends. He was trying to get some skiing in before traveling to Florida to be with his family for Christmas.

"I had just heard about some severe weather that was forecast for Tahoe, even whiteout conditions with frigid temperatures. I asked my boss if he was sure he really wanted to ski with such unpredictable weather. Being a former Marine, a runner, and an avid skier, his response was, 'No, I'll be fine.' I asked him for the hotel information, and he responded, 'Linda, don't worry. It's a personal trip. All you need is my cell number.' Although I understood it was a personal trip, I said, 'You are the CEO. It's my job to know where you are in case I need to reach out to you.' He said, 'Calling my cell should be good enough. I'll see you on Monday before I go to Florida.' That was the end of the conversation, and we wished each other a great weekend.

"On Monday morning, I arrived at the office around 8:15 a.m. and the CEO's office was dark. Immediately, I knew something was off, as the CEO always arrived at 7:00 a.m. with his typical Marine precision. Usually, if he was going to be late, he would send an email or leave a voicemail. I called his cell phone. It went straight to voicemail. I called the home phone and got voicemail there, too. I checked again for messages. Nothing. I remembered one of the friends he was going to meet, so I gave the friend a call. Luckily, he picked up the phone.

"I asked him if he had connected with my boss over the weekend and explained that he hadn't arrived at the office and wasn't answering his phone. His friend was immediately alarmed. He explained that the weather was so awful that he hadn't arrived until Saturday morning. He had tried to connect with my boss, but with no luck. With the weather conditions getting worse, he decided to drive back home early Sunday morning. I blurted out, 'So you left him there? Did you even search for him?' He was silent for several seconds. Before he could answer, I said, 'What was the name of the hotel? I want to call to see if he ever came back to his room. Maybe there's a chance he is still there.'

"I dialed the number for the hotel, and the front desk told me that he had never returned, so his things were in storage. I quickly called back the CEO's friend and gave him the news. He was already in his car, driving back to Tahoe. It was time to check in with the CEO's wife. His friend and I decided to divide and conquer. He called the CEO's wife, and I started calling different resorts. Maybe his car was sitting in one of their parking lots. After several calls with no success, my phone rang. It was the CEO's friend calling to let me know the hotel had the license plate number of his car.

"It didn't take long to learn that his car had been towed from Squaw Valley. Finally, we knew where to look for him. It was now 11:00 a.m. and time to call the search and rescue team. I gave them all the information I knew. They did a quick check-in with the CEO's wife and off they went. With the low temperatures and the whiteout storm, they weren't optimistic.

"At 1:00 p.m., search and rescue found my boss by helicopter on the opposite side of the mountain from where he had started. He had lost his way in the whiteout conditions and found a mountain ledge that managed to protect him from the storm. He ate snow to stay alive and tried to burn his paper money to stay warm. His cell phone didn't have coverage and soon the battery was dead. The search and rescue team were amazed at his resilience. When he was found, he even ran toward the helicopter.

"Once at the hospital, the CEO called to thank me for taking immediate action to find him. He was exhausted and had felt himself fading fast. Seeing the helicopter had given him renewed hope. From that time on, he always shared his whereabouts."

## What assistants wished leaders knew

**JEREMY BURROWS,** *EA to the CEO of Capacity, author of*
The Leader Assistant
"You want to know how to grow your business in a postpandemic world. And you *really* want to know how to find, hire, and retain top talent in such a competitive market. But what if the solution to both problems is one and the same? How do you grow revenue, reduce costs, and retain your best people? You embrace automation so your team is free to do their best work.

"No one wants to answer the same questions over and over. Your team doesn't look forward to days full of repetitive, manual processes. Sure, you can pay well (and you should), but if you can't automate the mundane—so your team can focus on meaningful, creative, and engaging work—you're not going to make it. So let your team be human again. Embrace automation. Build a business people *want* to work for."

**ANONYMOUS**
"I wish leaders really understood how many hours outside 9:00 a.m. to 5:00 p.m. involve work and how much personal time is interrupted by calls, emails, and requests. Understand that the "simple request" might involve hours of work behind the scenes. Often, we spend time on our vacation keeping up with work, as we don't have backup staff covering for us. If leaders put in crazy hours, at least they are paid fairly. We are not only underpaid, but very often underappreciated for all this extra work."

## How it really is: Assistants are a company's "Google"

In our workshops, I show a clip from the 1997 film *Air Force One*, starring Harrison Ford as the President. When the hijackers take over the plane and cut the communication lines, the President and his advisors try to figure out how to reverse the situation. Through a group of men emerges a female assistant; she tells everyone the hijackers likely overlooked the second phone line, which turns out to be the case. The assistant knows better than anyone else on that plane. Yes, this is fiction. However, most assistants have had situations in which they knew better than anyone else how to solve a problem. They know who to call, where the file lives, and what password to use. Why do they have these answers? Because people talk to them, and the nature of the work is that they need to know. They are often referred to as the go-to person in a company, or the company's "Google."

## What salaries do Executive Assistants make?

According to Melba Duncan, President of the Duncan Group in New York City, Executive Assistants in the C-suite in 2022 who are functioning as strategic business partners and life managers are earning base salaries of $150,000–$200,000 in the major geographic markets of New York City, San Francisco, and Chicago. At lower levels of responsibility and in smaller geographic markets, starting salaries of $100,000 are the norm.

Incentives for high performers can include signing bonuses, annual bonuses, training budgets, stock options, and flexible work arrangements.

## What about Personal Assistants, and how much do they make?

Personal Assistants provide support on a personal basis for a principal and their family. These assistants are referred to as private service professionals (PSPs) and they typically work out of their employer's home, but not always. Private service professionals include butlers, estate managers, chefs, nannies, and any staffer who works in the home. In the current workplace, a hybrid role referred to as a PA/EA—Personal and Executive Assistant—has emerged. This is someone who handles both professional and personal responsibilities for their principals. In my work with Olympia Dukakis, I functioned as a PA/EA. Salaries for Personal Assistants range broadly but can go as high as $400,000.

## The future for Executive Assistants and Executive Business Partners

Since 1992, the World Administrators Summit has convened, helping the leaders of global administrative and office professionals, their associations, and stakeholders to design informed plans for the future of the administrative profession. The WA-Summit is now managed by the World Administrators Alliance, which produced the Global Skills Matrix in 2021. I serve the WA-Alliance in an advisory capacity, with special emphasis on combating workplace bullying.

The Global Skills Matrix is a framework for career progression for the administrative role in any given company. The matrix offers levels 1–5, making it possible to associate degrees of work responsibilities with each level. In addition, the matrix identifies career progression opportunities to realize the potential of an effective administrator to an organization. The higher the level, the more responsibility and compensation accompanies it. The Global Skills Matrix is free for anyone to access and is designed to be easily customized to any company or organization, no matter where in the world they are located.[28]

See Job Descriptions for an example of a C-suite Executive Assistant job description.

## Training for Executive Assistants and Executive Business Partners

In a workplace that is changing by the day, especially with major advances in computer technology and artificial intelligence, it is increasingly common for administrative professionals to be encouraged to take ongoing professional development training to stay up to date. Annual training budgets of $1,000–$10,000 per year are commonly included in the overall compensation package.

The assistants of today hold undergraduate degrees and some have additional degrees that are paid for, partially and wholly, by their companies.

Some organizations work on both PCs and Apple computers; therefore, assistants may need to be fluent in both. It is very common for assistants to attend training for certification in the Microsoft Office Suite and other specialized workshops required for their particular roles. For example, a course in graphic design may be desired for work in marketing and on websites.

Supporting assistants as they get advanced training means creating budgets to pay for registrations and giving paid time off to take that training. These commitments are an increasingly important factor in job satisfaction and employee retention. Training is also helping Executive Assistants enter the pipeline for promotion into other areas of the company, such as Chief of Staff and project management. These are important developments in the evolution of the role.

**ANONYMOUS**

"In my thirty-five-year career as an EA, I have learned that training is paramount to the success of an assistant. I have rarely been supported by the companies I've worked for to get outside training, but I have made it a priority within my own personal budget to get whatever training I deemed necessary. Company leaders would be best served by investing in training and making sure that the time is counted as paid time off (PTO)."

## Technology training for assistants is a must-have

Job postings for an assistant role will most likely include "must be tech-savvy" under the "Qualifications" heading. That term is too broad, according to Vickie Sokol Evans, founder of RedCape and one of the top technology trainers in the world. Together, we have taught everyone from corporate executives to the staffs who support them at our Be the Ultimate Assistant workshops.

The majority of our students report that they are self-taught and admit that when they don't know something, they go to online videos. While many companies offer their own online video library for technology, our students say that they are too general and do not address their needs. Further, students say that after their companies roll out new software, they receive little to no training on how to use it.

Given how fast new software and apps are proliferating, the self-taught strategy is not working anymore. To maximize efficiency, ensure accuracy, and save precious time, specific and relevant technology training is a must-have.

Many job candidates claim to be tech-savvy. But what does that mean? Vickie defines a tech-savvy person as someone who "uses and embraces relevant technology to successfully execute their role and continually increases their technology skills through informal and formal learning. They develop an ongoing plan to maintain their skills with their manager or independently each year as technology evolves."

On the flip side, if a hiring manager is not specific about the tech skills expected for the role, then that manager may end up hiring a social media–savvy employee for a role which actually needs spreadsheet expertise. This is a setup for failure. No matter the position, what's missing after "tech-savvy" are the specific computer skills required for the role.

Questions to consider: Is your company using the Google or Microsoft platform? Is the role in marketing? Are design skills needed? Do they want someone who is fluent on both PC and Mac systems and can support an executive who practices BYOD (bring your own device)?

When leaders are asked what is keeping them up at night, an area of high focus is about accelerating digital transformation in their companies. Spending millions of dollars on the latest computer hardware and software won't do anyone any good if the staff behind the keyboards don't know how to use it. Just like high-performing athletes, members of your high-performing team must keep building their skills, especially tech skills.

Use RedCape's tech-savvy core and specialty skills charts to identify the needs of your role.

## Advice for assistants looking to advance their careers

1. **Create your own accurate and detailed job description
   highlighting your achievements and skills.** If it needs to
   be five pages, so be it. This document must be fact-based,
   data-driven, and void of emotion. This description is at the
   heart of changing the perception of the role.

2. **Do the research on your salary.** Ask HR for a pay evaluation. Have a serious conversation about the future of your career growth at the company. Given a choice, advocate for salary versus hourly compensation and understand the difference between exempt and nonexempt. Take control and be the CEO of You, Inc.

3. **Be present in your manager's email signature.** Include a line that gives your name, title, and contact information. This sends a powerful message to the recipients of your executive's emails. If your current title does not accurately reflect what you do, officially request a change. Titles matter. They matter a lot.

4. **Know your allies.** Ask them to write letters of support for your portfolio. Keep their emails telling you how amazing you are and thanking you for your hard work.

5. **Be visible and audible.** Make excellence super cool and rewarded. Celebrate the achievements of your peers publicly and privately. Participate in awards in your company and your community. Find ways to toot the horns of others and they will do it for you. This is a challenge for women, but my best advice is to begin. It's not bragging if it's true. Fight the imposter syndrome at every turn.

6. **Dress the way you want to be viewed.** Do you have a signature "look"? Whatever it is, be intentional about your brand and reputation in person, in writing, and on social media. It's up to you how you show up every day.

7. **Commit to ongoing training to keep sharpening your saw.** Ask for an annual training budget and make your case for why a particular training program is useful for your role. Calculate the ROI in terms of saved time and resources, which equals money. For example, if getting your Excel certification will save your manager one hour of time per week, calculate how much money that would save the company. That dollar figure will more than cover the cost of certification. Make your business case for training. Tell your leaders what's in it for them if they support you.

If they still say no, pay for it yourself. Don't allow money to stop you from getting the training you need.

8.  **Be proactive.** Ask to sit in on meetings and volunteer for projects that will stretch you, including managing others. Don't wait to be asked. Be ready to say why you want to do these things. Assistants are volunteering to help with onboarding, re-onboarding, offboarding, disaster planning, reentry to the office, cybersecurity, and succession planning, to name just a few projects. Don't hesitate to offer an idea if you have one that will solve a problem! Be ready to articulate what's in it for them if they say yes to you.

9.  **Read what your managers are reading.** This helps you stay up to speed and ask relevant questions to bolster your knowledge.

10. **Don't limit yourself.** Don't allow your lack of a college degree stop you from applying for a job that you know you can handle. Let your skills do the talking. The data shows that women, especially, self-limit.

## Conclusion

The administrative staff in our world's companies are needed more than ever. Their roles need to be viewed in an increasingly strategic way as part of a career progression that can create a pipeline to other areas of the company. Whether employees are working virtually or in person, an ultimate new workplace will be one that fully utilizes and leverages this rich natural resource, the administrative staff.

"We have a very high retention rate. It's common sense, really. Our goal is to treat people like people. We work to find ways to have our people take full ownership of their own careers. They are free to be who they are and to explore areas of interest."

**Senior HR Director**

# PART 3

# HR–Human Resource Professionals' Voices

Human resources (HR) professionals are vital constituents and stakeholders in the new workplace and they hold responsibilities not only for recruiting, hiring, and supporting employees, but also payroll, compliance, health and safety, and disciplinary inquiries. In the new workplace, the spotlight is on HR, as the scope of their work has expanded quickly into diversity and inclusion programs, advanced training and development, employee resource groups (ERGs), and mental health and wellness initiatives. Spoiler alert: It's a lot.

A major challenge in the work of HR professionals is that they are generally not viewed as allies by staff; and as such, they are often not trusted. HR is seen as either overwhelmed or out of touch, or sometimes both. When issues arise, staff is reluctant and often refuses to turn to the human resources professionals in their organizations. I am troubled by HR's negative reputation with staff. A very real us-versus-them dynamic exists, and I want this book to help change that. HR has an important voice in the workplace, and their voices need to be heard in collaboration with the other constituencies.

When I spoke about workplace bullying at the HRSouthwest Conference in 2018, I had many discussions with HR professionals who also want to make things better. When I shared the general perception that HR is not considered an advocate for assistants, one responded, "Tell the assistants that they are absolutely right." Others nodded in reluctant agreement.

In a world and workplace turned upside down in the pandemic, with stress and anxiety at high levels, we can clearly see the glaring areas of need from the staff. We have urgent and serious work to do. These characterizations, these perceptions of HR left over from a prepandemic world, are not helpful or productive as we try to find solutions for the very real new problems that exist in our workplace. We need strong bridges to support positive communication between all the constituencies of staff. In the current workplace and for the foreseeable future, a bright spotlight is on HR (a.k.a. People Operations and People and Culture) as the people responsible for sorting out the chaos in the new workplace. Other names for these professionals are People Officers and Talent Managers. For the purposes of this chapter, I am going to use the term "HR" to refer to this job function.

It is a profession in great transition as some HR functions are outsourced to external companies and some HR staff are based in another country. Some are "fractional" staff who work for only a fraction of a full-time position.

HR has a mammoth responsibility to coordinate response to a workforce that is now working both from home and in brick-and-mortar offices. Even these offices may look very different physically, due to many new safety and health protocols. Structural renovations have provided the ability to stay physically distant.

For clarity, here are the departments that typically comprise HR:

- Recruiting and Staffing
- Health and Safety
- Training and Learning Development
- Compensation and Benefits, a.k.a Total Rewards
- Labor and Employee Relations

Pre- and postpandemic, the pressure on HR has been enormous. One exhausted HR professional described 2020 as "grim day-to-day torture filled with death and destruction," and he is not alone.

He represents thousands of frontline HR office workers who were shaken to their core by the Covid-19 pandemic. It has been a traumatizing experience with long-lasting impact. No class in HR school prepared them for this crisis. He commented that HR finds itself challenged to meet every new situation each day "with optimism, hope, and truth."

Another HR professional commented, "Overnight we were expected to be infectious disease and vaccination policy experts, and it just was chaos. It wasn't fair."

If HR is viewed by assistants as adversaries in the workplace, it is most definitely not the ideal circumstance for breaking down silos. However, in conversations with assistants and HR professionals, I have found that these two constituencies have much in common and they use similar language in speaking about their roles.

## Areas of commonality between HR and assistants:

- Both groups want to be strategic business partners with their leaders.
- Both groups want to have a seat at the leadership table and be a respected voice there.
- Both groups say that they received little to no formal training for the job and that they fell into the profession.
- Both groups say they often feel their role is misunderstood and/or not respected.
- Both groups say they have been asked to do things that are illegal and/or unethical in their work.
- Both groups say that they are mostly self-taught and have often had to pay for their own professional development training. Given how complicated the workplace has become, both groups believe their training should be paid for by the company.

At the beginning of this chapter, I wrote that staff have a trust issue with HR professionals and that this is a global problem. I have asked HR professionals directly how we can build back trust and credibility.

## Empathy for HR

Much more empathy is needed for HR. To be clear, there were already plenty of complex challenges on their plates prepandemic. They included:

- Active shooter plans
- Creating meaningful diversity, equity, and inclusion programs
- Workplace bullying investigations
- Sexual harassment cases
- Salary evaluations and surveys
- Performance evaluations
- Job description creation and updates

Over lunch at the HRSouthwest Conference I referenced earlier, a group of HR professionals were talking about how they learned to conduct workplace bullying investigations. The consensus was clear. One told me, "No one trained us. We hope that someone on the staff has done it before so we can ask them how to do it."

It was these kinds of conversations that made me think that HR and Executive Assistants have much more in common than not. For one thing, both groups are tasked to perform important responsibilities with little to no training. We can do better.

Experts from all sectors are weighing in on the work that HR needs to do in a new and uncertain landscape.

## What salaries do HR professionals make?

Depending on the size of the company, level of responsibility, education, and the number of direct reports, salaries range from $70,000 to $140,000.

**JOHNNY C. TAYLOR JR.,** *President and Chief Executive Officer, Society for Human Resource Management*
HR is on the front lines of today's workplace challenges and that is why I reached out to Johnny C. Taylor Jr. of the Society for Human Resource Management (SHRM) headquartered in Virginia. Taylor's

background as an entertainment lawyer in Hollywood created an easy way for the two of us to relate to the staffs who run offices, specifically the administrative staff.

Taylor said, "In my career, I have worked with many assistants and what I know is that they function as the glue and the way things get done. Historically, I can see how they are a group of people, in general, who feel marginalized and forced to play by a separate set of rules compared to other staff. In the postpandemic workplace, I believe that Executive Assistants will be critical in stabilizing companies. My advice to HR and to managers is to activate them, enlist them to solve problems, respect them, and pay them fairly so they stay."

**CHRISTINA BELL,** *twenty-year HR leader in healthcare, Dallas*
"How do we build trust between HR and the staff? In response to that question, I would ask two others: What is the business trying to accomplish? What do the leaders value? In 2022, we are in a very employee-friendly workplace environment, which is motivating leaders to value ways to retain and reward high-producing staff. The bottom line to having trust in the workplace is to be trustworthy.

"From the beginning of my HR career, my organizations paid for my training. One important course I took was on learning how to conduct bullying investigations. I referred to David Ulrich's work and books. This training empowered me to sit in on leadership meetings, and when certain questionable ideas would be presented, I remember asking my executive after the meeting, 'Isn't that illegal?' I would be right. What most people don't understand about HR is how much there is to know legally, combined with understanding the leader's hiring philosophy at any given company. It takes hard work to have the right answer, and I admit it makes me frustrated when HR professionals get it wrong.

"As I look to the future, I am concerned about burnout and lack of work-life balance. The logical question to ask leaders is: Are you properly staffed? We must do better to build resilience in our staff, and the strongest teams are the ones who built resilience before they needed it.

"Sustaining a strongly defined culture with more staff working from home now takes skilled collaboration between leaders, HR, and the staff."

## War for talent?

McKinsey & Company advises us to "treat talent as the scarcer capital," and Jenny Johnson, the CEO of Franklin Templeton, says, "This is becoming a massive war for talent. If you haven't started thinking about whether your employees are going to be remote or not, well, your competitors are, and they will pick off your talents."

Richard Edelman, CEO of Edelman Public Relations, reiterates that point by saying that "employees are now considered a company's key to long-term success." Frankly, I would argue that it has always been that way, so I am happy to know that staff is now being openly acknowledged for the valuable position they occupy.

In today's workplace, staffers who are not offered the right combination of flexibility, salary, and benefits, such as professional development, are resigning and finding new work in companies where the culture suits their needs.

Andy Bird, CEO of Pearson, commented, "We have seen a massive increase in the need for corporations to reskill and upskill their employees. In many ways, companies are becoming the universities of the future."

Goldman Sachs President John Waldron says that their strategy for addressing burnout and resignation is simply to hire more people to handle the heavy workload. He stated that during the pandemic, they were underresourced and he wishes they had acted sooner. "We want people to stay here longer and feel really good about their career opportunities."

Fran Katsoudas, the Chief People, Policy, and Purpose Officer of Cisco (the number one best company to work for in 2021) is tackling burnout as a serious risk factor. She is an advocate of Zoom-free Fridays and using retention bonuses as rewards for going above and beyond. They conduct frequent mental health surveys to keep her team's fingers on the pulse of how employees are honestly feeling. After a prolonged period of high anxiety and overwhelming worry, her teams make mental health a high priority.[29]

Says Katsoudas, "Many of the best ideas come from our employees." For example, in response to feedback that staff were worried

about their children's education, the company initiated tutoring benefits. They also make life coaches available to the staff.[30]

The questions that leaders are asking HR include:

- How do we sustain employee productivity and engagement in a virtual environment?
- How do we measure success?
- How do we motivate our staff to genuinely want to go back
  into the office?
- How do we anticipate and prevent burnout, which leads to
  resignations and costly turnover?

McKinsey recommends a focus on creating a clear company culture defined by a unique set of values, practices, rituals, symbols, and
experiences. Staff who will be loyal and consistently high producers
are ones who find the culture simple to navigate, meaningful, and en-
joyable. Make the physical office environment attractive, comfortable,
and safe.

## Case study: Director of HR for over thirty years

A Director of HR shared her ideas with me about the core value of staff
knowing that they have the freedom to be who they are and to do work
that utilizes their subject matter expertise.

She discussed the importance of choosing words that accurately
describe the staff. They use "leader" over "manager" because the term
is people-focused, rather than about managing a project. They use the
word "talent" rather than "employees" because that's what they are—
talent. They have "task forces" rather than "committees."

She said that the heart of having high retention is creating a culture where the staff feels free to be who they are, and to do work that is
purposeful and means something to them. As Director of HR, she sees
that her job is to stay closely connected to the staff so that leaders can
be alerted to issues in real time.

## Building an ultimate new workplace: Advice from the experts

**AMY WRIGHT,** *Managing Partner of IBM Talent & Transformation*
"Employees now expect that their employers take an active role in supporting their physical and emotional health and providing training in the skills they need to work in new ways. Our research finds a significant disconnect in how executive leaders and employees believe companies have been addressing these gaps. There is an increased urgency for HR to drive this transformation inside organizations, but to do so, HR itself must be reinvented and the Chief HR Officer (CHRO) role must evolve as the CFO role did in 2008. This is an opportunity for organizations to rethink their workforce strategy and gain urgent buy-in and adoption from senior leadership."[31]

**LAURIE RUETTIMANN,** *host of the* Punk Rock HR *podcast,*
*https://laurieruettimann.com/podcast/*
"HR has a deserved reputation for disliking conflict and doing all we can to avoid it, but in 2020, we saw how much HR should really be redoubling our efforts to teach people how to communicate with respect and dignity. Doing this would positively impact not just day-to-day communications within departments or cross-functionally, but it could also benefit society as a whole."

**MICHAEL FENLON,** *Chief People Officer, PwC*
In a workplace where the competition for high-value employees is fierce, Fenlon has led PwC in making the professional services firm a great place for everyone to work. PwC invested $3 billion in 2019 on an upskilling program for all of its 275,000 employees over the following three to four years. Employees who agreed to participate in the training were guaranteed a job at PwC even if their roles are lost to automation.

**MAYA MARCUS,** *Vice President of People, Palo Alto Networks*
From *Business Insider*: "Palo Alto Networks was one of the first companies in the cybersecurity industry to publicly share its diversity data and commit to improving it. Marcus led the organization in partnering with the Girl Scouts, the National Society of Black Engineers, and

Black Girls Code to educate the next generation of diverse cybersecurity professionals.[32]

"Marcus knows that company culture doesn't change overnight. She said, 'Culture comes to life in the everyday choices made by each and every employee in how we treat each other, our customers, our partners, and the candidates we interview.'"

**CHRIS WINTON,** *Vice President of HR, FedEx*
"My aim every day is to help connect the dots between an individual's personal goals and how they can help the company's goals. We developed the Employment Pathways Program to prepare young people eighteen to twenty-four years old for IT and STEM jobs."[33]

**BETH F.,** *HR professional*
"Paid staff is not 'family.' Leaders do their staff a disservice to lead them in this personal direction. It is irresponsible, dangerous, and manipulative for leaders to sell company values using this manipulative language. This causes a blurred sense of reality, which ultimately produces results that are heavily weighted toward the employer's gain. It lulls employees into a false sense of security, purpose, and responsibility.

"Inevitably, the business situation changes. When negative feedback is given, hard times befall the employee, or, for a myriad of other reasons, staff are unceremoniously let go. Being fired is always hard, but to the employee who has been told they are family, it feels even harder. It results in feelings of disillusionment and betrayal, and it can be destructive to their self-worth. The unfortunate truth is if you were to die tomorrow, your job posting would be up before your obituary. We need to do better by our staff."

## In real life: What staff thinks about HR

### ANONYMOUS
"For financial reasons, our local HR department was outsourced from the United States to Asia. The results have been chaotic and frustrating. For example, it depended on the person you were finally able to

reach to determine how many paid days you could take off for the funeral of a grandparent. Now, first you get a robot, which usually replies that it doesn't understand your question, then you need to wait for a reply from a human, and often the reply is incomplete. Outsourcing may seem like it is saving money, but the reality is that getting complete and accurate answers takes more time and is less customer-friendly than having local colleagues."

## Moving forward

The new workplace is demanding the creation of new and trustworthy organizational structures and systems responsive to the changing world. Human Resource professionals are tasked with designing them while they are "flying the plane." Just as there is a need for the restructure of the administrative staff in organizations, so too is there a need to restructure HR operations. My hope is that HR staff will have an important voice in building the new structures in strong collaboration with their leaders and fellow staff. Doing that will build trust and be a setup for ultimate success.

"Everybody is a genius. But if you judge a fish by its ability to climb a tree, it will live its whole life believing that it is stupid."

**Unknown**

# PART 4

# Recruiters' Voices

Recruiters who are both internal and external to companies know that in order for job candidates to be as marketable as possible, the candidates need relevant, focused, and intensive training. When the candidates receive training, they are more ready to command the highest salaries in their market. That is why they send their assistant candidates to me.

What does a Recruiter's job actually entail as they work to find the right candidates for staff roles? The Recruiters of the world are an important constituency in the new workplace, and just like Leaders, Assistants, and HR professionals, Recruiters have a tough job, too. Yes, they can make big money on commissions from their placements (20 percent of a candidate's annual salary is not uncommon), but they work extremely hard for those commissions and sometimes have to split the fees with other recruiters, not unlike realtors.

Let's walk in the shoes of a Recruiter.

## What Recruiters want from candidates

1. Resumes that are up to date, with no typos or grammatical errors. Pay attention to the minute details like consistency in formatting with font sizes, periods after phrases, etc. Dates of graduation and employment matter and they will be checked. Inconsistent dates are grounds for dismissal and rescinding

job offers. Be sure your resume matches your social media profiles exactly.

2. Do your homework on the company and the recruiter. Read the websites and mass media coverage. Come prepared with good questions.

3. Be honest about your technology skills.

4. Do not badmouth former employers. To do this tells the recruiter that you would behave similarly with your next employer.

5. Protect your personal brand on social media. Be mindful of the images of you that appear online.

6. Be prompt for appointments; if you are going to be late, call ahead. Dress for the role you seek, even in the virtual world. It matters. Show up as professionally on a webcam as you would for an in-person interview.

7. Stay in touch with Recruiters. They can receive hundreds of resumes each day for one posting. They do not intentionally "ghost" candidates, but the sheer volume of email is difficult to juggle.

## What candidates want from Recruiters

1. Candidates want Recruiters to do better communicating with them. They get frustrated when recruiters go silent on them, a.k.a. ghosting. It feels disrespectful and like they are simply a warm body rather than a real person worthy of meaningful interaction.

2. Candidates want Recruiters to advocate for higher salaries when the job description requirements do not match the compensation.

3. Candidates want Recruiters to advocate for improved packages, including annual training budgets, signing bonuses, stock options, and generous vacation time.

4. Candidates want Recruiters to post real jobs, not ones that are just meant to generate resumes.

5. Candidates want Recruiters to post salary ranges with job openings.

## What frustrates Recruiters

1. Incorrect or incomplete information about a job description sourced from HR or from leaders. That impacts everything about the search for a proper candidate.
2. Hiring managers and/or principals who change their mind about the requirements of a position.
3. Hiring managers who insist on making a college degree mandatory rather than preferred.

**LENI MILLER,** *President of EASearch and author of* Finding Right Work: Five Steps to a Life You Love
"Over my career, I have seen a dramatic shift and change in business infrastructure and the profession of executive support. In my work consulting and recruiting senior-level Executive Assistants, I know that the acute shortage of good professionals is based primarily on limited educational opportunities. Critically needed are training opportunities in technology, communication, finance, business operations, administrative operations, and management.

"Thanks in part to this shortage of trained executive support staff, salaries in northern California have risen 20+ percent since 2017. However, compensation is still far lower than the level of their contribution merits.

"Executive Assistants have now emerged as members of a profession unto itself, just as accountants, paralegals, lawyers, doctors, nurses, and architects have. It is time that there is training and development in this profession just as there is in all other professional specialty areas in our culture."

**CHRISTOPHER BAKER,** *Recruiter*
"The best part of my job is making great placements that last for ten or more years. This is what I strive for every day. One of the toughest parts of my job is having to tell an amazing candidate that my client decided to hire the other amazing candidate.

"What most people don't understand about recruiters is that if we had our wish, we would place every single candidate whose resume we receive. Our very livelihood is dependent on making placements, and our clients are very specific about who and what they want. We do our best to get them to broaden their horizons about candidates when it comes to salaries, years of experience, and skills requirements, but the clients will only go so far, if they budge at all. In a sense, we are personal shoppers of human capital.

"The stakes are high. If we don't deliver who and what they want, they will sever their relationship with us and move on to the next recruitment firm.

"Some HR professionals don't give us enough detail and nuances of the job opening, and there is an absence of a well-crafted and comprehensive job description. In addition, some are slow to respond, and when they do, we receive very little feedback about what might be lacking in a candidate.

"My contention is most established CEOs didn't get to be CEOs without knowing the fundamentals on how to hire, reward, and retain top-notch employees. Whether the CEOs respect and follow these fundamentals is another matter entirely, unfortunately.

"My advice for leaders? I recommend creating a line item in comp packages providing every opportunity for continuing education and training. Pay them generously and encourage key hires to share their suggestions/input so they feel their opinions are valued. Be in tune with staff morale and come up with creative ways to increase it when it needs a boost.

"To my clients who are seeking the best of the best in who they hire, I tell them that there is rarely such a thing as a 'perfect' candidate and as long as they understand that first class always costs more, we will endeavor to come as close to their ideal as possible."

Still another recruiter tells clients, "It costs more to go first class."

"I was a proud workaholic and for most of my life, I wore that title as a badge of honor. And now in my forties, I barely remember my thirties. I traveled over 200 days of the year to exciting and exotic places. I loved my work, but I learned that the work does not love you back.

"In that love of work, I lost myself. Simon saw my workaholism and threatened to not give me my bonus one year if I did not stop sending emails at 1:00 a.m. I almost gave up the money because I could not stop myself. My self-worth was so completely tied to my work. Looking back, I wish I had given more time for me. I paid a dear price. Watch out. You can easily trick yourself to justify any behavior. I'm living proof."

**Monique Helstrom, former Chief of Simon (Sinek)**

# CHAPTER SIX

# Secrets

"Anything that's human is mentionable, and anything that is mentionable can be more manageable. When we can talk about our feelings, they become less overwhelming, less upsetting, and less scary. The people we trust with that important talk can help us know that we are not alone."

**Fred Rogers**

Everybody has secrets. Our secrets are sometimes referred to as our "baggage." They are our past, our DNA, and the things that make us who we are. This chapter highlights how our histories—our secrets—show up in all kinds of ways in the workplace and impact whole company cultures.

I have a theory that people put one another in boxes. We size people up as we get to know them, and we assign labels. For example, let's talk about Sue, who is a well-respected C-suite executive. She is also a mom of three kids and she is devoted to them and to her husband. Sue hosts all the family holiday dinners and loves to cook. Sue's direct reports know she is committed to a work-life balance and makes it a high priority. That's Sue's box.

But what we know about Sue is only a small part of her story. My theory is that as much as we know about Sue, there is much more that we do not know, nor should we. These are the things that are outside of the box.

Sue allows the world to see the parts that she wants to be seen. Don't we all?

I do. I have many examples from childhood and beyond of moments that that directly impacted the way I respond in the workplace. These events happen to us in a heartbeat, and then they can live inside us. Sometimes forever.

## Case study: My story

As a Jewish kid in a mostly non-Jewish New Jersey school, I experienced anti-Semitism. From age seven, I was called a "dirty Jew" and other derogatory terms. One time on the junior high school bus, a kid tried to set my faux fur hat on fire with his cigarette. I smelled the burning and heard the laughing. I quickly removed the hat, but the cruel laughter and looks on the other kids' faces remained. On a few I saw pity and helplessness. Luckily, I was not physically hurt, but I have never forgotten how it felt to be treated as different and as something like an alien. I did not feel that I belonged. I also remember using small scissors to snip off the scorched part of the hat so that my mother would not find out. I'm not sure I ever told her what happened.

The result? I never rode the bus after that day. It felt safer to walk home alone, even in the rain or snow. This event also created a hyper-awareness in me of those who are uncomfortable or who appear like they don't belong. I am drawn to sit with the loners at lunch or to begin a conversation with people who choose to sit at the back of the conference ballroom.

At my own workshops, every one of my students knows that the expectation in our space is that every person is equal and that if they are in the room, they belong there. I have zero tolerance for anything less.

I am living proof of the universal phenomenon of the power of memories; even though decades have gone by, the event on the bus lives on, along with all the feelings that came with it.

The school bus story is only one of the stories that helps define who I am and explain how I behave in the workplace. It is a story that is not obvious as I move in the world, but it can show up fast. I share it to make the point that all of us have events in our pasts that impact our present. It is important to acknowledge that if this is true for ourselves, it is true for everyone else, too.

## Case study: Anonymous

Dramatic deathbed confessions don't only happen in movies. "Rose" had been a mid-level manager for the majority of her career. She had two grown sons who adored her, as did her four grandchildren. Over the years, Rose volunteered at a women's shelter and was active in causes that impacted young women. As a soft-spoken and talented manager, she hired young mothers, often against the advice of other managers. She was known for her steely determination. That was Rose's "box."

During Rose's final days at age ninety-five, she told her sons that she had to tell them something very important and that she could not die without telling them her story. Rose shared a secret that she had been carrying with her. At age seventeen, Rose had gotten pregnant and had an abortion. The shame was so great that she tried to commit suicide by jumping off a bridge. She was saved, and her second chance convinced her to spend her life helping others, specifically single moms who needed a break. This secret had weighed heavily for decades and drove many of her daily decisions.

Life's traumatic events can and often do have a direct connection to how we behave at work and in life.

These events have a broad spectrum of severity, and what may seem catastrophic to one person could be considered just a difficult day for someone else. From my coaching conversations, I know that many people are functioning in emotional pain every day. What varies is how close to the surface the pain is. We must be sensitive to triggers that may bring a strong response front and center when we least expect it.

The Holmes-Rahe Stress Inventory lists the following ten life events as the most stressful for adults, to such an extent that they can potentially make you sick—physically and emotionally.

*The Holmes-Rahe Stress Inventory of the Ten*
*Most Stressful Life Events for Adults*[34]

1. Death of a spouse
2. Divorce
3. Marriage separation
4. Imprisonment
5. Death of a close family member
6. Major injury or illness
7. Marriage
8. Job loss
9. Marriage reconciliation
10. Retirement

Most of us can easily relate to one or more of these stressors. However, while some people around us may have been directly impacted by 9/11 or the Sandy Hook Elementary School shooting or Hurricane Katrina, or the Covid-19 virus, the signs may not obvious. It is impossible to tell on the surface what someone is wrestling with on the inside.

Most of us don't know what traumatic events have happened to others, how long ago any particular traumatic event occurred, or to what degree an event is preoccupying them.

To build an ultimate new workplace, it is important to acknowledge what holds us back, what stops us, and what motivates us like nothing else. Those are our secrets. Different people have different tolerances for adversity and trauma. They do not provoke the same reaction from everyone, which is what makes the workplace complicated and tricky and endlessly fascinating.

Leaders and every person in our workplace can help others simply by understanding that there may be forces at work that no one else can see.

## And then there's more real life

Many have heard about the Holmes-Rahe Stress Inventory. However, based on my work all over the world, I've learned there is much more in play for people in our workplace.

We can't assume the same event will impact everyone the same way. For example, an assistant at a large company in Texas was a superfan of the music legend Prince. It was well known among her colleagues that she would take vacation days to travel to see him perform. The news of his sudden death in 2016 hit the assistant very hard and she was distraught. Her colleagues and managers took up a collection for her to attend the funeral in Minneapolis. The assistant was moved by the kindness and sensitivity of her coworkers, and it helped her to have support in her grieving. It made all the difference and the whole team felt a part of the experience.

The following traumatic situations are weighing on some of your coworkers' minds. They distract and preoccupy and come to the surface when triggered. While I hope none of the following apply to you, I suspect you know people that have been impacted by them.

These situations are in alphabetical order and are not organized by severity, which is different for everyone.

- Abandonment as a child or adult
- Abortion
- Abusive parent(s) or guardian(s)
- Adoption
- Affair with a married person (sometimes with a coworker, sometimes not)
- Alcoholism
- Bankruptcy
- Being arrested
- Broken home
- Bullying in the home
- Bullying in the workplace by a manager or coworker (experienced or witnessed)
- Coming out as an alternative gender
- Criminal record
- Death of a beloved pet
- Discrimination (age, race, gender)
- Divorce
- DNA test proving you have a different parent/ family than you thought
- Domestic violence
- Drug addiction/substance abuse (illegal or legal drugs)
- Eviction
- Getting fired (made worse if via text message, being walked out by security, etc.)
- Health issue that no one knows about
- Hiding a sexual orientation

- Mental illness
- Natural disaster (hurricane, tornado, blizzard, etc.) destroying home and lives
- Partner/family member absconding with all the family money
- Phobias
- Premature or violent death of a parent, spouse, child, sibling, relative, friend, or partner
- Prison time
- PTSD: post-traumatic stress disorder caused by military service, loss of loved ones from 9/11, the pandemic, or another traumatic event
- School violence: experienced or witnessed an active shooter event

- Serious and/or chronic illness of yourself or someone close
- Sexual assault as a child or at any age by someone who was trusted (family member, friend, clergy)
- Sexual assault in the military (In 2018, more than 20,000 military service members were sexually assaulted)[35]
- Sex change procedures
- Sexual harassment
- Spouse living a double life, having multiple families
- Suicide attempt
- Weight issues (anorexia, bulimia, stomach stapling surgery, etc.)
- Workaholism

## Case study: When a loved one dies

An assistant's mother passed away on a Thursday. The assistant called her manager to tell her the news and to say that she needed a few days to make plans. The manager's annoyed response: "How soon will you be back? We have a lot of work to do." The manager's insensitivity resulted in the assistant finding another job within a year.

Our reaction to life events matters in the workplace. Most of us remember the kindnesses we received, but we also remember when people were not there for us. Those reactions can mean the difference between loyalty and going above and beyond or getting the air sucked out of you.

If a coworker has an unusually strong reaction to a personal or world event, like the pandemic, allow some space for these feelings to be processed. Leaders can demonstrate sensitivity by connecting one-on-one to gently ask, "How are you?" and "How can I help?"

I teach my students to look at everyone in their lives with fresh eyes and to know that as much as you know about them, there is at least an equal amount that you have absolutely no idea about. For that reason, choose to release automatic judgments and instead consider why someone might experience a strong reaction to an event. There is rarely a bad time to genuinely say, "I care about you and hope you are OK. If you need help or someone to talk to, I'm here."

We will be well on our way to an ultimate new workplace if we choose to slow down our responses and become more thoughtful of others' behaviors.

Given the breadth of stress and anxiety-provoking events that staff are silently handling, it is increasingly important for companies to offer top-notch mental health services and resources to address them. Removing the stigma around these issues is necessary, appreciated, and highly motivating to staff.

## STAFF MATTERS QUESTIONS

1. What did you learn in this chapter about secrets that you can use?
2. How do the secrets you hold trigger certain behaviors and responses? Can you see how the secrets we hold can trigger behaviors in the workplace?
3. What mental health resources are available at your company for the staff? Is more needed to improve them?

We all remember our first kiss, our first car, our first job, our first day. Firsts are really important because they stay with us for a lifetime. Lasts are pretty important, too.

# CHAPTER SEVEN

# Firsts

We remember our firsts forever and reference them often. In the workplace, we refer to the five firsts: first hour, first day, first week, first paycheck, and first year anniversary. We remember all of these in detail. Thus, it is important to devote time and attention to firsts for all staff. In companies of all sizes, however, that is not happening. Poor onboarding chases good new hires away.

In conversations and in workshops, I ask attendees about the onboarding processes at their companies. I am eager to find out which companies are doing it really well and what that looks like. Unfortunately, the news is not good. The majority of my students feel their entry to the company was rocky and that they were set up to sink or swim, with no lifeguard or raft. The message they received was loud and clear: you are on your own—figure it out somehow. That makes for an unstable work experience from day one.

How does that serve anyone? It doesn't.

Onboarding is the beginning. It has the power to make or break employee retention. I discovered that the endings (offboarding) need improvement, too.

My mother, Ruth Low, worked as a secretary in New Jersey. She passed at the age of eighty-nine in 2009. As I grew up, I witnessed the old paradigm of a staffer being hired and shown to her desk. There's your phone, your filing cabinet, and your typewriter. See you in twenty-five years when you receive your gold watch at a farewell party.

You might be surprised to read that when this story is shared in class as "the way it used to be," students respond by saying that what I described is how it is right now in their company. One student works as an Executive Assistant for one of the biggest firms in the world.

Ideally, we want our staff to acclimate happily and effectively as quickly as possible so that they can do the work they were hired to do in the first place. We want staff to feel confident and fully prepared, not only for their first day, but for the entire experience of working at the company. Part of feeling like they are on solid ground and being set up for success involves removing uncertainty and confusion about where they should go, what they should do, and who they should contact with questions. These factors apply whether the job is in person or remote.

Pretty basic, right? On the surface, those seem like realistic or reasonable expectations. However, my students report the following situations in some of America's most prestigious companies:

- On day one, no one knew they were starting, so they sat in an outer office while annoyed staffers tried to sort things out.
- Little to no orientation.
- No tour of the building.
- No training.
- No introductions to fellow staff.
- No instruction on how to use the phone system or to log in to their computer.
- They felt like they were bothering other busy staffers by asking questions.
- Ambiguous rules about when it's okay to work at home and when it is not.

If you have had this onboarding experience, of course you remember it and talk about it. The downsides of allowing these oversights to occur in your company are numerous, including negative word of mouth and reviews on online crowdsourced job sites. At its extreme, some staffers feel disillusioned and disappointed that the company is disorganized, and they look for another job. That is a big waste of money and time for everyone, a lose-lose situation.

## The pandemic fallout

If in-person onboarding has been problematic, then onboarding people virtually (sometimes across time zones) has caused a seismic shift. HR departments have been severely challenged. In fact, some companies simply enacted a hiring freeze early in the pandemic because they had no way to onboard new staff remotely.

In response to these changes, one trend is to involve the administrative staff in the onboarding of other administrative staff and some managers. The administrative staff require minimal training to step into onboarding responsibilities. Another trend is the creation of re-onboarding plans for staff who were hired during the pandemic and now are back in person and require new acclimation.

At one large company, the onboarding is not handled by HR, but by each department individually. The assistants in each department onboard other assistants and the managers. This is a system that works for them, and it will work as long as there are several people who know how to do it. Without this knowledge base, the system will fall apart if the onboarder leaves the company.

## What's the fix?

Many companies offer a SharePoint, Teams, or other internal shared online platform where staffers can view videos on onboarding subjects. Those are definitely helpful as part of the process.

However, think back to your first day of a job. You were perhaps nervous, excited, anxious, and more than a little scared. Are you really in the mindset to watch videos and learn from them?

Humans need humans to show them the ropes, even if it is virtually.

Novartis is a company that handles onboarding simply and effectively. It's called the Buddy System. Longtime Senior Administrative

Assistant Jocelyn Williams is a "buddy." She explains that new staffers are assigned a buddy from the first day to give them a tour, introduce them to other staff, and show them the ropes about "the way things are." This buddy functions as a lifeline and a willing support system, someone who totally gets why coffee is important and can tell you the best place to order lunch. A staffer can have this buddy well beyond the first day, for as long as necessary. At Novartis, not everyone is a buddy or wants to be a buddy. People need to apply to be a buddy. Buddies can be mentors, but not always. More about mentors in chapter 12.[36]

I am keenly aware that no onboarding system is perfect, and all systems sometimes break down and make staff frustrated. However, in general and in principle, the Novartis staff I spoke with love the simplicity of the system and believe it is a contributing factor to employee satisfaction, retention, engagement, and general happiness at the company. The people who are buddies love doing it. They feel useful and important.

Here are elements of a strong and effective onboarding system, which, of course, need to be customized for each job's function.

1.  Planning: Serious thought needs to go into what the experience of day one, week one, month one, and year one look like. Certainly, preparatory materials (documents, videos, etc.) can be given to staffers before they begin work. The goal is to have 100 percent clarity on the basics of where to go, what to do, and who to see on the first day.

2.  Meetings: Organize face-to-face and/or videoconferencing meetings with managers and fellow staff. These meetings help reinforce the company culture on meeting etiquette, dress code, and level of formality. Do not make your new hires guess about any of these important details. Starting a new job is stressful enough.

3.  Social strategizing: Focus on social interactions so staffers get to know the players as quickly as possible and schedule a mix of formal and informal interactions that help develop easy rapport. Sharing organizational charts help with understanding who reports to whom, etc.

4.  Training: Plan for training in week one. All computer

systems are not made alike and there are often glitches that occur. Have someone literally sit with your new staffers (in person or virtually) to get them comfortable with the devices being used and the way passwords are managed.

5.  User manuals: One current trend that I really love is the creation of "user manuals" that managers and staff write themselves to help their teams know them better. They serve to shortcut and fast-track the building of rapport and trust, which is especially important in a virtual world.[37] The topics include, but are not limited to:

    • SME: top three areas of subject matter expertise
    • Time of day when I am the most productive
    • Preferred communication style (text, email, phone, 1:1, videoconference)
    • Attitudes about meetings (how long, how many in a day/week, how many people max?)
    • Hate the phone/fine talking on the phone
    • Coffee or tea? Favorite place to get it? What size and how do I take it?
    • Top three qualities I look for in my team
    • How do people win with me? (behaviors I value)
    • How do people lose with me? (pet peeves and gripes)
    • Top five things to know about me that may not be obvious

## Onboarding for executives

While a user manual is a great idea to expose personality and preferences, it is a best practice for Executive Assistants to design and complete a more formal and comprehensive onboarding form for each executive they support. The information contained in this document is about travel preferences and confidential information such as passport number, driver's license number, credit card numbers, PINs, passwords, etc. The form also can include preferential information, such as people on the "interrupt" list. These forms are not one-size-fits-all because they are as unique as the people whose names are on them.

The sooner an Executive Assistant can obtain this hard data before beginning to support an executive, the faster they can get up to speed with completing tasks. Some assistants refer to this document as their "bible" for their executive.

## Orientation for executives

Orientation is a specific aspect of onboarding, especially for executives, which deserves its own section because of its importance and newness. What I see all over the world is that *everyone* needs orientation to a new company. A welcome trend is the implementation of an orientation for new and even current executives, specifically around the *ways to utilize their assistants.*

Doing this is a setup for success. Here's why: assistants report that executives and HR have very little idea what to expect of an assistant or how to best leverage their time together. These issues are complicated by the trend of assistants supporting multiple executives; therefore, their working time is split into fractions. All of these factors cause confusion for executives.

Sometimes assistants experience frustration from being underutilized or undervalued by executives who have not been trained on how to work with them. This frustration sometimes escalates into quitting.

The companies implementing orientations for executives are experiencing very positive results. Ideally, these sessions are not longer than an hour and are in person. These sessions are led by an experienced Executive Assistant and/or an HR staffer and can be delivered one-on-one or in a group. Executives welcome the information because it reduces stress and anxiety not only for them, but for the assistants, too. The reality is that most executives have never received training on how to utilize an assistant.

One of the most successful orientations for new executives at a financial company in New York City includes the following points. Some may appear minor or superfluous, but I assure you they are not. These details matter. They are remembered and can make all the difference in staff retention. The orientation begins with a clear conversation about the specific kinds of tasks and responsibilities that assistants will do at this company. Unless there is a protocol against it, these responsibilities often include personal tasks as well.

1. The importance of saying
   - Good morning/Good night, [first name].
   - Hello/Goodbye
   - Please
   - Thank you
   - You're welcome
2. Pronounce first and last names the way the assistant wants them pronounced. Nothing is more personal than someone's name, and data shows that humans thrive when they hear their own name. True story: after two years of working with an executive who intentionally mispronounced her name, an assistant quit because of how disrespected and insulted she felt.

After one such executive orientation, an assistant called the person who had led the session and said, "What did you say to my manager? I can't believe that he now says 'good morning' to me every day and calls me by my name! Awesome job. Thank you."

On the surface, these suggestions may seem trivial and unimportant. I would encourage you to give it a try and see what happens. Orienting all executives who have people reporting to them about the best ways to utilize and leverage their team is a smart best practice and it deserves serious consideration as required training. The time spent up front with orientation will pay off in the long term.

## STAFF MATTERS QUESTIONS

1. How effective is your company's onboarding plan?
2. What ideas from this chapter could work at your company?
3. Who needs to get involved to build a better onboarding plan?

*All the time, we hear that our people are the backbone of the company, a leader's right arm, the face of the company culture, the brand ambassadors, the eyes, the ears, and the glue. Leaders openly say that there would be no company without the staff. We painstakingly vet, interview, and hire them. Why then, after all that trouble, if our people are so valuable, are too many treated so poorly?*

# CHAPTER EIGHT

# Hiring & Firing

One of the workplace's biggest conundrums is the gaping disconnect between what we know about how staff should be managed, developed, and compensated, and how staff is *actually* managed, developed, and compensated. This chapter is meant to outline the hard truths of the situation.

## The reason to hire is the search for subject matter experts (SMEs)

Hiring is a search for a "SME" in at least one area—and most likely many areas—that address a company's needs. The search for a SME happens through the gathering of resumes and interviews. This process is costly, especially if an outside recruiter is enlisted. The fee to the employer (candidates don't pay a fee) is 20 percent (give or take, depending on geography and the recruiter) of a candidate's annual gross salary. Not a small or insignificant amount of money. After a certain number of weeks or months of marketing, vetting, interviewing, and checking references, a person is selected for the position. This "chosen one" joins the rest of the team (the other "chosen ones"). It is important to acknowledge that every company, no matter how small or large, is populated by SMEs. One issue is that SMEs don't usually know the expertise of their colleagues, and making this information more easily accessible is imperative in the new workplace.

Since all staff members were painstakingly chosen, they are deserving of respect on that basis alone. Every staffer is there for a reason, a purpose. One powerful platform for sharing this information is Office365, which offers the opportunity to create profiles for members of a team that can be shared with the whole company. However, it is one thing to have the tool and quite another to use and leverage it. That happens when leaders see the value in connecting their SMEs.

I strongly urge you to create an easy way for staff to understand who they are working with because the benefits are numerous. After all, staff does not walk around with their resumes for everyone to see, and not everyone has a LinkedIn profile. Staff can choose to check out the social media profiles of colleagues, but the system can be streamlined. Women, in particular, are not encouraged to talk about themselves and their areas of expertise. This behavior is viewed negatively, as bragging and tooting your own horn, so most will resist doing it.

Globally, one of the biggest complaints I hear is that companies are not fully leveraging the SMEs whom they have painstakingly hired and placed on the payroll. These humans are a company's most valuable natural resource, and money is lost when we use only a fraction of their abilities.

## Handwriting exercise

At workshops, I conduct an exercise to highlight the subject matter expertise on a team.

> Step 1. On a piece of paper, each person signs their name the way they would on any document.

> Step 2. Each person puts the pen in the other hand and does the same thing.

There is a dramatic reaction! This exercise has been done dozens of times, and each time students laugh and groan and express how awkward it feels to write with their *other* hand. Writing with the hand you always write with represents your areas of expertise, the tasks that are automatic and in your control because you know exactly what to do. These tasks are easy. These are the things about which people can feel confident and even cocky. However, writing with the other hand is out of your comfort zone. It is very unfamiliar and awkward, making you feel like a little kid again. Like most new skills, it would take time, practice, and training to gain expertise.

This exercise is useful in a group because it enables everyone to share with one another both the areas in which they are a SME and the areas in which they are not. Hearing about their fellow SMEs encourages teamwork and mentorship because the tasks that come easily for some of our colleagues feel completely different for others. An awareness of everyone's individual gifts and talents generates enthusiastic support for one another in their areas of expertise. The most productive and effective teams agree to do this generously and without keeping score, and the best managers support them to do so.

> **BEST PRACTICE:** Leaders who see the value in sharing subject matter expertise are finding ways to bring the staff together to share what they know. They are creating spreadsheets that are included on the company website. The spreadsheets contain contact information and the one, two, or three areas of expertise in which the staffer would welcome helping others. Even international companies are doing this with great success.
>
> Until staff is overtly encouraged to know and access the subject matter expertise of their coworkers, they will not be fully leveraging the internal natural resource each person represents.

## "Hire slow. Fire fast." Jeff Hoffman, Cofounder of Priceline

Hoffman's words are prudent and important to heed. Slowing down the process of hiring for the right fit is a setup for success. Speeding up the process just to cross it off the list and put a warm body in a seat is a shortsighted and wasteful business practice.

In our fast-paced world, all the constituencies in our workplace are pressed for time to produce results. Here are some examples of what happens in the hiring process.

1. A leader wants a new assistant yesterday, if not sooner.
2. The HR team scrambles to find candidates using generic job descriptions.
3. External recruiters are pressured to find suitable candidates, despite having inadequate information.
4. Current assistants are pulled into the process to screen resumes and help interview the candidates in hopes of finding a good match for the leader.

As a result of the rush, a host of problems can occur.

## Incomplete, generic, outdated, and nonexistent job descriptions

Detailed job descriptions are critical in the hiring process. It cannot be overstated how important they are in targeting the right candidates and ensuring a proper fit. The hard reality, though, is that not enough time is given to fully describing the job at hand. This description requires getting detailed information directly from the executive, and it would be time and effort well spent. Unfortunately, it is a step that is too often skipped.

Some candidates report that the job description is generic and dated. True story: an assistant in HR said their department is using job descriptions that are ten years old! This is not an uncommon report worldwide, even in large companies.

Other candidates report they are not given a written job description at all during the hiring process. Instead, the recruiter or hiring manager verbally describes the job and the candidate accepts it. I urge against doing this because of the danger of "scope creep," in which job responsibilities are disorganized, confusing, and out of control. The assistant inevitably says that the job description they were told verbally bears very little resemblance to the job they are actually doing. Recourse is limited if there is nothing in writing. My best advice to anyone considering taking a new job without a written job description is to write one yourself based on the information from the interview.

The most successful hires are ones who utilize a detailed and accurate job description based on current, firsthand information from the executive being supported.

> **BEST PRACTICE FOR CANDIDATES:** Insist on a written and detailed job description, even if you have to write it yourself based on what you hear in the interview. Ask follow-up questions to gain further clarity about what will be expected of you.

## 2021: Year of the job description

The pandemic caused major upheaval in the workplace, so it follows that job descriptions have changed, some drastically. For this reason, 2021 was dubbed "The Year of the Job Description." HR is tasked with revamping and updating job descriptions. My advice for HR is to ask the people doing the jobs to revise them because no one understands a job better than the person doing it. Here are a few other factors to consider when revising job descriptions.

1. Does the title fit the role? Titles matter.
2. Are the educational requirements still relevant? Do you really need to require a degree? Would it serve the work better to see candidates taking certain workshops or certifications?
3. What kind of experience is now needed for the role? Do you need to address the new demands of the virtual world?
4. Does the job description clearly outline the expected results?

5.  Does the description identify the title of the person to whom the candidate would report? Is the role realistic, as in, can it be humanly done by one person? This question speaks to the reality that some job descriptions are the equivalent of two full-time jobs, not one.

## Words matter: The language in a job description

Data shows that when women assess a job posting, they feel they need to possess 95 percent of the listed qualifications before applying for the job. This is in contrast to men, who apply even if they only possess 60 percent of the stated qualifications. Therefore, the language used in job descriptions is extremely important if a company is looking to hire more women. The language will consciously or unconsciously either attract or discourage women applicants.[38]

Language that encourages women to apply:
  • Post the salary range. This kind of transparency signals a commitment to fair compensation
  • Make a college degree "preferable but not mandatory"
  • Offer a flexible/hybrid schedule
  • Promote a culture that is committed to work-life integration

Language that discourages women from applying:
  • Must have a "thick skin" (indicates bullying)
  • Physical labor (must be able to lift twenty-five pounds)
  • Words like "superstar," "rock star," or "ninja" can feed into insecurities

At the 2019 Next Gen Summit, Rana Yared, a partner at Goldman Sachs, said, "We changed the vocabulary around recruiting. We used to talk about whether the candidate was 'aggressive' enough to do the job. We removed the word from our recruiting vocabulary. I don't know what 'aggressive' means other than 'obnoxious.' Instead, the questions we ask now are: Are you intellectually curious? Are you assertive when you form a view? And do you have an insatiable desire to learn?"

To decrease gender or racial bias, one HR director removes candidates' names from the top of resumes during the screening process.

## College degree?

One of the results of the Great Resignation of 2021 is the awareness that a college degree is not necessary for all jobs. Job candidates tend to self-eliminate if they see a college degree requirement on the job description, even if they possess all the other qualifications. Hiring managers are realizing they are missing out on stellar candidates. My advice to candidates is to apply anyway, and to highlight their relevant experience and skills.

A March 2018 Society for Human Resource Management (SHRM) survey of six hundred HR professionals found that nine out of ten companies will consider candidates without a college degree, especially if they have relevant certifications.[39] In the new workplace, the trend of companies not requiring a college degree is becoming increasingly common in order to not lose out on stellar candidates.

## Common mistakes in the hiring process

*Mistake no. 1: Accepting a job without even knowing who the person is*

Sometimes candidates are asked to interview for positions without knowing for whom they will be working. This is especially true for high-profile and famous executives. Someone representing the "principal" will interview the candidate.

> **BEST PRACTICE:** Do not accept any job without knowing to whom you will report. Sign a confidentiality agreement if you need to in order to find out this vital information.

*Mistake no. 2: Accepting a job without meeting*
*the person you are meant to support*

I worked for the Oscar-winning actress Olympia Dukakis, and I know dozens of celebrity assistants. It doesn't matter how rich or famous a person is—a candidate needs to meet that person first, before agreeing to work with them. If the candidate will be working with the spouse and/or the children or parents, etc., the candidate should insist on meeting them, too. These meetings can happen via videoconference if necessary. These face-to-face conversations are a very important part of the hiring process; while skipping them might seem like a time-saver, it is actually a setup for failure.

There are many stories of an assistant who goes to work for an executive but does not meet the spouse ahead of time. A few months in, the assistant is fired because the spouse did not like them. This situation may have been avoided had they met before the assistant was hired.

> **BEST PRACTICE:** A candidate needs to insist on meeting all the people and fellow staff they will be working with before agreeing to accept the position. Ideally this meeting will be in person, but at the very least, meet them on a video call.

*Mistake no. 3: Accepting a job after only one interview*

I don't believe either party knows enough about the other after just one interview. A trend that I fully support is to conduct a "working interview" or a "shadowing interview." If, after the first interview, both the executive and the assistant think this might be a fit, assistants are invited to go in on another day for a few hours to observe, to shadow the executive and the current assistant. Some candidates will do some work to demonstrate their abilities even more.

Think about it. Everyone is on their best behavior during a first interview. It's a whole other experience to feel the vibe on a different day, to watch how people interact, to observe the culture in action in real time. People reveal more of who they really are during a second and third interview. This trend is like dating before you get married. It is worth spending the time and energy to ensure a successful match. Recruiters are beginning to suggest it, as well. Most recruiters get paid their commission after a hire has been employed for thirty, sixty, or ninety days. A working interview can cut problems off at the pass, before anyone says "yes."

> **BEST PRACTICE:** Don't accept a job after only one interview, if at all possible. Don't be pressured into making too fast a decision. A working interview is a responsible strategy to ensure success.

*Mistake no. 4: Accepting a job without a written offer*

It is bad enough for a candidate to not be given a written job description. It is an even bigger recipe for failure to not have a written job offer. I have heard too many stories of recruiters being pressured by the hiring manager to give a candidate a verbal offer over the phone and expect an answer on the spot or within the hour. This practice is unfair, inappropriate, and unprofessional.

The stakes are high for everyone in our complicated workplace. For a candidate at any level, this is their livelihood, their career, their life. Their families depend on them. It is too important a decision to be forced to make quickly.

Job offers are not real until they are in writing. It is reasonable to take three to seven days to review an offer with a lawyer, an accountant, and a partner.

Data points in written job offers:

- Annual salary
- Overtime policy
- Annual training budget
- Timetable to discuss future compensation at annual reviews
- Bonus structure
- Vacation time in first year and subsequent years

- Sick days/personal days policy
- Equity plan and stock options
- Health insurance details
- Flex time to work at home
- Perks such as cell phone and/or company car
- Reimbursable expenses such as commuting costs

---

**BEST PRACTICE:** Get all job offers in writing. The time to negotiate is *before* the contract is signed, not after. If in doubt, ask. If still in doubt, ask until you are satisfied with the answer.

---

## Aptitude and personality assessments

Recruiters say that candidates often lie on their resumes and overstate their skills and abilities. That may or may not be true. Either way, it is totally appropriate to ask candidates to take a skills assessment. Of course, this increases the cost and slows down the hiring process, but the benefits are clear.

> "The most important quality in a person is integrity."
> **Warren Buffett**

Another way of determining fit is personality assessments such as the DiSC and CliftonStrengths, two mainstream tests. I include the DiSC Assessment as part of the Be the Ultimate Assistant workshops. The tool gives our students tremendous insights about their own personality as well as the personalities of the people around them. What I particularly like about the DiSC are that the questions are specifically about a person's workplace personality and that the assessment only takes ten minutes. I love the simplicity and the accuracy. Is it 100 percent accurate? No assessment is, but it is a powerful tool in hiring.

Personality assessments are being used as a mainstream tool by many companies to determine fit. They are best used as just one valuable piece of the hiring puzzle.

There is value in having staffers read one another's reports, with mutual consent. This objective data provides a safe resource for conversation and a fuller understanding about another's workplace personality. In fact, some companies value these results so much that a summary graph is posted outside a staffer's office and on their profile, so that everyone entering can see exactly what personality type the staffer possesses. Brilliant idea. My students who have taken the DiSC Assessment report feeling positive about the insights it offers. I believe that personality tests are certainly worth a try in an effort to build a strong and cooperative team.

## For candidates: Resume details matter

About your resume/curriculum vitae: spend time creating a resume that is factual, illuminating, and a visually interesting example of your work product. Your LinkedIn profile should exactly match your resume. Recruiters are checking this. Be hyperdetailed and truthful. If you don't have a college degree, don't say you do. People lose jobs when lies are discovered on these important resource materials. The seemingly small details matter, such as the year of college graduation.

On the LinkedIn free version, include a great headshot and a banner image that tells the story of who you are and communicates your tech savviness. The goal of your resume and your online profile is to inspire the reader to learn more and to call or bring you in for an interview.

*Advice for candidates from* **CHRISTOPHER BAKER**, *Recruiter for Executive & Personal Assistants*

- No typos or spelling errors in resume or cover letter, or on social media (example: there/their/they're, fare/fair, etc.).
- Use professional and appropriate photos on LinkedIn for the kind of role you are pursuing.
- Be sure your resume aligns with the LinkedIn profile and include every single computer proficiency.

- Make sure your skills are sharp, with up-to-the-minute technology.
- Do not lie or embellish your resume about anything, including education. Employers will check employment dates, and lying about this may cause retraction of the offer.
- While some design elements are good to have on a resume, don't overdesign it or have a graphic designer create it. Let it be an example of your work product.
- Be careful not to violate an NDA (nondisclosure agreement) with the details about a previous job on a resume.

## Ageism

From the time I began teaching, I have been hearing my students speak about ageism, which is discrimination on the basis of age. In a post-pandemic workplace that has been massively disrupted, a candidate's age has become less important than the relevant skills and proficiencies they bring to a role. Therefore, a college degree that was achieved over twenty years ago (an indicator of someone's age) may have less value than a technology workshop certification that was earned in the past year. Conversely, candidates may experience ageism because they are young and fresh out of school.

In the current workplace, candidates can avoid and overcome ageism by focusing on their relevant skills, related experiences, and enthusiastic desire to work at XYZ company. Hiring managers tell me they often hire on personality, attitude, and their gut feeling, rather than solely on the resume.

## About the job interview

Have a story and/or explanation ready for everything on your resume. Do your homework on the company and the people interviewing you, including the support staff. You never know who is going to exert the most influence on the decision to hire you. It is a mistake to disregard the receptionist, the assistant, or the security guard. They all talk.

Have you ever been asked what you thought about a candidate? Take good notes, including who you met with and what outfit you wore. Offer to come in on another day for a "working interview" when you can observe and shadow key staff.

If you can, ask for a tour of the office, keeping an eye out for diversity and networking-friendly spaces. Listen to the tone of how people speak with one another. Do your homework! Ask questions, but don't ask anything that can be easily found on the company website.

> "Candidates who find ways to tangibly demonstrate the ability to scratch their executive's itch and ease their pain points will stand out from the pack and rarely, if ever, be unemployed."
> **Nancy Fox, business coach, The Business Fox**

*Candidates can ask questions like:*

- What is your biggest problem at this company and can I offer how I would solve it?
- How do I win with you?
- How do I lose with you?
- What does success look like for this position?
- When I learn information that I feel you need to know, how do you prefer I share it?
- What is the performance review process?
- How does onboarding happen and is there a training period?
- What have been the career paths of others who have held this role?
- What would you consider an unsuccessful hire? What happened?
- How would you describe the company culture and what do you like best about working here?
- How soon can I expect to hear about how you would like to proceed?

*About social media*

Know that hiring managers are reading what you share on all social media platforms, so be careful about the photos you post and the details you reveal about your life, even if your accounts are "private." These impressions can make or break candidates and serve as justification for hiring or disqualification.

*The application process*

In the interest of time, most companies want candidates to apply online. What if a job description asks for a college degree and you attended college but didn't earn the degree? Apply anyway. Including this requirement is one way hiring managers are weeding out candidates. If you are qualified, give them compelling reasons to bring you in for an interview.

What if you are absolutely perfect for a job, but your resume has been rejected? Don't take no for an answer. Give the hiring manager a call, send a snail mail letter, send an email, send a LinkedIn message, send cookies with a clever note, or even (in certain situations) show up in person to drop off your materials. During an interview, one candidate learned that her prospective employer had recently rescued a dog. In her thank-you note, she included several helpful links for new dog owners.

Find someone inside the company who can walk your resume into HR. If you really are perfect for the job, they just don't know it—yet. Find a way. These acts make you stand out, and recruiters are impressed by them.

## How do you hire the best people in the new workplace?

In a postpandemic workplace, the highly prized qualities are grit, adaptability, and resilience. The volatility of the workplace is revealing employees' ability (or inability) to respond smoothly to the ever-changing landscape. Simply put, the question is: How do you respond to adversity?

One Chief of Staff answers that question this way: "When I am evaluating candidates, I think of our team as high-performing airplanes. If our team agrees on a speed of 500 mph as the pace we will maintain with the highest accuracy possible, then it is very important that every member of the team keeps up. If someone begins consistently working at 450 mph and then slows to 400 mph, you can see how certain deadlines will be missed and the work will get slowed down. You can also see the impact on the work if multiple people work at a slower speed. I need to know a candidate's work ethic and commitment to the team. All things being equal, I hire for pace and focus on those kinds of questions during the interview process."

## Case study: Robert Alvarez, former COO and CFO of BigCommerce, Austin, Texas

I had the good fortune to interview Robert Alvarez, the former Chief Operating Officer and Chief Financial Officer of BigCommerce in Austin, Texas, and his Senior Executive Assistant. The company has over six hundred employees. Alvarez believes in servant leadership (that a leader's primary goal is to serve), and he has a strategy for hiring the best people—or at least the best people to work inside the culture he and the team have designed. He talks about looking for candidates who are "humbitious," a combination of humble and ambitious.

First of all, Alvarez interviews almost every new job candidate. His hiring strategy is to assign people to two "buckets" with an emphasis on values.

Bucket 1 is a candidate's qualifications, experience, and skills. These are the things that appear on a job description and reveal if a person is qualified for the job.

Bucket 2 is a candidate's DNA and the way they interact with the world. Bucket 2 holds values such as ambition, humility, ethics, trustworthiness, and integrity.

Alvarez's secret to hiring the best people is to ask questions designed to reveal the contents of their Bucket 2. The questions also reveal the values of the company. Through this process, candidates can then decide if the job is a good fit. Alvarez knows that when tough decisions need to be made, he wants to rely on people who won't hesitate to put the best interests of others ahead of their own. These qualities are in Bucket 2 and cannot be faked. They embody who a person is.

The key to keeping this bucket system working is having leadership and recruiting teams that live and breathe this philosophy. According to Alvarez, it won't work any other way.

*To reveal Bucket 2 qualities, ask candidates the following:*

1. What are the top three factors to which you attribute your success?
2. What fuels your fire?
3. How will this job serve your life?
4. On a scale of 1 to 10, how lucky are you in life?
5. Tell me about a time you were at a company and disappointed someone.
6. Tell me about a time when you were at a company and someone disappointed you.
7. Tell me about a time at a company when you felt your values or beliefs were being compromised. What did you do?
8. If you were starting a company tomorrow, what would the top three core values for your company be?
9. Did you build any lifelong friendships while on past teams?
10. Tell me about a time when you've wanted to quit or did quit. Why? What did you do?
11. Tell me about a time when you witnessed company culture go bad.
12. Tell me about a mentor or coach you've had in the past.

*Here are more questions to consider asking:*

1. How do you learn best?
2. What is one of your favorite stories from your career highlight reel?
3. Did you ever have to deal with a team member who wasn't pulling their weight? What did you do?

4. How do you stay up to date with what is happening in the profession?
5. What's your way to plan for the week ahead?
6. Tell me about a workplace problem that you correctly anticipated. How did you handle it?
7. How would you describe the pace at which you work?
8. Tell me about a time you discovered that you had made an error or a mistake. What happened and how did you handle it?

Hiring is both an art and an inexact science. It is messy matchmaking of a very special kind. It is a complicated two-way street. Leaders in our workplace would be well served to slow the process down. If we work on getting it right the first time, companies can save a lot of money by not having to replace bad hires.

## Stay interviews

I am a big fan of stay interviews. These are different than performance reviews. In stay interviews, staffers and managers meet several times a year to discuss and document what a staffer thinks about their future at the company and what issues may need to be addressed, such as professional development plans. The message sent to the staffer during this interview is that the manager cares about what they think and that it matters if they stay. Managers get to ask questions like, "What is a rule or policy that you would change if you could?"

In a postpandemic workplace, the stay interview results in lower turnover and a higher percentage of loyal, engaged, and committed staffers.

## And then there's ... firing. Isn't there a better way?

Do you know someone who has ever been fired? Have you ever been fired? I have. Just like we remember our first day on a job, we also remember our last day—especially if it was not our choice. The truth is that every job ends sometime. One way or another. The question is: *How* does it end?

My story: In high school, I didn't have many friends or hobbies except for reading and watching movies and television. I was fascinated by the world of modeling and fashion. Early role models were women like Cheryl Tiegs and Cybill Shepherd. I wanted to be them. At age fifteen, I attended the Barbizon School of Modeling and went on to earn money working as a fashion show model.

Fast forward to my freshman year at Rutgers University. When I came home on weekends, I earned extra money teaching modeling until they fired me. Like many college freshman, I had gained the "freshman fifteen" (as in pounds). I was fired because I was too heavy.

As you can imagine, this hurt. Of course, I knew that the world of modeling centers around extraslim women, but this had not been an issue before. I licked my wounded ego and promptly found another job selling cosmetics at a local mall. They didn't care about my extra pounds.

While unforgettable to me, my story is not in the high-trauma category.

I can tell you from stories told in our workshops that one of the most traumatic things you can go through is to be told you are being fired and then have a security guard (who you have known for years) accompany you back to your desk, then stand over you as you quickly put your personal belongings in a box. Your fellow staff watches in stunned silence. It is hard to not feel like a criminal in this situation and it can be traumatizing.

Sometimes the staffer is told the news and then is immediately walked out of the building. They are not given the opportunity to say goodbye to anyone. Personal belongings are mailed to them.

From speaking with dozens of staff around the world, I have learned that this experience is excruciatingly painful and humiliating. The trauma of it lasts a very long time.

Isn't there a better way to fire people? Can we put the humanity back into this inhumane practice?

There is value in rethinking how we fire people. In some cases, both parties want the business relationship to end and it is a relief for everyone. Leaders may want a staffer to leave, but the smartest leaders work to support the staffer to not have a reason to do damage on the way out or after they have left the company. If the employment ends traumatically, the staffer is going to talk about the experience, and the negative word of mouth can be toxic and destructive long after the staffer has been fired.

It is a choice to make firing mean, nasty, and loud. It's stressful and bad enough when someone needs to be fired. After all, it is one of the top ten most stressful situations a human experiences.

There is no easy way to let someone go. Whenever and however possible, choose kindness, compassion, and humanity during the process. Those actions will be remembered and talked about, too.

Imagine your daughter or son is the one who is to be fired. How would you want it to be handled?

## STAFF MATTERS QUESTIONS

1. What are the employee retention numbers by department at your company?
2. How can your hiring and firing processes be made better?
3. Would you want your children to work at your company? Why or why not?

"When I first graduated from law school, I worked as a law clerk for a federal judge in New York City. On my last day at the two-year job, I found a present on my desk. Inside was a pair of gold cuff links from Daisy, our office cleaning lady. I was very surprised and moved by this extravagant gift. When I saw her to thank her, Daisy told me that she gave me the gift because I said 'good morning' to her every day. It was one of the nicest presents anyone ever gave to me. Sometimes you can make a big difference in someone's life without even realizing it. My saying good morning apparently did that for Daisy and Daisy's present did that for me as well."

**Nick Katsoris, author of the Loukoumi**
**book series, New York City**

# CHAPTER NINE

# Culture

"I've learned that people will forget what you said, people will forget what you did, but people will never forget how you made them feel."

**Maya Angelou (also attributed to Carl W. Buehner)**

What does it mean to work at your company? What is the experience like? Company culture is the values that shape how an organization is perceived by the staff and the world. When leadership expert Peter Drucker said, "Culture eats strategy for breakfast," he was referencing the importance of culture and the need to make it a high priority.

Cultures are not all made alike, and staff agree that for a company's culture to have staying power, it must have the support of top leaders. Culture can make staff quit, or it can be their main reason to stay. Since the staff is populated by humans who have strong and specific feelings about how they experience their day-to-day work environment, leaders need to care about these feelings.

Everyone on a team can be well served by a large dose of empathy, of imagining themselves in another's place.

"The key to everything is empathy, because
nothing is more effective and fruitful than the
ability to walk in the shoes of others."
**Satya Nadella, CEO of Microsoft**

Nadella's ideas on empathy explain the huge success of the television show *Undercover Boss*. In the show, CEOs go undercover in
their own companies to see the culture of the company from the staff's
point of view. At the conclusion of every episode, the CEOs reveal who
they are and what they have learned from this powerful experience of
walking in the employees' shoes.

**UNIVERSAL TRUTH:** We all want the person in charge to see
who we really are and what we really do.

## Diversity, equity, inclusion, and belonging

An ultimate new workplace will have companies with strong, focused attention on hiring and retaining a diverse workforce and
policies that create an equitable pipeline for hiring, compensation,
and programming that openly addresses the concerns of staff. It is
not enough for companies to create these policies and programs;
it is vital to be transparent and publish the data. One such hiring
practice is to remove names from resumes during the screening
process, thereby removing information about the applicant's gender
or ethnicity.

In the aftermath of the #MeToo and #TimesUp movements,
companies are offering "civility training" for all employees, designed to build cultures of respect. The reality is that in many companies, the primary motivation for investing in this training is to
reduce the initiation of costly lawsuits and the way that happens
is by reducing cases of harassment through training. Insurance

companies offer preferred rates for companies that incorporate these kinds of trainings because they prove to be effective in reducing harassment claims.

## Bad manager/good manager

I often ask managers to think back to one of their first jobs and to remember the worst manager they ever had. I ask, "What qualities made them a bad manager?" I observe that the body language changes immediately. Fire in some eyes, sadness in others, slumped shoulders. They remember how their bad manager made them feel. I can visibly see it. In workshops, attendees share what comes to their minds about what makes someone a bad manager. Here is what they say:

- Micromanaging
- Out-of-control ego
- Arrogant language
- Humiliating people in front of others
- Lying
- Angry yelling
- Throwing things in the office
- Sexual harassment
- Playing favorites
- Unfair rules
- Making it hard to take time off so employees had to lie
- Neglect
- Unreliability
- Lacking integrity—did not keep their word

I ask, "What effect did these behaviors have on you?"

Answers: "It made me want to quit." "They made me not want to work hard." "It made me call in sick even when I wasn't sick."

Then I say, "Think of the best manager you ever had. What qualities did that person have?"

The body language of the audience shifts again. Leaning forward, smiles, big hand gestures, and even some glistening eyes from the memories. They remember the acts, behaviors, and words that made a best manager. Here is what they say:

- Helped me advance in my career
- Gave me flexibility
- Taught me a lot about the business
- Was happy for my success
- Paid for extra training
- Openly acknowledged me in meetings
- Trusted me with sensitive information
- Showed up at my father's funeral

I ask, "What effect did these behaviors have on you?"

Answers: "I would have laid in front of a truck for my manager." "I was loyal." "I went above and beyond every day, even when no one was watching."

Since culture begins with leaders, it is valuable to spend time asking yourself which category you are in: bad or good? Another useful question is, "Would you want your daughter, son, or best friend to work for you?" Ask the managers this question.

> "Don't keep your people in the dark because
> that's where suspicion grows best."
> **Anonymous**

All staff knows that culture starts at the top, as in the CEO. Meaningful change only occurs with their overt support. Here are a few examples of how C-suite leaders built the culture at their companies.

**Douglas Conant**, former CEO of Campbell Soup Company, wrote in *The Blueprint* that your staff sees everything. When he took over as CEO of Campbell Soup in 2001, business was down and the headquarters in Camden, New Jersey, was in disrepair from aggressive cost cutting and neglect. Conant and his team decided to send a powerful message to everyone associated with Campbell that a new day was dawning. A day of optimism in the face of extremely challenging circumstances. They cleaned up the campus from top to bottom, repainted neglected areas, replaced the razor wire surrounding the complex with tasteful estate fencing, and much more. Over time, these tangible actions, combined with important strategic initiatives, made the future appear both increasingly real and promising for all associated with the company. Conant says the key to the Campbell turnaround was "Civility, starting with the work environment and then advancing that mindset into every nook and cranny of the culture."

**Deanna Mulligan**, former CEO of Guardian Life Insurance Company in New York City, was one of the first corporate leaders to send the staff home to work when the pandemic hit in March 2020. Staff was supported to buy the equipment they needed to work from home, and senior leaders communicated updates to staff regularly. These actions let the staff know that the leaders genuinely cared about them and their wellbeing.

**Joyce Mullen,** President and CEO of Insight Enterprises since January 2022, said that she learned a valuable lesson about being a leader early in her career from a United Auto Workers plant manager. The manager said, "Just paint the bathrooms, Joyce." She did. "In giving the bathrooms a fresh coat of paint, I sent the message that I am willing to spend money to make their physical day-to-day environment better."

She commented, "Figure out what is making their job hard and what issues are getting in the way of having a great day."

## Time off and flexibility. Hold the guilt.

Given the vast age range in our workplace and the fallout from the pandemic, it is no surprise that employees need schedules that can accommodate childcare, special events at school, aging parents, sick partners, and a myriad of other circumstances.

> **UNIVERSAL TRUTH:** A company culture that genuinely supports staff to be good parents, children, and people is the one that is going to be chosen every time. Staffers who are not forced to lie in order to take their child to the doctor or to fly across the country to attend to a dying relative are more loyal, more productive, and more satisfied in their work. They are more willing to go above and beyond because their managers are willing to do the same for them. Kindness is remembered forever. So are slights.

## Absenteeism/presenteeism/quitting

You may have heard the saying, "People don't leave companies, they leave bad managers." Poor managers hurt a company's culture and reputation. If a company is having trouble hiring top talent, management is an important place to look to find out why.

If an employee has decided to leave a job, there is usually time between the decision and the actual departure. There may be damage done by the staff in that period of time *before they leave*. This is passive-aggressive retaliation or punishment against bad managers and real or imagined ill treatment.

These are some of the ways that staff retaliate against poor managers:

- Absenteeism: As a direct result of their bad managers, employees miss work to interview or to have "mental health" days or to enjoy "retail therapy" days. The thought is: my manager treats me badly and this is a way of getting back at them.
- Presenteeism: It is common for an employee who feels

they have a bad manager to think, "Well, if I am not appreciated, why should I work so hard?" The employee is at their desk but doing the bare minimum to get by.

- Stealing: Pilfering either physical objects or information.
- Sabotage: Intentionally deleting or altering information, or not sending information on time.
- Spreading poison: Exerting a negative influence on the morale of other staff.

All of these behaviors cost companies money and cause damage to the culture.

What does culture look like? How does a company communicate its culture? Here are some key questions to help you find out:

- Do the leaders walk the talk of the company's mission and vision? Do staff even know what the company's mission and vision are? On a flight to London, I asked the flight attendant, "What is the number one reason you are so loyal to this airline?" He didn't hesitate. He stood up taller and said, "Pride. I love what our company stands for. This is my home and these people are my family. And I don't care that other airlines pay better. They don't have what this one has. Leaders who treat me like a person."

- Is it a culture of respect or disrespect? One way to tell is if there is a zero-tolerance policy about workplace bullying. Workplace bullying is an epidemic around the world and tolerating it is the fastest way to chase good people away. It is easier for demoralized staff to quit than to confront a yeller or a manager who leads by intimidation and uses public humiliation as a management strategy. Fear creates a suffering-in-silence mentality. When staffers quit, they will rarely share the true reasons at their exit interviews. This is a culture of disrespect. The smartest leaders are the ones who hold bullies and harassers accountable—no matter who they are. Bullies cannot survive in an authentic culture of respect.

- Is the use of profanity accepted or not? Some companies

make clear their point of view on the use of profanity in the workplace. It is much better for potential employees to know this up front, so they can decide if that is the environment that works for them.

- Is it a culture of inclusion or exclusion? Are staffers encouraged to involve their families/pets in their work? Do leaders have a true open-door policy? Are leaders a visible presence? Do leaders hold town halls and ask for input from any and all staff? Is training offered to all staff or just some?

- Do staffers work remotely/virtually and to what degree? In a postpandemic world, working from home is much more the norm, and it is especially helpful for staff who are caring for children and the elderly. The more open leadership can be about setting realistic expectations and flexible policies about working from home, the higher the productivity and loyalty. It is vital that leaders are transparent about the policies and set a guilt-free tone about them to eliminate any dissension among the staff.

- Is there flexibility? Can staff work at home when they want and within workable and agreed-upon parameters? On that same London flight, I asked the flight attendant about the company culture. He shared that the flexibility of schedule and routes motivates him to not seek employment elsewhere. He cares less about the money than he does about the freedom and flexibility.

- Is free food offered as part of employment? Food is a big part of the culture in many companies and attention is being paid to the kind of food choices being offered, such as healthy and culturally diverse options.

- Is there a commitment to employee safety and privacy as reflected by the physical office floor plan?

- Is physical and mental wellness encouraged and openly supported? Meditation rooms, yoga rooms, lactation rooms, nap rooms, gyms, and massage rooms are examples of what might be available.

- Are vacations genuinely supported? Is there unlimited time off or is the culture one of expected workaholism? There is a very real fear, especially among American workers, that if they take a vacation, their time away may reveal that the company can do without them. The result might be getting fired when they return to work. Their solution is to not take vacation or to do work and be accessible during the vacation.

- Is diversity of ethnicity, age, and gender celebrated and embraced or viewed as externally imposed and possibly even inconvenient?
- Is the environment informal or formal? Is it loud or quiet? Are leaders encouraging games like ping-pong or volley-ball and team-building activities such as escape rooms?
- Is there a strict dress code? Any dress code? Rules on tattoos, body piercings, or hairstyles? It is important to share this information up front to avoid any confusion.
- Are there rules on fragrance use and smoking?
- Are there rules on vaccinations and/or face masking?
- Are there rules on how staff can decorate their area? Are personal photos allowed?
- Are birthdays acknowledged or celebrated?
- Are work anniversaries acknowledged and celebrated?
- Is there a separate lunchroom for executives that is off-limits for non-executives? I can tell you that staff deeply resent this setup where it exists.
- Is the culture friendly to nursing mothers and people with physical limitations?
- How generous and flexible are the family leave policies?

Culture is not one-size-fits-all. The fact is that some staff flourish in a more formal environment and others don't. That is precisely why companies need to be specific about the culture, and staffers need to be clear about what they need to thrive.

## Respect is number one

No matter where on the planet I have traveled, the quality of respect is, hands down, the number one thing that employees want in their work.

For people to feel respected and appreciated is even more important than money.[40]

The top four things that staff want most in the workplace are:

1.  Respect
2.  Feeling of belonging/being valued
3.  Fair compensation
4.  Professional development training

Respect can be demonstrated in a myriad of ways. They include:

*   Fellow staffers say, "Good morning, [first name]." This acknowledgment is vitally important because, otherwise, you run the risk of staff feeling like they are merely a number or chair filler.
*   Names are pronounced and spelled correctly. There is nothing more personal than someone's name.
*   The words "please" and "thank you" are important words to use, both out loud and in written communications. The few extra seconds it takes is the difference between a feeling of partnership or dictatorship.
*   Management is transparent and leads "town hall" type meetings to keep the staff updated about the latest news in the company.
*   There is fairness and transparency about rules and policies. Staff knows when things are not fair.
*   Staffers have the opportunity for regular feedback about their performance, and they are also asked for feedback about their managers. It is human nature to want to know how we are doing. Feedback should be given on a regular basis and more than just once a year. Staff should not be blindsided or surprised about their performance.
*   Birthdays and work anniversaries are acknowledged and celebrated in some way which communicates that staffers matter.

- Staffers have a voice in their own destiny; they have a say in what projects they work on.
- Companies with strong cultures of respect set a clear expectation that destructive and toxic behaviors will not be tolerated and that if they exist, swift action will be taken by management. For example, some companies ask all staffers to sign and recommit to their "code of ethics" on an annual basis. This is a key component to their culture of respect.

> "People support a world they helped create."
> **Dale Carnegie**

## Tools that communicate culture

*Company website*

Any person looking to work at a company or do business with a company will go to the website as an obvious first step. The language, images, and videos found there are powerful ways to communicate culture.

*About the Careers tab*

It surprises me when I go to a company website in search of the Careers tab only to find it buried in a submenu or placed at the very bottom of a long home page and in the teeniest font. It seems counterproductive to make this information about culture so hard to find. To do this sends a message that inspiring people to work at this company is not a very high priority for the leaders, or at least the people who designed the website.

The Careers tab is a vital place to articulate culture and what it would mean to work at the company. The companies who do this best write about the value of the staff and what they mean to the company as a whole. This tab highlights the perks of working there and can offer videos featuring actual employees speaking about their experience at the company.

*Employee resource groups*

Employee resource groups (ERGs) are also known as affinity groups. They are designed to bring together staff who have a particular shared interest. Participation is voluntary. These groups are supported by the company's leadership. They play an important role in representing the culture of a company, as they can offer a safe place for self-expression, support, positive action, and social engagement. ERGs might focus on one of the following topics:

- Ethnicity and race
- Anti-racism and discrimination—Black Lives Matter, Stop AAPI Hate, Unidosus
- Anti-sexism/sexual harassment—#MeToo, #TimesUp
- Nationality
- Religion
- Military veterans
- Sexual orientation
- Working parents
- Gender
- Age/longevity in the company—the over-twenty-years-of-experience groups
- Job function—increasingly, the administrative staff has its own ERG
- Remote staffers
- Physical and mental differences (use of mobility devices, neurodivergencies, hearing deficits, etc.)
- Social causes—community volunteerism
- Shared interests—exercise, cooking, meditation, sports teams, etc.

*Time-off policy and backup strategy*

An ultimate workplace is one that acknowledges that people need breaks, time to rest, and vacations that are free of guilt. While some companies offer unlimited time off, sometimes staff are reluctant to take it. Why? Lack of proper backup. I can tell you that employees worldwide are choosing to not take vacations or feel that they must work on vacation because important work won't get done otherwise.

We all can participate in the solution. Wouldn't it be great to go away and know that you could completely unplug and really not have to work? Even better would be if your job were still getting done, so you don't have to return to an avalanche of work and dozens of urgent emails.

*360-degree performance reviews*

It is a given that all staff—no matter who they are—want, need, and crave feedback. The way companies handle this is an important part of the company culture. The true value of these reviews comes down to how the feedback is being delivered and whether the staff trusts the process.

360-degree reviews are popular because they democratize the process of feedback. In theory, everyone gets a chance to weigh in on the performance of their peers and their managers. On one hand, these reviews are time-consuming and pricey, but on the other hand, staff can receive genuinely useful and constructive feedback. One staffer comments, "360s provide a holistic view of performance, rather than a singular avenue between the leader and assistant. I appreciate my colleagues' perspectives and advice to help me sharpen my skills and enhance my capabilities."

Staff warn of the following concerns, which are important for leaders to take note of when soliciting reviews:

- Staff worry that these reviews are not really "anonymous" as advertised, and that their comments end up being used against them. At worst, these reviews are seen as "professionally dangerous." Comments included, "No one at our company believed—even with a third party processing the results—that they were ever entirely confidential."
- "If you want a true 360, you have to select your reviewers from a 360 perspective, which should include an equal balance of your supporters and detractors. Those who self-select reviewers often skew results by choosing those who they perceive as their supporters."

- Staff report that in some companies, the 360 reviews are only for managers, not for lower-level staff, which contributes to an us-vs.-them dynamic. Assistants say they are asked to give input to the reviews for their managers but not vice versa.
- Staff comment that 360 reviews are more popular in the United States than in other countries.

*More tools that shape culture*

- Company electronic and written communications (job descriptions, manuals, emails, newsletters, physical and online bulletin boards, etc.)
- Social media channels featuring posts, images, and videos
- Mass-media personas of CEO and executive team
- Word of mouth by staff, clients, and customers
- Social activities for the staff, such as volunteering and team-building activities
- Professional development training offered to the staff
- Actions in the larger community, such as social justice and charity events

## It's your life

I will conclude this chapter on culture with information about one of the most common hot-button topics that I encounter. It is the quest for work-life balance. Other terms for this are work-life presence and work-life integration. Whatever words you use, this is about making the most of our precious 24 hours each day, 168 hours each week. Most people struggle to get everything done, and the experience of striving for balance is different for everyone. If you are wondering if a particular person is struggling, ask them. Then listen.

Successful cultures are ones where leaders care about the staff. Remember what it was like to be a child, a teen, a new parent, the caregiver of a sick relative. Kindness matters, especially in dark times. Kindness and generosity will inspire profound loyalty, and it is remembered.

Slow down long enough to imagine yourself in someone else's shoes. It can make all the difference in designing a sustainable culture for an ultimate new workplace.

## STAFF MATTERS QUESTIONS

1. How does the staff at your company understand and embrace the company culture?
2. What makes you proud of your company culture?
3. What ideas from this chapter could work at your company?

"Only the people who really care about you tell you the truth. It's too much trouble for everybody else."

**Olympia Dukakis**

# CHAPTER TEN

# Is It Safe?

"What would you do if you weren't afraid?"
**Spencer Johnson, author of *Who Moved My Cheese?***

Full disclosure: I am a big fan and student of psychology and talk therapy. My students know that they get to benefit from my thousands of dollars of therapy and now you do, too. I have consulted with psychologists and leadership experts for this chapter.

I call this chapter "Is It Safe?" because humans in our workplace are seeking the answer to that question. They want to feel safe and free to be who they are and to say what is really on their minds. Freedom to be who we are may be the biggest and best gift of all.

However, the humans in our workplace do not feel safe. Many feel they are in danger physically or psychologically. Their worry is real, preoccupying, and time draining, and it can be physically debilitating. Psychological safety is all too rare in the workplace, and that reality is hurting us all.

## What does psychological safety mean?

Psychological safety is the belief that you won't be punished or humiliated for speaking up with ideas, questions, or concerns.

### Abraham Maslow's Hierarchy of Needs

One of my most useful classes in college was psychology. Anyone who deals with people in the workplace should study some psychology. Right up there with Freud and Jung is Abraham Maslow and his hierarchy of needs—five, to be exact.[41] In my work, I have often thought that if all managers could understand one thing to make the workplace better, it would be the hierarchy of needs.

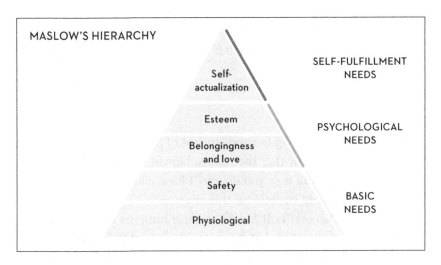

As humans, we need certain things for our essential survival: food, water, air, clothing, sex, sleep, and shelter. Those are the first two levels of the hierarchy.

The next two levels are at the heart of what every staffer wants in the workplace: belonging and respect.

### Belonging

Staff are hired for a reason, and they want to feel that they belong, that they are included, welcome, special, and important. They need to matter.

They want to have a clear idea of how they fit into the organization and why they are there. The antithesis to this idea is feeling like they are "just a number" and that their presence does not really matter at all.

*Respect*

Respect is hugely important in the workplace and in life. Simply put, when respect is present, most everything is possible. When disrespect is present, it overrides everything else. Respect is demonstrated in all kinds of ways in an ultimate workplace, from pronouncing names correctly to providing transparent and fair compensation to asking a staffer's opinion on decisions.

The hierarchy says that if these four levels are solidly in place, a person can self-actualize and be free to become the person they want to be.

Respect and belonging are more important than money. Respect and belonging are the keys to getting the best out of people in the workplace and in life. These things make humans feel safe. If that is what you seek, I encourage talking with your team about how to manifest them.

## The silencing effect of fear

**UNIVERSAL TRUTH:** When people feel psychologically safe, they will tell you everything. When people feel unsafe, afraid to be who they really are, terrified to say what is really going on, fearing backlash, repercussions, and retaliation, they will tell you *nothing*. Job number one for leaders is to make it safe for your staff to talk to you because if you keep shooting the messengers, they will stop coming.

Silence and the fear in the workplace are hurting staff badly. They hurt individual staff and a company's bottom line. Fear is rampant in the global workplace and it drives many of our decisions. Fear slows us down and stops us dead in our tracks. Fear can cause humans to shut down. Fear preoccupies and distracts us. Fear wastes valuable time. Some fears are irrational, but others are rooted in reality. What issues have staff so scared that they stay silent?

- Losing their job
- Being demoted
- Losing stature and prestige
- Not being liked
- Looking stupid
- Failing
- Being wrong
- Being judged
- Being seen as an impostor (others will find out that you are not really qualified for your job)
- Being ostracized or left out
- Being publicly humiliated

There are many ways fear manifests itself. One way is for staffers to rarely/never take a vacation or days off. The fear is that when they return, they will find that they were not missed. Another example is the fear of falling out of favor with the leaders or even of being fired after asking for a raise. Fear takes a big toll on physical health, mental health, and family/friend relationships.

Human nature and the world tells staff to play it safe because it is dangerous to be the messenger. We learn to not say too much and to not rock the boat. We hope that someone else will speak truth to power and say the thing that everyone else is thinking. The stakes are very high, especially in a postpandemic landscape that is slippery, vulnerable, and unreasonably changeable. The global workplace is filled with single parents who are the main breadwinners in their households. These parents are reluctant to make waves when they perceive a direct connection between speaking up and taking food out of the mouths of their children.

I cannot overstate the omnipresence of fear in our workplace. There are many reasons why this is an unacceptable state of affairs. Fear is taking up large lots of real estate in the brains of our staff. We have a finite number of hours in our workday and a finite amount of energy to accomplish what needs to be done. If a staffer is preoccupied with fear, imagine all the work that is not being done. It is easy to see the damage this would cause to the bottom-line profits. I will never forget an executive saying to me, "Bonnie, if no one is complaining, I think there is no problem."

Fear is quiet. Deadly quiet.

> **UNIVERSAL TRUTH:** Just because it is quiet and no one is openly complaining, it most definitely does not mean there is no problem. In fact, the opposite is probably true. Frightened staff do not speak. I implore leaders to listen to the silence and not assume nothing is wrong. It is a learned skill to hear what is not being said and to pay close attention to the quiet parts.

## Lessons from Olympia Dukakis: How to make it safe for staff to speak

"When is the tall one going to talk?" This is what my former employer, actress Olympia Dukakis, would ask the other staff members about me. When I began my work as the public relations director at the Whole Theatre in Montclair, New Jersey, I was twenty-nine years old. I was filled with fear, and my way of dealing with those fears was to be silent and vigilant. I was determined not to miss a thing. I would be a sponge and learn as much as I could from everyone else. I was scared to speak. I was scared about many things—being wrong, being unprepared, looking stupid, and making the other people in the room think that they had hired the wrong person.

Over a period of months, in meetings, Olympia would ask, "So, Bonnie, what do you think about that?" I would tentatively answer her question, and she would inevitably say, "Yes! That's it. That is exactly right. Let's do that." Then we would move on. Olympia would also encourage me by saying, "I may not always agree with you and may not always do what you say. But I always want to know what you think.

That is why I hired you." These words—and my doing my job well—
built my confidence. Others on staff began coming to me for answers
to their questions, which built my confidence even more.

Within a few months, Olympia joked that she couldn't shut me up,
and that was true. Her way of managing me was empowering. I am sure
she could see my hesitation. Olympia would often look me straight in
the eye and instantly convey the message, "I believe in you. I know you
can do this." Her belief in me was powerful and life-changing.

Looking back, I believe Olympia Dukakis saw something in me I
hadn't yet seen. She mentored me before I even knew the word "mentor," and I am forever grateful.

Olympia made it safe for me and everyone on the staff to speak
our minds. She made it clear she expected that from us and that if
we had questions, we must ask them. The culture that Olympia built
was one where the staff knew we had an obligation, a responsibility to
speak up and share any ideas that were in the best interest of the theater. Olympia also knew that mistakes were going to happen; the only
price to be paid for them would be if we were not honest about owning
them. After sharing one cringeworthy mistake I made, she responded
with a laugh, "Well, nobody is going to go to theater jail over that." I
will never forget that.

> **UNIVERSAL TRUTH:** Staff tend to beat themselves up over
> mistakes far more than their managers do. Staff can get con-
> sumed with worry and self-doubt, and the issue turns out to be
> nothing, or certainly not so serious, much of the time.

### About women

Women, in general, require extra encouragement to speak their minds.
This is because of the deeply rooted socialization from childhood that
tells young girls to be "seen and not heard." Therefore, as adult professionals, women typically need to be told "I want you to tell me what you
think" more than once. They worry the words are merely lip service

and insincere. In various ways, they need to hear, "I really am sincere when I say I genuinely want to know what you think. I am depending on you to do that. Will you commit to that?"

If in doubt, give it a try.

## About mistakes

The given in our complicated workplace is that mistakes are going to happen. As a leader, Olympia understood and accepted that the price she had to pay for delegating so much to me was that sometimes mistakes would happen. My own attitude toward mistakes was to commit to a "one-time rule." I would try my best to make each mistake only one time. I would own them, learn from them, and move on.

That was a lesson that took a very long time to embrace, especially the moving-on part. It came with age and experience. In our global workplace, I see so much time and energy wasted as staff beat themselves up about mistakes. The worry and fears are eating them from the inside out, wasting precious time in the process. I want to reduce that wasted time.

## What leaders need to know

**UNIVERSAL TRUTH:** It is human nature to protect the person in charge from the truth. The staff are the eyes and ears of executives. They see and hear everything. Other staffers usually feel safer and more comfortable speaking to a fellow staffer rather than to the person in charge. In my experience, not all leaders know this.

I ask assistants in my class if it is true that people say and reveal things to them that they would never say to their managers. The answer is a big fat yes and a sea of nodding heads. If that is true, it means assistants have information their leaders do not have. That information makes the assistants even more valuable and influential. The smartest leaders are the ones who know that people are talking to their staff and then use that knowledge by including assistants in meetings and making it known to the team that assistants are valued contributors. The smartest assistants are the ones who know when and how to share this information with their executives without naming names.

## Purpose

Part of the main driver for employees is a connection between their personal lives and their careers. Loyalty is built when a person's sense of personal purpose is able to strongly connect to that of the company. For example, in chapter 19, you will read the story of Executive Assistant Kristen Olmstead, whose purpose to give back in her community is in complete alignment with the goals of her company. In a world that is craving authenticity and evidence that we are making a real difference in people's lives, company leaders do well to pay close attention to their company's purpose and find ways to integrate the staff into the middle of it. Supporting staff as they combine their work with their purpose helps them feel connected and safe.

## When the going gets tough, create a safety net

When leaders become aware that staffers are having a tough time, here are some things to say that make things better and safer. It is important to keep in mind that sometimes the solution is for leaders to simply validate the legitimacy of the problem.

> *I'm so sorry this is happening.*
> *How can I best support you through this?*
> *Would XYZ be helpful or would something else be better?*
> *Thank you for sharing this with me. We will get through this together.*
> *Come to me anytime. I care.*

## Magic words that create safety

Here are some of the most powerful words we can say to one another in the workplace and in life. They are validating, empowering, and motivating. These words should be used in writing, in one-on-one meetings, and in front of others. Most humans yearn to hear these words, and when we do, they build confidence, self-esteem, and self-respect, ideal qualities to have in a strong staff. Use the person's first name—pronounced correctly—in front of the following sentences.

> *I believe in you.*
> *I trust you completely.*
> *I know you can do it.*
> *You're enough.*
> *I've got your back.*
> *I'm proud of you.*
> *You've got this.*
> *We depend on you.*
> *I have no doubts about your abilities.*
> *I have complete confidence in you.*

## Feeling safe equals freedom

The sky is the limit for companies when staff feels safe, respected, and accepted. Staff who feel genuinely supported are loyal and go above and beyond when no one is watching. I did.

To feel psychologically and physically safe at work means having the freedom to express who you are and what you think. It means being able to fully actualize your potential, your hopes and dreams for your career, your livelihood, your very life—without fear of backlash. It means having a long, wide runway to express your subject matter expertise, which leads to limitless potential for companies and the people who populate them. It means getting closer to the ultimate new workplace. That's worth shooting for, isn't it?

## STAFF MATTERS QUESTIONS

1. How do you feel safe or unsafe in your role?
2. How can you tell if the leaders in your company know what is really going on if they are too protected?
3. How could your company do a better job at opening up honest communication among staff?
4. What ideas from this chapter could make a difference in your organization?

## TRUE STORY

I had a morning phone meeting with a Be the Ultimate Assistant student who works for a well-known tech company. She sounded stressed, tired, and downright awful.

She said, "I was up most of the night. I support three executives, and they are all traveling right now in different time zones. I was keeping track of their flights to make sure everything went all right."

I said, "Is that the norm? How many hours a week do you work?"

She said, "Seventy to eighty."

I said, "That is not sustainable. Most every assistant knows what seventy-to-eighty-hour weeks feel like, but they are the exception, not the rule. Do your executives know about the workload you have?"

She said, "No, and I can't say anything. The culture here is to not complain. If you do, everyone knows that you get on the short list to be fired."

There is a lot wrong with this. However, this is an example of an element of a company's culture that is never written down and never present in an employee manual. It is referred to as the "invisible ink." **But everyone knows it is there.**

# CHAPTER ELEVEN

# Expectations

In the workplace, each constituency, each stakeholder has expectations for their roles, their careers, and their lives. They have hopes, dreams, and goals for their work. It is all staff's right to have clear expectations of what they have been hired to do. So why is it not happening? Why are many staff confused about what they are expected to do, and how can we fix that problem?

The lack of clear expectations is a major obstacle preventing an ultimate new workplace. To reiterate, the constituencies in our workplace are:

- Leaders
- Staff
- HR team
- Recruiters

There is a big gap between what people expect and what is actually happening in the workplace. But why is that the case? And most importantly, what can we do about it?

In general, I see much room for improvement when it comes to clear communication between these constituent groups. These communication gaps often break down completely, as evidenced by high attrition, job dissatisfaction, and a revolving door of staff.

In chapter 8, I covered the need to put things in writing, as opposed to relying on verbal communication. These include materials
like job descriptions and job offers. In this chapter, I will explore these
ideas further, taking a look at how expectations are set and met . . .
or not.

On one hand, it is not surprising that confusion and mixed messaging exist in the world, given the proliferation of so many communication channels. Plus, in a global workplace made even more remote
since the pandemic, we have many people working closely together
who have never been physically in the same room together and may be
thousands of miles apart.

## Communication: Are you getting through?

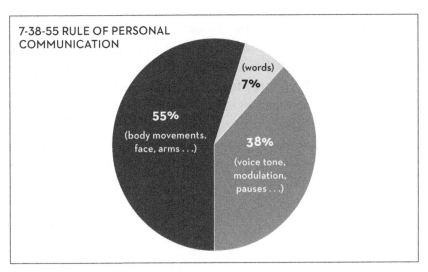

*7-38-55 Rule of Personal Communication developed by psychologist
Albert Mehrabian in his 1971 book,* Silent Messages

We communicate on three channels: verbal words, vocal tone, and
nonverbal body language.

The graphic above reveals the impact on human emotions of each
element and highlights the overwhelming importance of body language. This means that humans are watching facial expressions and
hand movements as a key way to interpret communication with others.

This graph is also a good indication of why emails and texts are so often misunderstood. An email only has words. Intended or not, **ALL CAPS IN BOLD** can often communicate the tone of those words—but only to a degree. An email removes 55 percent of the tools we use to communicate with others. This understanding about communication helps us to better control our ability to share our message the way we intend.

Building an ultimate new workplace depends on setting clear expectations for all the constituencies. This needs to be done through spoken words, written words, and body language. One solution that goes a long way to improving the 55 percent statistic is videoconferencing software. As the work-from-home culture has proven, webcams enable us to look into each other's eyes, hear vocal tone, and see body language (at least from the waist up), even when we are oceans apart. We know that effective communication can happen remotely, as long as we can see and hear each other.

The truth is that not everyone is good at communication, thus causing disconnections, hurt feelings, and misunderstandings. Like the handwriting exercise in chapter 8 demonstrated, setting clear expectations takes practice, time, training, and mentorship. Don't rush setting expectations. Look to your SMEs who are good at it.

## Commitment to consistency

All companies offer a brand promise to customers and staff. We expect companies to have a certain logo, a special look and feel that we come to depend on. The same is true for people. When we, as individuals, set expectations clearly and properly, all constituencies know what they are going to get from us. When we meet and exceed expectations, this builds trust, brand loyalty, and a sense of calm certainty.

Inconsistent messages create brand confusion and anxiety over not knowing what to expect. Confusion wastes time and money and sends customers to brands they can trust.

The following are places where expectations are shaped, influenced, and set. I am reiterating the points from chapter 8 about the company website and the Careers tab because of their importance.

*Company website*

This is a key place for setting expectations for everyone looking to do business with your company. The words and images you use matter. Videos are more common, and the 7-38-55 graph illustrates a big part of the reason why.

*Careers tab on the website*

These pages communicate how much a company values its staff. The words, images, and videos go a long way to setting expectations about what it means to work at the organization long before a candidate has an interview. I have read many company sites where, even on the Careers pages, the focus remains on the clients and customers, rather than the employees. These pages spend very little time explaining what the experience of the staff will be if they choose to work at the company. That is a serious red flag. Intentional or not, the message this sends is that the staff's needs are not a priority. Think about the message it would send to you as an aspiring candidate. Candidates want to be able to imagine themselves feeling respected and accepted.

*Social media*

The language used to describe the company and what it means to work there should be consistent across all social media platforms.

*Job descriptions*

I cannot emphasize enough the importance of these documents. Nonexistent or overly generic or glaringly obsolete job descriptions send a very negative message to potential candidates. The specificity and the language used to communicate the details of a position should echo what candidates read on the Careers tab. A job description can set clear expectations not only about the specific responsibilities of the position, but also about the company culture. A well-written job description can be a significant factor in targeting and attracting top talent.

For example, assistants are very alert to the bullet point that says "must have a thick skin." This prepares the candidate for a difficult personality, and it may signal the opportunity for "combat pay." Combat pay is extra money paid to those who work with a potentially demanding, irrational, and unreasonable executive. Deliberate or not, that reference to thick skin is a universally known red flag and it sets a strong expectation for a challenging personality. Some assistants report being told that if they "pay their dues" by working with a notoriously tough executive for a minimum of a year, they can "write their own ticket" for the next job. This is a tricky career strategy because of the traumatic price that frequently has to be paid. (See chapter 15 on disrespect.)

> **BEST PRACTICE:** Once a candidate agrees to join the company, they and the supervisor meet to go over the job description line by line. Goals for each responsibility are discussed. Ample time should be allowed for discussion and questions. Once the job description is mutually agreed upon, the new hire signs it, as does the manager. Each year at the annual review, that job description is reviewed, discussed, and revised as needed. Once every point and associated goals have been reviewed and agreed upon, it is signed again. This happens *every year*. I think this practice is brilliantly simple and smart.

## Job interviews

The job interview is a golden opportunity for company leaders to set and reinforce expectations and, truly, this is where interviewers and candidates can either shine or fail miserably. When a candidate arrives for an interview, they have set certain expectations via their resume and their own social media. From those materials, a hiring manager was motivated to go to the next step, the interview.

Example: Many leaders and staff openly complain "Those millennials are such a problem. They come in here and expect to be promoted in a month and to be making six figures within the first year. The nerve of them."

My questions in response are: "Who set those expectations with them? How did they get those ideas? Who wasn't clear about a realistic career path at the company?"

Why are these interviews handled so poorly? Here are a few thoughts based on my conversations:

- **Too rushed**—Hiring managers are pressured to get a "warm body" into the role as soon as possible.
- **No prep**—Interviewer is not prepared or briefed on what the job really entails.
- **Inexperience and lack of training**—Interviewing is a learned skill that takes time, practice, and training.

Around the world, I am continually struck by the staff who report that their job descriptions bear very little resemblance to the work they are actually doing. This creates obvious confusion, resentment, and disillusionment. A logical conclusion is to think, "I didn't sign up for this." In a strong job market, the result is that staffers quit in search of better-run companies.

Notes to candidates:

- Do your homework on the company and your interviewers.
- Prepare your questions.
- Interview the interviewers as much as they are interviewing you. Ask questions like, "How long have you worked here?" "What kinds of temperaments are successful here?"

Sites like Glassdoor provide crowdsourced reviews from people who have worked at the company. Most candidates know to take these comments with a grain of salt, but look for the patterns and commonality in the feedback. The best research is speaking to others who work at the company or who used to work for the company. LinkedIn is a great tool for this kind of research.

*Examples of disconnects in expectations*

- A written expectation that working at home is fine, but in reality, it is frowned upon and judged harshly.

- The "mommy tax" or "mommy penalty" that essentially punishes working parents for needing time for nursing or attending to sick children, sometimes resulting in an us-vs.-them dynamic between those who have children and those who do not.
- The expectation is set to "just get your job done" and the staffer is trusted to be accountable for the hours they work. The reality is that someone or a device is keeping track of every minute the staffer works, which sends mixed messages.
- Expectations say that unlimited time off is available. The invisible ink says to not take a vacation because the team may not miss you, and you will be out of a job when you return.
- Expectations say to follow the rules. The invisible ink says the end justifies the means, so it is fine to bend the rules if necessary. Reality and experience teach us that there are times when it is called for to lie and to break the rules. In my experience, staffers lie sometimes, and every person needs to bend or break the rules occasionally. And that's OK. One relatable example is telling someone on the phone, "Oh, they just left for lunch" when the person is sitting right there but did not want to speak with whoever was calling.

"Orville Wright did not have a pilot's license. Don't ever be afraid to bend or even break the rules."
**Richard Tait**

## Case study: Unreasonable expectations of a high-profile executive

An experienced Executive Assistant had concluded a three-week trial period with an internationally famous and wealthy high-profile executive in New York City. The trial paid $300/day. The EA spoke to me on the day she would be respectfully declining this opportunity. Here's what she said about the difference between what she was told the job would be versus the reality:

- The job description came through a reputable recruiter and said it was for an Executive Assistant. The reality was the job was really for a Chief of Staff/Personal Assistant. "I would have had five direct reports."
- The job called for eighteen-hour shifts, six days a week. There was no backup for vacations and no flexibility on work schedule. "I would be sacrificing all quality of life, not to mention my relationships with family and friends. Also, that schedule is a setup for failure, burnout, and for making costly mistakes. During those three weeks, I barely slept an average of three to four hours each night."
- "If I accepted the job, it would pay $125K." Even at double the salary, the job as outlined above is not sustainable over time.
- The recruiter did not know the reality of the role except for the base salary. She was not told what this job really entailed.

In this situation, the best thing that happened was the three-week trial period. It is very smart to do that, when possible, so all parties can figure out if the situation is a good fit. A major red flag was the knowledge that the prior assistant had stayed for four days, and there had been a revolving door of people before that. Clearly there is a problem with the system. The bottom line is that no one person could succeed for the long term with these unreasonable expectations.

To be clear, there is nothing wrong with the executive wanting coverage eighteen hours per day, six days a week, but that would be a three-person job. When the EA told the current Chief of Staff that the job was not as outlined and offered an alternative plan, the EA was told no. The EA respectfully declined the position.

One of the many issues with this kind of situation is that, oftentimes, people close to the high-profile principal are afraid to be the messenger and say that the job description and work schedule are not realistic or sustainable. I have also spoken with many recruiters who report they are not given accurate information about the role, which makes doing a paid trial period a smart idea for everyone. If you are a leader and decide that a trial period is a good idea, pay the candidates a fair daily rate.

## Expectation: Basic rights of dignity and respect

At the very least, employees of every company at every level should expect to be physically and psychologically safe at work. The hard truth is that, in general, staff do not feel safe at work; this largely explains why so many staff want to work from home.

In the era of #MeToo and #TimesUp movements, much attention is being appropriately paid to workplace bullying and sexual harassment in our companies. In fact, the hospitality industry in Chicago created one more hashtag to shed light on the harassment problem in hotels. It is #HandsOffPantsOn, meant to address the problem of hotel guests inappropriately touching the maids.

The data shows that an overwhelming majority of perpetrators of harassment/abuse are men, and the majority of the targets of abuse are women. It is not that women are never the harasser/abuser or that men are never the targets. The discussions in this book are not meant to reinforce a women-versus-men dynamic. But by revealing the truth about what is happening around bullying and harassment, women and men can work together to find real and long-lasting solutions. That is the only way we can build an ultimate new workplace.

The massive and pervasive exposure of abuses has caused some companies to create and enforce codes of conduct in order to get everyone on the same page. Staff are expected to sign and adhere to these codes.

Here is one example of a code of conduct that I created and share with my students:

---

### CODE OF ETHICS AND CONDUCT FOR EMPLOYERS AND STAFF

This is a mutually agreed upon list of fundamental givens for our work relationship designed to enable each of us to do superior work as a team and in collaboration in a positive, productive, and supportive atmosphere.

I, the employer, commit to the following:

1. Every employee will be treated with respect, dignity, and kindness.
2. Job descriptions will be agreed upon and signed by both employer and employee.
3. Every employee will have a mutually agreed upon compensation and benefits package that will be reviewed at designated times.
4. Expectations will be made clear either verbally or in writing.
5. Verbal and written feedback and acknowledgment will be given to staff.
6. Frequent and clear two-way communications will be the norm in order to make the best use of time and energy.
7. Staff are encouraged and expected to speak their minds regarding any issues that are deemed important to achieving our goals.
8. Verbal, sexual, or physical abuse is not permitted by anyone working for or doing business in our company. There is zero tolerance for workplace bullying, sexual harassment, or abuse of any kind.
9. No employee will be asked or expected to engage in illegal activity.

Signature
Date

I, the employee, commit to the following:

1. Perform excellent work in accordance with expectations that will be in constant flow and subject to change, while receiving ongoing feedback.

2.  Communicate in concert with the customized structures designed for our particular workplace and culture.
3.  Exhibit professional and respectful behavior at all times and expect to be held accountable for my actions.
4.  Exhibit good judgment and discretion regarding sensitive and confidential matters.
5.  Assist employer in every way possible to achieve their goals.
6.  Act as eyes and ears for my employer and bring matters to their attention.
7.  Work toward a positive, cooperative workplace; will not engage in negative or counterproductive encounters with anyone.
8.  Will not participate in verbal or physical abuse, nor be involved in any illegal activity on behalf of the company.

Signature
Date

## Commit to empathy on the road to an ultimate new workplace

As all the constituencies work to set clear expectations in our complicated workplace, let us commit to empathy and trying to understand the points of view of the others around us. Everyone in the modern workplace is under pressure to perform challenging and demanding jobs. Let us support one another by clearly discussing our expectations up front and in writing.

Slow the process down for as long as necessary to do it right. Taking this time at the beginning will pay off in the long run, and fewer staffers will feel the need to quit when their expectations are not being met.

## STAFF MATTERS QUESTIONS

1. How are staff given clear expectations at your company?
2. How could your online and printed materials about the company be improved to clarify expectations?
3. What ideas from this chapter could make a difference in your organization?

"You can't be what you can't see."

**Marian Wright Edelman, civil rights activist**

"You are the average of
the five people you spend
the most time with."

**Jim Rohn, personal development expert**

# CHAPTER TWELVE

# Mentorship

I am a strong believer in mentorship and have firsthand experience with the mighty benefits of it. In a world obsessed with success and megawealth, there is no person you can name who *got there alone*. Nobody. They all got to where they are because they had mentors.

> **UNIVERSAL TRUTH:** To be successful, we need mentors. They are our role models for life. Period. The best way to have a mentor is to be one.

## The words of mentorship: Advisor = teacher = sponsor = role model = coach = friend

There are numerous schools of thought about the words "mentor" and "coach." To me, they are interchangeable. They mean different things to different people. Other words that can mean exactly the same thing are advisor, teacher, sponsor, role model, guide, expert, SME, confidante, consigliore, and friend. All are valid and brilliant terms if they work for you.

A mentor can be your in-person colleague or someone oceans away with whom you communicate only via email, text, or videoconferencing. Sometimes mentors show up in the form of networking groups that turn into group coaching, also known as peer-to-peer learning. Our teachers can be everywhere, and all of them can offer nuggets of important insight.

Just as I believe the words of mentorship can be interchangeable, I also believe in flexibility about the structure of the mentoring. I do not support strict rules such as having to meet once per month or per week. This is not a one-size-fits-all subject.

"Virtual mentors" are gaining popularity in the work-from-home (WFH) environment. These are experts you follow on social media through their articles, podcasts, and videos, but who you do not necessarily know personally. These SMEs can be powerful mentors simply through the content they are posting, and unless you choose to pay for a class, this kind of mentorship costs you only your time.

Some discussions make a distinction between mentoring and coaching on the basis of money. The idea is that you pay a coach, but you don't pay a mentor. That can be true, but not always. Others claim that a coach has received formal training in coaching and has earned a license or certification. That also can be true, but not always.

I prefer not to get stuck in semantics, but rather to focus on the value of being supported by another human being, however it happens. With any group of people, it is important to be clear about which words you agree to use.

## Why are mentors important?

We are born and raised by humans, sometimes biological parents and sometimes others. The people who raise us are our first mentors, and we draw from those experiences, both good and bad. These earliest mentors guide us in most every aspect of our lives. Some people resist being mentors to others because it sounds like too overwhelming a time commitment. In the workplace, it is not reasonable or realistic to think we can mentor another person in every aspect of their working lives. That false expectation stops people from saying yes to being a mentor. However, because we are all SMEs—subject matter experts—we all have the ability to mentor others in our area(s) of expertise.

For twenty-five years, Olympia Dukakis would say, "Bons, you don't have to be an expert in everything. You just need to know who the experts are to get the answers we need. Fast." Olympia was right years ago and she is right now. In many cases, the experts she was talking about ended up serving as mentors to me. An example was one of her talent agents, from whom I learned most everything I know about movie and television contracts, and who also became a friend.

## What mentors do

They talk to you without any agenda other than that they care about you and want you to reach your goals to self-actualize. Mentors are experts in their own right and give you the benefit of their "been there, done that" experience. They refer you to resource materials or other experts. They offer advice and guidance. They tell you the hard truths and challenge your beliefs.

Big caveat: Mentors may not always be correct about whatever it is that they are giving advice and guidance on. At least, it may not be correct for you at this particular point in time. Even the smartest mentor/expert is not inside your head.

Mentors work with you in person, talk over the phone, or communicate through email, texts, or videocalls. The frequency of these communications is totally up to the two of you. There is no right or wrong way. Sometimes money changes hands and sometimes it doesn't. Sometimes there is a barter arrangement (service for service). There are no hard-and-fast rules for mentorship, and this has contributed to some of the confusion and debate about what it is.

Another false belief about mentors is that you should only have one. I believe in having multiple mentors and not always at the same time. In my career, I have had many mentors, including my parents; Olympia Dukakis; my life partner, Robert Sanders; my son, Adam Kramen; my business partner, Vickie Sokol Evans; my therapists; and many more. They have mentored me, and I know I have also mentored them.

Indeed, you can be a mentor and a mentee at the same time. By now I hope you are embracing the idea that you are a SME. It is very common for mentor/mentee relationships to be mutually beneficial through the generous sharing of expertise between both parties. A win-win situation, for sure.

Do you have to ask for mentorship formally? Sometimes yes, but not necessarily. Other mentor/mentee relationships are less formal arrangements that happen over an occasional coffee meeting.

## Reverse mentoring

I love the phenomenon known as reverse mentoring. While traditional mentoring has meant experienced staff (usually older) mentoring less-experienced people (usually younger), reverse mentoring flips that dynamic. There is a recognition in the workplace that our younger staff may lack work experience, but they possess a particular area of expertise that the rest of the team needs.

One example would be a marketing team that asked the younger (twentysomething) staffer for input about pop culture and the appeal of certain new social media platforms.

Another example is my thirtysomething student from Belgium. From the time he was a child, he worked in his family's security business, so he has become a SME in cybersecurity and hacking. His new employer is leveraging his knowledge and skill. He is consulting with the IT department, sitting in on high-level meetings that include the CEO, and sharing his knowledgeable advice.

I am a big fan of leveraging SMEs of all ages and levels of experience this way. Besides increasing productivity, it builds confidence, self-esteem, and respect on a team.

## So why doesn't everyone have a mentor?

In my classes for assistants, I ask, "Who has a mentor right now?" People who say yes are usually 10 to 20 percent of the room. I follow up with, "Who believes that having a mentor is important?" Almost 100 percent of the students raise their hands.

Why do so few staff have mentors, and yet so many want them? Here are the main reasons:

- Rejection: fear of being told no when you ask
- Vulnerability: fear of revealing what you don't know
- Retaliation/backlash: fear of being fired or punished when what you don't know is revealed
- Actions: fear of not being able to follow through with what you are being advised to do
- Time: lack of time to commit to the process
- Lack of confidence: belief that you are not worth having a mentor

## Who should you ask to be your mentor?

The answer to this question depends on what it is that you would like to learn. That might mean asking the CEO for a meeting to discuss their career because you want to hear the story firsthand. Many staff have asked for "mentorship" from the CEO or other C-suite executives, and guess what? Most of the time, the executive says yes. The executives are flattered by the request and despite how busy they are, they make the time for a meeting or two or more.

> **UNIVERSAL TRUTH:** Most leaders love hearing from staff about their ambitions and are flattered to be asked for advice. Plus, most people really enjoy talking about themselves. Admit it, don't you? The truth is that most people are afraid to approach the person in charge. Yes, executives are busy, but they still want to hear from staff. As a staffer, if you have a good reason to ask for mentorship, fight the fear and ask. After all, it's lonely at the top.

The main thing to remember is to have a specific ask. Be sure to convey the answer to this question: *Why are you asking them?*

There are no rules when it comes to how often you should meet with your mentor. It is customized to suit you, your schedules, and your lives. It also does not have to be a lifelong commitment. Mentoring sessions might be one and done, and that will have been exactly right.

You can ask someone for mentorship from inside or outside your company. With the help of technology, you can ask someone in another country to be your mentor. The more specific you can be about why you are making the request, the higher your chances of a positive response.

## Formal and informal mentoring programs

Formal and informal mentoring programs exist all over the world. I speak at many conferences. Often a small group of attendees will decide organically to create a networking group that enables them to get together (in person or virtually) every month or every quarter. This is mentoring. In a world where staff can often feel isolated and alone, these grassroots networking groups are impactful and powerful.

Some of these programs give themselves a name, such as Masterminds, or an acronym such as HEAT (Hillshire Executive Assistant Team) or CAPS (Campbell's Administrative Professional Staff). Some create a logo for the group and make T-shirts, baseball hats, and other products to encourage a strong sense of team.

Mentorship programs can be informal or formal inside companies. Informal mentoring programs most often occur through the ERGs (employee resource groups). Formal programs would be ones where a staffer would register, be assigned a mentor, and follow the rules set by the program.

### Online mentoring groups

Social media, specifically LinkedIn and Facebook, is filled with groups to join that serve as online resources. There you can not only read and express opinions with people in your profession, but you can also find a mentor. Online app platforms like Clubhouse (audio-only group meetings) and Lunchclub (one-on-one video meetings according to interests) are powerful parts of the networking and mentoring landscape.

*In-person mentoring groups*

Most communities are offering plentiful opportunities for networking, and those events are great places to find mentorship. A best practice is to arrive at these events thirty minutes early and stay after it is over to meet people more easily. In all of these conversations, be sure to offer help to others even more than you ask for help.

**Just do it.** Whichever mentoring system appeals to you, I strongly urge you to pursue it. In a world that is increasingly complicated, mentorship is your way to stay current and ready for whatever challenges come your way. Mentorship can make all the difference for your career advancement and achieving your highest goals. It is a cornerstone to the future and to building our ultimate new workplace.

## STAFF MATTERS QUESTIONS

1. To what degree is mentorship encouraged in your company?
2. How could mentoring work in your organization to strengthen the pipeline of talent?
3. Who needs to be involved to build a mentorship program inside your company?

"Pay them as well as you can afford to. Pay them fairly. And then do everything in your power to take money off of their minds."

**Alfie Kohn, author, social science researcher**

# CHAPTER THIRTEEN

# Money

In April 2018, I watched the CBS show *60 Minutes* when Salesforce CEO Marc Benioff was the guest. It was a revelation. It was the first time I had heard a corporate leader speak openly in the mass media about the wage gap. I listened to his determination to make sure that women were paid as much as men at Salesforce.

Benioff talked about the head of HR, Cindy Robbins, coming to him to tell him there was, in fact, a wage gap between women and men at Salesforce. To get clear on the situation, they conducted a pay study that revealed there was a $3 million gap. Benioff authorized filling that gap and committed to continue filling the gaps going forward. CEOs like Benioff have made front-page news with their commitment of millions of dollars to close the wage gap between women and men. At the World Economic Forum in 2017, he said, "Every CEO needs to look at if they're paying men and women the same. That is something that every single CEO can do today."[42]

I am grateful Marc Benioff has been a role model for increased transparency, accountability, and awareness about the wage gap. Since that interview, I have witnessed a pattern of employees sharing how there is increased attention being paid to salary evaluations at their companies. I see the veil of secrecy and confusion about compensation coming off slowly but surely. I am happy I lived to see the day.

Money—the pursuit of it and lack of it—dominates the thoughts, the minds, and the hearts of people in the global workplace. Next to workplace bullying, the subject of money is one of the hottest-button subjects in my workshops for assistants all over the world. Money preoccupies us.

How do I know this? In classes, I ask how high the stress level is about the issue of money on a scale from 1 to 10. They shout back, "10!" "12!" Rarely do I hear a number lower than 7. The subject of money is on people's minds. Is it on yours?

In this chapter, we'll cover what I know about money and compensation, and specifically, what the staff of the world are saying and feeling about it. Historically, the subject of money has been taboo, forbidden, and usually shrouded in secrecy. Especially for women, talking about money has been considered a bad thing, an off-limits, touchy subject that should not be discussed, except in low voices behind closed doors.

## It's personal

Money is a very personal subject. If we were talking together, I would ask if you've ever lived paycheck to paycheck. Have you ever known what it feels like to not be sure you could pay your rent or buy food? If you have, you never forget it. I certainly haven't.

I remember a time when I was making decisions about whether I should use the gas I had in the car to go to the grocery store or just wait two more days until I had to drive to work. I remember spending fifteen dollars on a new blouse from a sale rack because I couldn't remember the last time I had anything new. The guilt was oppressive, but I don't regret buying it. My thought at the time was, "Is this all life is?"

I became determined that when my financial situation improved, I would help others improve theirs.

## Case study: How I learned to negotiate from Olympia Dukakis. "Can they get me more money?"

I graduated college without learning how to negotiate a salary. This is why I understand how difficult it can be to do. Looking back, I would have handled money very differently. I hope this book will help others not step into the same financial ditch.

As you already know, my first job out of college was working in the box office for $4.25 an hour. It wasn't until I worked with Olympia Dukakis as her Personal Assistant that I got a front-row seat for one negotiation after another, for twenty-five years.

Each time Olympia received a project she was interested in doing, her first question to her agent always was, "Can they get me more money?" She was never embarrassed or shy about asking. I would sit there and think I wanted to do that for myself, but how? What I observed was that it was easy for Olympia to ask for more money, in part because she was not the person who had to do the asking. I would think about myself and all the staff who do not have agents or managers or lawyers or even assistants to ask for more money on their behalf. What about us? Who is advocating for me? The answer, of course, is no one. It follows that every working person needs training in how to advocate for themselves to negotiate a fair and respectful salary.

## Speaking up about money

It's time to break the silence about money and, more specifically, the disparity between what men earn and what women earn. In an economy and society that depends on the work of both genders, money is a people issue, a family issue, and most definitely not only a women's issue, as it is sometimes painted.

I have been face-to-face with men who told me there is no wage gap. One said matter-of-factly, "The wage gap is BS. I don't know what women are complaining about. What's the problem? Women have it really good." Clearly, there is a disconnect in education.

The secrecy and silence around these issues about money are significant contributing factors to the lack of accurate information about the current economic state for women. There is most definitely a wage gap between women and men.

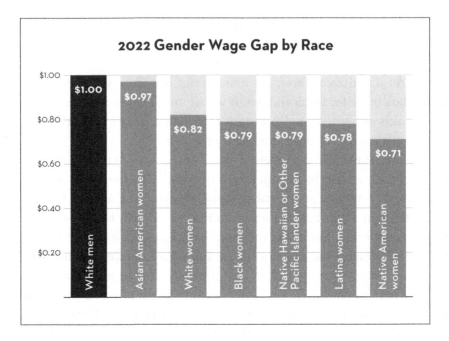

## We've come a long way to closing the wage gap, just not far enough

Despite the following legislation, the wage gap persists.

- **1963**—Equal Pay Act, which protects against wage discrimination on the basis of race, origin, color, religion, or sex.
- **1964**—Civil Rights Act, which prohibits discrimination on the basis of race, origin, color, religion, or sex.
- **1996**—The first Equal Pay Day was originated by the National Committee on Pay Equity to bring attention to the wage gap. This day in any given year represents how much more time into the next year a woman needs to work to make the same money as a man made in the preceding year. For example, Equal Pay Day in 2022 was on March 15. A hypothetical woman would have to keep working until March 15, 2022 in order to earn what a

man made in 2021. Equal Pay Day for Latina women was December 8, 2022.[43]

• **2009**—Lilly Ledbetter Fair Pay Act was enacted to eliminate wage discrimination.

• **2019**—The campaign Equality Can't Wait was founded by Melinda French Gates to accelerate gender equality. The campaign conducted a poll that found that men don't consider the problems of gender inequality to be as severe as women do.

**Progress:** As of this writing, twenty-eight states in America have made it illegal to ask job candidates their salary history.[44] At present, there is a proposed Paycheck Fairness Act pending in the United States Congress, which seeks to ensure protection to employees who discuss their pay.

I reiterate that these deeply disturbing facts about the wage gap are not only a "woman's problem." These are family issues. These are human issues that impact all of us. For these reasons, both men and women in our workplaces have a responsibility to act.

Note: Because my area of expertise is with assistants, I will focus on the compensation of administrative staff. The principles are relatable to other professions and industries.

## The facts

• Assistants are 93 to 97 percent female. The global workforce is 48 percent female.

• If no major wage change initiatives are enacted, *Time* magazine estimated that it will take 135.6 years to close the wage gap.[45]

• One in three women believe the wage gap will never close.

• Most assistants are not making the money they deserve to be earning. Many are severely underpaid.

• Most women want to change the situation but don't know how and feel frightened and intimidated by the whole process.

## Bonuses for Executive Assistants

**ANGELICA CANALES,** *former EA to a Fortune 250 CEO,*
*New York City*

"As an EA for twenty-five years, I know that receiving an end-of-year bonus can be life-changing money. I know this from experience. Many assistants in corporate America are not bonus eligible, for whatever reason. Sometimes it is because they are undervalued and the job title isn't thought of as 'important.' I have even encountered executives who don't consider their EA a direct report. The reality is that many EAs are supporting multiple executives, which is a lot of responsibility and results in over sixty-hour workweeks. This is occurring without extra compensation and without a year-end bonus. There is a way to have assistants receive bonuses that would not cost the company any extra money. When executives are earning five- or even six-figure bonuses, HR could set aside a percentage, even $5,000 of the executive's bonus, for their EA. The executives would barely feel it, and it would promote tremendous goodwill with their EAs. Of course, having all administrative staff eligible for bonuses would be ideal. It would be a key differentiator for companies wanting to attract top talent."

## How things are changing

The #MeToo and #TimesUp movements have highlighted the treatment of women in general, not only bullying and sexual harassment. These include the issues of gender bias and salary inequality.

In Hollywood, actors Benedict Cumberbatch and Bradley Cooper have both stipulated they would not sign onto a project unless their female costars received the same salary. It worked. This is a trend.

Actor Justin Baldoni hosts a web series called *Man Enough*. In it, he says, "TimesUp and MeToo and all these things are amazing, but the issues are not new. The problem is they're new to men." Baldoni makes the important point that many men are resistant to the fact that gender inequality exists in the first place. As a result, when male allies overtly support women, especially around issues of compensation and advancement, they experience some negative backlash from male naysayers.

Given the dominance of women in the administrative profession, I will be using the pronoun "she" to discuss these issues. What I am sharing can most definitely be utilized by men, and I enthusiastically welcome them to do so. I am happy to note that I see an increase in the number of men in my workshops and audiences. That is great news for many reasons, including the fact that a more diverse workforce is a stronger and more innovative, creative, and productive one. A current reality is that the presence of more men in the administrative profession will drive salaries higher simply because they are male.

## Reality check

I hear from women who feel stuck and paralyzed in their jobs. They are living paycheck to paycheck. They have trouble making ends meet and putting food on the table. They are preoccupied with worry and fear. Many are single parents.

A 2019 study by Child Care Aware of America reported that the average cost of childcare ranges from $5,760 to $20,880 per year, depending on the city. The costs increase if there is more than one child or if that child has special needs. These facts should concern every CEO, executive, HR professional, and recruiter reading this because that worry is preoccupying your staff. The worry is taking up valuable real estate in brain power and time. It is easy to see that if a person is consumed with worry, it is more difficult to perform work.

Without coaching, women are not asking for the money they deserve. They hope their hard work will be noticed, acknowledged, and rewarded. It's not happening like that. In the meantime, assistants are functioning as Executive Business Partners. They are servant leaders who are the right arms of their executives, the backbone of the company, and the face of the company culture. On top of all that, they are taking work home to do at night and on weekends—and not telling anyone. Many are burning out, getting sick, and staying silent all the while.

In general, women are loath to complain about anything, especially about money, to leaders. Women are reluctant to make even the smallest of waves if they fear their jobs could be on the line. Therefore, they are silent. Yet in our heads we know that you don't get if you don't ask. That is absolutely true about money. Women, in general, have not been trained how to ask for what they want, including money.

What exactly are women afraid of? What stops people from asking for the money they deserve? Here are a few reasons.

- Fear of rejection and being told no
- Fear of not being liked by managers and the people in charge
- Fear that our coworkers will judge us harshly
- Impostor syndrome: we feel like frauds and that we don't deserve more money
- Afraid of losing our jobs if we ask
- Fear of success

If all these things are true, why aren't leaders taking action as Marc Benioff is doing?

When I speak with executives all over the world, they essentially say, "Bonnie, if I don't hear there is a problem, I think there is none." I respond by saying that just because people are not talking, it does not mean there is no problem. Quite the opposite, actually.

This set of circumstances is complicated by the fact that assistants report they absolutely "love" their jobs and are passionately committed to them. Recent data shows the most passionate people in the workplace are the easiest to take for granted and take unfair advantage of. The real-life consequences of this are women who are burned-out and suffering from record levels of stress as they work to pay their bills with inadequate and often unfair compensation. Their love for their jobs is not paying the bills.

Given the serious wage gap, coaching for women around issues of salary and compensation is especially important. According to Carnegie Mellon University, only 7 percent of women will negotiate their salaries, contrasted with 57 percent of men. Most women have a profound fear of asking for money. In general, women have never been taught how to negotiate. Coaching is a game changer for women.

I have seen an average of 20- to 40-percent increases in pay for women who receive coaching about negotiating salaries.

## Best practice: Speak up

The annual review is not the only time to talk about money. Bring up the subject of money in your feedback sessions so that your manager knows it is on your mind. Say things like, "I want to be sure about the kinds of things you would like to see me doing in order to be considered for an increase/bonus/benefit." You are planting seeds and communicating that you are ambitious and willing to do the work to earn more money. Staying quiet can be misinterpreted as satisfied and complacent.

> **UNIVERSAL TRUTH:** In general, women are not trained to negotiate and therefore find it excruciatingly difficult to ask for a raise. The result? They don't ask. Some find it easier to quit a job and get a new one than to ask for an increase. A new job gives an opportunity to safely discuss the starting salary. Data shows that women are better at negotiating starting salaries than men.

## Women speaking up and fighting back— Hollywood assistants #PayUpHollywood

Olympia Dukakis would return to New York City after shooting in Hollywood and half-jokingly say, "Bons, you are so lucky to work with me. People treat assistants like crap out there." At the time, part of that treatment of assistants was to grossly underpay them and expect them to put in fifty-to-eighty-hour workweeks as the norm.

Former Hollywood assistants Deirdre Mangan and Liz Alper created #PayUpHollywood, and in 2019 they exposed the entertainment industry's flagrant abuse of labor practices.[46] These practices include low wages of \$11.25 per hour, few benefits, no reimbursement for gas or expenses, discouragement of submitting overtime pay, and severe verbal abuse. The assistants viewed these jobs as a way of paying their dues to break into show business and therefore saw no option but to withstand the treatment. Most felt fortunate to find their jobs.

In 2021, a longtime talent agent told me, "It's a new day and all of this media attention about the abuse is causing the heads of agencies to change the culture for the better. I see a difference. It will take time, but I am really happy that the abuse is stopping."

## UNIVERSAL TRUTHS THAT LEADERS NEED TO KNOW ABOUT WHAT THE STAFF IS SAYING ABOUT MONEY

The staff know what their leaders and their peers receive in compensation. Leaders may think this information is secret, but it is not. Certainly, rumors abound.

When staff find out what their colleagues earn, they decide if it is fair or not. They do the math. They know what leaders earn per hour versus what they earn per hour. For this reason, it feels like an inappropriate expectation for staff to work over fifty hours each week and be told to not submit for overtime. This disparity can lead to unspoken resentment and anger, which in turn leads to attrition and a decrease in engagement and productivity.

It is not constructive to deny there is a wage gap. It is math, not myth. Staff need the leaders to speak up on their behalf when misinformation is being shared.

There is much confusion about the laws that guide whether to pay people by the hour or by a set salary. Staff are not clear about the policies around exempt versus nonexempt payments and overtime. Even HR professionals are confused by these rules. I am advocating for more transparency about these policies and decisions.

## The fix: Commitment to pay equity and pay transparency

I urge leaders to openly and honestly talk with their staff about money and to be as transparent as possible. A big dose of empathy is useful here. Most everyone has known what it feels like to struggle to make ends meet, even if it was a long time ago.

If it is accepted as true that money is on most everyone's mind, then it serves companies to support their chosen staff with this obvious pain point. One way to do that is to take the subject out of the shadows and move it into the light. Offer financial counseling. Schedule open discussions about compensation as it relates to career growth. Staff are not only concerned with what they are earning today, but also about next year and the next five years. I assure you this conversation would be profoundly welcomed.

Nickle-and-diming is a way to save money in the short term, but it is extremely demotivating, humiliating, and demoralizing for staff. Generosity goes a long way. The bottom line is that leaders who commit to paying fairly or generously are the ones with companies with higher employee retention, increased productivity, higher staff satisfaction, and higher profits. Staff who are fairly paid are the ones who go above and beyond every day, even when no one is watching.

## Case study: Base salary plus incentive

**SAM R.,** *CEO in New Jersey*
Sam runs a successful business and realized he needed to employ an Executive Assistant in order to fully leverage his time and energy. Working with an assistant is something he had never done before, and the only way he knew to start was with me. I asked if he had a number in mind that he wanted to offer as a salary for this position, and he replied, "I don't know. Around $45,000." Given the scope of the full-time role he described and the cost of living in 2021 in New Jersey, I told him the salary was too low and more appropriate for a new college grad. He clearly wanted more advanced communication, tech skills, and experience than the salary he quoted could attract. I suggested creating an incentive plan that would be the base salary plus

a commission on certain kinds of sales. This structure could support the right person in the role.

## Case study: Newly famous celebrity with a lean team that is well-meaning but green

A high-profile newly famous celebrity needed a Personal/Executive Assistant who could travel with her. Interviews were happening haphazardly and there was no real plan to find someone. Her small team, comprising the business manager and the financial manager, were talking to friends and people they knew. My student is an experienced EA who heard about the position by chance via Instagram when the celebrity herself responded to one of his posts. Interviews began, although there was no written job description. I advised my student to write his own job description based on the two interviews he had. The team was very impressed with this work and came back with a revised job description based on the one the candidate had presented. The new job description expanded the role even further. Everyone was very excited, and my student was told to expect an offer.

My student and I knew the role was worth over $100,000 per year, especially with all the travel. The CEO extended an offer of $60,000 per year, which I believe came from a desire to solve the problem quickly without doing any research on the true market value of the role. My disappointed student crafted a well-reasoned, fact-based professional response, including a counterproposal of $100,000. Based on the respectful responses, it was clear the team knew he was the right one for the job. They settled on $90,000 per year and an excellent benefits package, plus a plan for future increases.

My student and I believe that part of his job will be to teach the team how to approach these kinds of hires as they move forward.

Lesson for all concerned in negotiating compensation: Do the research on market value for the job description in the geographic region. Find out how much a role is worth by speaking with a local recruiter and researching job websites like Indeed, Glassdoor, and Comparably.

## What to do: The strategy to make the money you deserve

If your experience mirrors some or all of what I have written, here is what you can do:

- **Decide.** Set your intention. Look at the calendar and decide that today is a new day to take action about money.
- **Worth.** Work on a detailed, factual, and formatted resume that outlines your skills and expertise. Find out how much your role is worth in your geographic market, given your experience, responsibilities, skills, and education/certifications. It is impossible to negotiate if you don't know the number. Visit a local recruiter as a great resource and check out Glassdoor, Indeed, and LinkedIn for examples of current compensation ranges in your city.
- **Value.** Chances are very good your current employers do not want to work without you and do not want to replace you. Seriously, I have numerous stories of assistants who finally quit their jobs, only to learn they were replaced with two or even three people. This is no exaggeration.
- **Create a fact-driven business case.** Your work has a return on investment (ROI). Create a written business case which functions as your professional summary. Doing this in writing communicates the seriousness with which you are treating your career. A friendly and professional cover letter accompanies the document.

The business case typically contains:

- Current resume/CV;
- The job description you were hired with and your current job description. They often look very different;
- Quantifiable achievements from the last year;
- List of projects coming up in the next six to twelve months;
- Three to five kudos letters from people telling you how wonderful you are and how you helped them;

- Salary history;
- Salary proposal based on your research. Name a number that is 5 percent higher than you know is fair. Include other things you want: increased vacation time, approval to work at home one or more days each week, stock options, and an annual training budget ($3,000 to $5,000 average), for example.

I suggest sending the business case document with a cover note to your manager(s) seven to ten days before the meeting to discuss salary. This way managers have a chance to absorb the information and to think about it. No one wants to be blindsided when faced with important decisions.

Essentially, this business case document does the talking before you ever have to say the words out loud to your executive or HR professional.

My students have experienced tremendous success using this strategy since most assistants are champion researchers. Executives respect and appreciate that their assistants are taking charge of their careers and handling themselves as the leaders of their own livelihoods. Many assistants report that their executives had no idea how underpaid they were and are eager to correct the compensation.

When we break the silence to finally talk about realistic ways to approach negotiation, stress levels automatically come down. Strategies, such as creating a written proposal outlining your current situation and justifying the changes using data and metrics, work.

## Case study: Leaders often don't know the details

One of my students has a strong relationship with her executive, who is the owner of the company. She had been working at the company for three years, and her responsibilities had grown substantially in that time. She had been receiving cost-of-living increases, yet felt she was underpaid. She did her research and found out what her salary should be in her geographic market, given her responsibilities and experience. She created a business case document sharing the data and outlining her value to the company. When her executive read the document, he was mortified and embarrassed. He said he had had no idea how grossly underpaid she was. The executive set the wheels in motion to adjust her compensation and thanked her for bringing it to his attention. This decision resulted in not only a $20,000 increase but also a plan for some retroactive compensation and future increases. The bottom line: Sometimes leaders do not even know what their staff earns. Tell them.

The assistant is now being paid fairly for her job description. The silence was broken between her and her executive, and they are both committed to discussing compensation on an ongoing basis.

## Case study: Written business cases work

One of our Be the Ultimate Assistant students is Laura from California. She was hired right out of college as the CEO's Executive Assistant at a small company. She accepted an extremely low salary because of her lack of experience and her youth. Within two years, at age twenty-four, Laura was totally up to speed, and the CEO and everyone else at the company could not manage without her. In addition, her efforts had contributed to the increased profits of the company.

Laura prepped for her annual review by doing her research and creating a written business case. In it, she proposed an increase of $15,000 in order to bring her more in line with what was appropriate for her level of responsibility. She also proposed including an additional budget for training and another week of vacation. Laura anticipated that the CEO would read her document and ask her to compromise on some or all of her proposal. His response? The CEO was very impressed with the document and gave her *everything* she asked for. Needless to say, Laura was ecstatic. Best of all, she will be much less anxious for the next negotiation.

Even better news? Laura's story is not an isolated situation. Staff all over the world are creating fact-driven business cases, asking for more money and getting it. When the justification is made crystal clear, leaders are responding in positive ways. If they don't, it is important to find out why. The answer to that question will tell you if it is time to leave or to work things out another way.

If you are being told no after making your case, the questions to ask are "What would you like to see me do that would enable me to earn that salary?" and "Is there anything I can do?" The answers to those questions will support you to make prudent decisions about how long you are going to stay at that job.

## HR trends: Pay equity and pay transparency

In 2022, HR professionals are more inclined than ever before to adjust salaries. In a workplace turned upside down by the pandemic, there is a talent shortage as staff are resigning in search of a better culture. In the effort to stabilize companies, money is one important tool. Pay equity and pay transparency are front of mind, which is great news for the staffs of companies, and the effort to retain excellent staff is driving salaries up for both women and men. There are three factors supporting these trends.

1.  **The job market is hungry for top talent.** Supply and demand—the strong demand for skilled staff is motivating leaders to look at compensation as a major way to retain people.
2.  **Proliferation of and free and easy access to crowd-sourcing sites for compensation data**. Indeed, Glassdoor, Salary, LinkedIn.
3.  **#MeToo and #TimesUp.** These movements have resulted in company leaders taking a new and hard look at the treatment of women in all ways, not only regarding workplace bullying and sexual harassment. Women have become more vocal about what they need in the workplace, including compensation. Leaders are listening and responding.

More companies are following Salesforce's lead by doing voluntary internal salary evaluations. Increasingly, staff are receiving salary increases without even having to ask for them because of these initiatives to close the wage gap. If your company is not already doing this, present HR with the data and your business case and ask for a salary evaluation.

## Exempt vs. nonexempt and salary vs. hourly

One of the elephants in the room in the American workplace is the mystery surrounding the way decisions are made to pay staff hourly (nonexempt) or a salary (exempt). The official rules for this are found in the Fair Labor Standards Act (FLSA).[47] The fact is that company leaders have a lot of leeway in the interpretation of these rules, and every employee could be an hourly employee if leaders decided to make them so. This would apply to everyone from the CEO on down the line.

Laws were created to make sure employees were not taken advantage of, but that is not necessarily happening in real life. Big questions loom regarding what criteria are used to make someone a salaried employee or an exempt one. Exempt in this context means they are exempt from receiving overtime. The rules have much to do with how many hours it takes to do your job and how much decision-making responsibility you hold. Therein lies part of the problem. If a job description is not accurate, leadership has little chance to understand the true scope of a given employee's level of responsibility, influence, and impact.

Note to all employees: Make sure your job description is 100 percent accurate and keep it updated. Your compensation—hourly or salary—is riding on this.

## The bottom line: Job description equals money

In general, employees are seriously confused over how these decisions are made, and I urge HR professionals to be as transparent as possible with this information. Many HR staff admit that these rules are confusing, even to them.

I can tell you that the hourly-vs.-salary debate is about more than just money; it is about an us-vs.-them perception that gets established in a company. An Executive Assistant may, in fact, make a great deal more money being paid hourly than if they were on salary, but the perception at the company is that they "just punch the clock," therefore the role has lower status and value than those of salaried employees.

Note to everyone: In general, everyone despises punching a clock, digital or otherwise.

Another issue is in play. If employees are being paid hourly, it means they officially are eligible for overtime if they work more than forty hours. However, in real life staff receive the message "Don't put in for overtime, even if you are working more than forty hours. If you do, there will be backlash." This conflict between the official rules and what is really happening destroys morale and productivity. It also causes tension and resentment between the staff who put in for overtime and the staff who don't want to make waves.

The best course of action for leaders and HR is to make these policies easy to understand and easily accessible to all staff. Accountability and transparency around all issues involving money is a big win for companies.

If we truly want to turn this compensation ship around sooner than 136.5 years from now, we must have collaboration among all the constituencies of our workplace—leaders, staff, HR, and recruiters. We must break the silence around the issue of money and deal with hard facts, not fiction. It's time to appreciate the importance of money in the workplace and keep the conversations open and honest until the wage gap is closed.

There will not be an ultimate new workplace until that happens.

The following article addresses these issues. The piece originally appeared as the cover story in *Executive Support Magazine* in 2020 and is reprinted with permission and with some adjustments to the text here. I am sharing it at the risk of repeating some of the ideas I have already conveyed. While the focus of the article is on Executive Assistants, the information applies to everyone who is on a payroll.

---

## How Is HR *Really* Deciding How Much $$$ to Pay You?
## The Hard Truths about Compensation
By Bonnie Low-Kramen & Jeremy Spake, CCP, GRP

*Note from Bonnie:* The title of this article had been a burning question for me for years. I finally found an expert who gave me the answer and a whole lot more.

Did you ever have a conversation that feels like a pivotal turning point moment somehow? I want to tell you about the one I had with Jeremy Spake in August 2019. Jeremy is a compensation expert and before we spoke, I knew that he had delivered two mega session presentations on this subject at the June 2019 Society for Human Resource Management (SHRM) Conference in Las Vegas.

After a series of emails about the current state of compensation in the United States, I requested a phone conversation which happened in August. This conversation, frankly, blew my mind. That talk was the most honest, clarifying, validating, and fact-filled discussion about money that I have had with anyone. What Jeremy shared with me substantially changed the content I teach about negotiating for salaries for assistants, for women, and for anyone who earns a paycheck.

Spoiler Alert: There is great news to share about the future of compensation for Executive Assistants in America, so if money is a burning issue for you, read to the end.

### Where we are right now
In our emails, I shared the following information with Jeremy.

In general, Executive Assistants in the United States are underpaid, some severely underpaid, to the point of not being able to support themselves. Despite the low salaries, these assistants hold a tremendous amount of responsibility in their roles. There are many contributing factors as to why the disconnect exists.

1. The role is populated by 93-97% women.
2. They don't ask.
3. They don't know what the role is worth in their market.
4. They are not trained to negotiate.

5. There are genuine fears about asking for more money.
   • Fear of losing their job
   • Fear of approaching HR
   • Fear of rejection and being told "no"
   • Fear of not being liked and viewed negatively
   • Fear of not being worth more money because of not holding a college degree

While some of these fears are often irrational and do not have a basis in reality, many of these fears are, in fact, possible outcomes.

The reality is that in 2020, there are EAs who are functioning as true executive business partners and viewed as part of the ELT—Executive Leadership Team. They are the right arms to their executives, the backbone of the company, the face of the company culture and as such, are a powerful, influential, and key constituency in the modern workplace.

Despite this reality, the hard truth is that EAs are not only underpaid, but they also report that their companies are using obsolete job titles, outdated job descriptions, and salaries that have not been adjusted, in some cases, for years. CEOs say to me, *"Bonnie, if I don't hear anyone complaining, I think there is no problem."*

Given this landscape, I asked Jeremy this question:

*How is HR really deciding how much to pay Executive Assistants?*

**Jeremy:** First of all, I see what you see, which is that there are pronounced pay equity issues across all industries, jobs and geographies. The good news is that there is an increasing push by corporate HR departments to not be simply reactionary regarding these issues, but to proactively address—and correct—them. So there is an increasing focus right now around compensation practices and ensuring they are equitable.

Here's the hard truth. Part of the answer is complicated, and another part is very simple. For many small to mid-sized companies, HR and compensation departments are working with obsolete job descriptions and market data.

Therefore, we have found that all too often, salary bands are set using vast aggregates of market data from jobs that are sometimes functionally incongruent.

**And many times, compensation is being set arbitrarily—based more on the minimum compensation that people will accept for a role than on hard data.**

**Bonnie:** OMG. "Arbitrarily." You are validating what I am hearing all over the world. So, what I am hearing you say is that the decisions about what to pay people are essentially educated guesses?

**Jeremy:** In many cases, that is true. In larger companies that have bigger budgets, leaders buy surveys for "job families" of particular jobs or functions—"Executive Assistants," for example. The main vendors that provide these surveys are:

- AON
- Culpepper
- Deloitte
- ERI (Economic Research Institute)
- Mercer
- Pearl Meyer
- Radford
- Western Management Group
- Willis Towers Watson

The cost of these surveys ranges widely—often between $5,000-$15,000. Therefore, these surveys are often cost prohibitive for smaller companies and explains why many will only refresh their market data every few years. HR professionals consider this type of survey information as the most reliable data available, even if it is several years old because we can typically age the data from one year to the next based on average salary increases from that year.

In fact, I have worked in the past for multiple compensation survey firms, so I am very familiar with the data collection and reporting processes from both the participant and vendor side.

*[Bonnie in stunned silence.]*

**Jeremy:** When it comes to the C-suite Executive Assistants and the women and men who work for CEOs, *this job family does not* *appear in most surveys.* And when it does, many participating companies either don't know it is there to pull data from or to match their internal roles to or are lumping all their salary data into one larger "Admin Professional" bucket.

*[More stunned silence.]*

**Bonnie:** So, this would explain why C-suite assistants do not currently have a data source that reflects the high organizational level at which they work and the commensurate salaries that they receive.

**Jeremy:** Generally speaking, that would be correct. Another contributing factor to insufficient salaries is that the role has a perception problem. All too often, women particularly have been socialized to not highlight their talents or speak openly about their achievements.

The simple truth is that HR professionals do not fully understand the EA role. Thus, there is an inconsistent perception about what EAs actually do and at what level they function. Many people in leadership and HR still think of assistants in the old paradigm of answering phones, filing, and typing. The reality is much different—but not enough people know this reality. EAs need better PR!

**Bonnie:** How do we fix this? Where does the U.S. Department of Labor fit in all this with their job codes and salary ranges for C-suite EAs?

**Jeremy:** The DOL is not a viable or useful resource for current salary data because the job categories are too wide—meaning you can't really pull out an EA salary data point from the larger set of data—because they're lumping everything regardless of scope into one set of job data. Because of this lack of specificity, HR directors typically do not rely on information from the DOL as a primary compensation data source. In fact, most organizations I work with do not use this data at all to guide their salary structure development. HR prefers to rely on these market data surveys and what candidates will accept for a role to identify a salary threshold for both a job and a level.

The real long-term fix that I see is to collaborate with the survey companies to add current job family descriptions and salary ranges for the C-suite EAs. If these job families exist in these surveys already, we should partner with these survey firms to better advertise their existence and push companies that subscribe to these surveys to report data for these roles. That is how we build a true market data snapshot of salaries for commensurate roles.

The bottom line is that high level EAs are not being offered the money they deserve because historically there has been so little hard data available about the role.

### Pay Equity & Pay Transparency

**Jeremy:** Here is the good news about what is happening right now. There has recently been a flurry of state and local legislation that makes it illegal to ask new job candidates their salary history. Currently, 17 states and 20 local city governments across the U.S. have enacted this legislation. What does this mean for HR? It means that if we can't base new hire salary rates off their previous pay elsewhere, how will we know what a role is worth? Enter market data.

Companies will increasingly need to rely on market data from compensation survey vendors to not only validate their current salary rates, but to drive new salary structure development.

So, it is more important now than ever before for EAs to ensure your job descriptions adequately reflect the level and scope of the EA role, so that the right market data is used to drive salaries for these roles. Having the job description fully reflect the realistic scope of the EA role will help when requesting a salary review of these roles and the function.

### 3 Factors Driving Pay Equity and Pay Transparency

**Jeremy:** There are three factors contributing to new trends around Pay Equity and Pay Transparency. These issues are now front of mind for leaders and HR professionals and cannot be overstated.

**Bonnie:** *[I now jump out of my seat because I am so excited by the ramifications of what Jeremy is saying.]* Really? To use positive and hopeful words like "Equity" and "Transparency" is music to my ears. These words are polar opposites and so different compared to the negative words that have been commonly applied to compensation issues for decades: words like off-limits, taboo, secret, and forbidden. Assistants have historically felt isolated in the process of asking for salary increases and not encouraged to discuss it. What's happened? What's changed?

**Jeremy:** In 2020, the following three factors that will be driving compensation practices for the foreseeable future are:

1. **The strong job market which is increasing the competition for skilled talent**

   The skilled and experienced EAs are in high demand and currently, there are more jobs for EAs in the U.S. than there are people to fill them. In response to the pressure to retain this talent, HR professionals are having to review salaries more frequently, adjust job titles and job descriptions. What this means is that companies are voluntarily conducting pay evaluations, and staff are receiving increases without even asking for them.

2. **Easy and free access to crowdsourced salary data websites like Glassdoor, Blind, Payscale, and LinkedIn**

   Assistants are talented in doing research and are easily finding, documenting, and presenting real-time current compensation data in their geographic market. With more and more millennials in the workforce, they have never known a world without apps to crowdsource information and therefore, it is simply a new "normal." It should be noted that crowdsourced site data is self-reported and not verified, therefore, the data is not considered "clean data." As a result, HR professionals take this data with a grain of salt and do not use it as their primary or sole resource, but they still do review it seriously.

3. **The movements #MeToo #TimesUp**

   In 2017, the #MeToo and #TimesUp movements began in response to systemic, pervasive reports of sexual harassment and bullying in the workplace. One other result of these movements has been to shine a light on all issues related to workplace advocacy—including **compensation**. Leaders have become highly sensitive to the front-page news outlining the large wage gap between women and men and are working to make it right. CEO Marc Benioff of Salesforce is just one of many examples of company leaders investing millions of dollars to close the gap, not only to retain their people and because it is the right thing to do, but also because these actions attract the best new talent. Smart.

**Bonnie:** What do we recommend assistants do with this information?

1. Create your resume/CV and written job description that is finely detailed and specific. These documents are critical to justifying higher compensation.
2. Do your research on what your role is worth in your market. Visit with a local recruiter to get as close as you can to the right number based on your responsibilities, experience, skills, and education.
3. Gather and organize all your data in writing and format in a way that it is easily reviewed.
4. Set up a meeting with HR to present the data and respectfully ask for a "salary evaluation" to see how you are measuring up in the marketplace.

The ramifications of these developments cannot be underemphasized. The time for open conversations about compensation is right now.

**Jeremy:** Most HR professionals are inclined to cooperate with requests to conduct a salary evaluation as a part of their desire to retain excellent staff. Research shows it is more expensive to recruit and train new talent than it is to retain your high performers; so we should encourage employees to feel empowered and ask for this type of review—either on an ad hoc basis or as a part of annual performance evaluation processes.

In fact, many HR professionals in companies have begun conducting voluntary salary evaluations due to the increasing legislation and workplace advocacy efforts around pay equity and pay transparency. In these cases, employees and managers don't even have to present any data—comp departments all over are taking these evaluations seriously. If your organization is not conducting these evaluations, ask for them. Now is the time.

---

It is a new and exciting day in our workplace. We are encouraging open conversations between staff, HR, leaders, and recruiters about the following:

- What EAs really do
- How EAs contribute to the bottom line of a company
- What EAs deserve to earn based on their job descriptions

It turns out that the saying "You don't get what you don't ask for" has never been truer. Jeremy Spake and I highly recommend that you do ask. In a new workplace, where the stakes are high, there has never been a better time than right now.

## STAFF MATTERS QUESTIONS

1. How are leaders making pay equity and pay transparency high priorities in your company?
2. What can HR do to provide more transparency around compensation?
3. How is the latest compensation survey data for job families made available in your company?

# CHAPTER FOURTEEN

# Respect

The thing that people want most is to feel respected. When they do, everything becomes possible. When they don't, the opposite is true. Disrespect is poison and the fastest way to chase people away. Sometimes the poison is invisible, but it is most definitely there. You see it in people's eyes and in the way they walk.

Aretha Franklin's 1967 smash hit "Respect" is considered to be one of the best songs of all time. Why? The word hits a nerve. In my view, respect is one of the words that hits the biggest visceral nerve in the global workplace. I know that is a bold statement, and I also know that it is true.

I notice that social media posts that contain this word in the headline usually get high views. When I began working with Olympia Dukakis, neither of us dared to wonder how long our work together would last. At the core, we worked together for twenty-five years because of mutual respect. That bedrock of mutual respect carried us through every storm, every crisis, and every adversity, including deaths, divorce, mistakes, and much more.

Olympia believed that every person was very important and deserving of respect. That was the given, and she expected me to execute my work with respect as a core value.

I've lost count of the stories of people who are quitting their jobs and coming to me looking for new work because of how disrespected they feel. But I'll get to that in the next chapter. In this chapter, I focus on the impact of mutual respect and the realistic and actionable ways to respect staff and all the constituents in our workplace, including leaders. The staff are referred to as crucial body parts—the backbone of the company, the right arms to managers, the face of the culture, the eyes, the ears, and the lifeblood, not to mention the glue. If any of these attributes ring true regarding your staff, they are more than deserving of respect.

I speak about how respect and belonging are the top two most important things that staff want and need for job satisfaction. They want it even more than money. Surveys show this to be true, but how do I *really* know? In my workshops and conferences, I see the nodding heads of recognition when I discuss respect. I watch the body language in the audience. Staff come up and tell me how much it means to them when I even *speak* the word. Readers of my book show me the word highlighted with exclamation marks in their copies. It means a lot to them and it means as much to me. I hope respect means a lot to you, too.

## Why do it? The impact of respect

The results and benefits of a culture of respect are shown in the following ways:

- Higher staff retention, which saves money. A lot of money.
- Improved productivity.
- Increased engagement—staff's desire to go above and beyond.
- Increased job satisfaction.
- Increased happiness and creativity. Staff generates new ideas that work!

- Increased loyalty, confidence, morale, and teamwork among staff.
- Stronger and more resilient working relationships.
- Staff encouraging their talented colleagues and friends to work at the company.
- Higher company profits.

## How to demonstrate respect: Words matter

Be polite and courteous. This may seem elementary, as we learned it in early childhood, but in today's world, good manners are lacking. "Please," "thank you," "excuse me," and "how can I help you?" are magic words that open doors and calm nerves. Saying them costs not one penny. Some think skipping over manners is a sign of the 24/7 frantic-paced, virtual times we are in. Some say being polite is old school and not needed anymore. *Untrue.*

My mother said they were "magic words" and she was right. The benefits of speaking the magic words are valuable. Literally. The average cost of replacing a $50,000 employee is $62,500–$70,000 according to the Work Institute.

Feel the difference between "Get me the Smith file" and "Please get me the Smith file, Laura. Thanks."

My student Christina wants to be called by her full name—not Chris or Chrissy. Her executive insists on calling her "Christy," which irks Christina, but she has decided to tolerate it. My student admits it feels disrespectful, but it is not a battle she wants to fight . . . not right now, anyway. The executive may believe this issue is trivial and no big deal, and it may not be—to them.

Every leader must decide the degree to which they consider the concerns and preferences of their staff and the actions they are willing to take to address them.

We all need to decide which battles are worth fighting and what things we simply tolerate as part of the job. Recognize that whatever subject is preoccupying us is taking up valuable brain space, time, and energy. That is time that cannot be retrieved, and it is time when other work is not getting done.

## Respect others' time and feelings

Very few people enjoy having others hijack their time. Let us not presume that others have time for us at the particular moment we want their attention. Here are a few examples of the words to say to show respect about time.

"Do you have five minutes to talk?"

"I have an idea. Do you have a few minutes to hear it?"

"I have something on my mind. May I share it?"

Apologize when you have made a mistake or offended someone. If you are not sure whether you have, ask. There is never a bad time to own your behavior.

Just ask. "Did I do something to offend you or make you angry?"

Be proactive. If you see something, say something. Don't wait until someone says, "I'm drowning. Can you help?" Instead say, "It seems like you may be having some trouble. Can you use a hand with that?"

Whatever words you say, speak calmly and with a cool head. Loud and aggressive voices generally make other people shut down and render them literally incapable of hearing anything.

## Respectful everyday actions

*Written thank-you notes*

Students in my classes confirm they have landed jobs because they sent a handwritten thank-you note in addition to an email following an interview. I have heard this same success story many times. This expression of respect via snail mail and attention to detail matters. The extra effort can mean the difference between getting hired and being looked over in favor of another candidate. After all, the potential employer, recruiter, and hiring manager all want to feel respected and special, too.

*Turn off the tech*

You will stand out from the rest simply by being the one to power down your phone at an interview, at dinner, and in a meeting. The ability to give another person undivided attention in today's frantic 24/7 instant-access world is a game changer.

### Hold the door! Hold the elevator!

Even if it is going to make you a little late. These respectful acts are remembered and modeled. You never know who is watching. Be sure to say thank you.

Giving up a seat on the subway, bus, or train—whether it is for a pregnant woman, an elderly person, a young child, or anyone who looks like they are struggling—is respectful. It is noticed and remembered. When I see someone doing something kind, I look them in the eye: "I think what you did for that person was really cool. Thanks."

### Surprise acts of kindness and respect

On long flights, I bring a bag or two of individually wrapped chocolates or candy for the flight attendants. I give it to whoever greets me at the front of the plane and say, "I know you and the team work really hard, and I want to say thank you." The reaction is worth everything. Every flight attendant makes it their business to come by and say thank you. The action makes the crew feel respected and valued.

### Respectful actions in the workplace

- Ask, don't demand.
- Invite staff to meetings and introduce them to others.
- Help others generously and without keeping score.
- Do favors when you can and give advice when asked, whether you have something to gain or not.
- Connect people who should know each other because you can.
- Show up a few minutes early for meetings. Sometimes that is when relationships are built and enhanced.
- Honor starting and ending times for meetings.
- If you send emails or texts in the middle of the night, be absolutely sure the recipient knows that it need not be

responded to until the next day. Have an agreement about how to reach each other in the case of a real emergency.

- Don't interrupt conversations. If absolutely necessary, say, "So sorry to interrupt but . . ." Be intentional and judicious about doing this.

- Help others who have been interrupted. You can say, "George, I had a question about/I was really interested in what you started to say a bit ago. Can you finish that idea for us?"

- Walk the talk. If you have high standards as an expectation, model those high standards yourself.

- Create, communicate, and implement transparent and fair policies for all staff, whether they work in person or remotely.

- Hold people accountable for what they agree to do.

- Apologize when you make a mistake. Don't accept blame when it is not your fault.

- Show grace when others make mistakes. This is a potent and remembered show of respect.

- Show empathy for others. Put yourself in their shoes and imagine what their situation would be like.

- Don't prejudge or second-guess why someone is behaving in a particular way or saying/doing something. Ask.

*Respectful actions: Especially for executives/leaders/ managers/supervisors*

- Stand behind your team as opposed to throwing them under the bus. You hired these people for a reason. Back them up, especially when the situation is messy and complicated. This is an important test of respectful leadership.

- Commit to fair compensation for all staff.

- Invest in the professional development of the staff.

- Give your staff a voice in their own career paths. Care about and support their ambitions.

- Be clear in direction and expectations. Give context, not only content. Say why you need what you ask for, and you will get a better work product.

- Delegate and get out of the way. Trust your staff to do the work they were hired to do.
- Be a person of your word. Do what you say you will do. If you say it, your people can take your word to the bank.
- Be visible and accessible to your team.
- Talk with your team. Know their names.
- Give regular feedback, both positive and negative. Be specific and detailed.
- Give credit. Publicly acknowledge your team. Name names and be specific about their accomplishments. This matters more than you know. Leaders need to appreciate that their team is listening for acknowledgment, and when it comes, it is treasured and remembered. In the celebrity assistant world, it is well known which celebrities include their assistant's name in their acceptance speeches.
- Make it safe for your team to screw up. Be quick to forgive mistakes and openly urge your team to learn from them and move on. No progress is ever made without mistakes. One CEO says, "Mistakes are gifts." Another says, "Done is better than perfect."
- Write. Send personal birthday cards, holiday messages, condolence cards, etc. to your staff.
- Call. Pick up the phone and call your staff on special and not-so-special occasions. Assistants are particularly helpful with this kind of information for their executives.
- Show up. You really know who is there for you if they show up when times are hard. It's easy to show up for a party but not as easy for a funeral. In my classes, I ask students who they want to be and who they want to be around. I urge them to be the person known to move toward a problem or a tough situation rather than away from it.

True story: The assistant to a CEO had a sick father who passed away after a six-month illness. The CEO was compassionate and completely supportive of his assistant taking the time she needed to care for her father during his illness. The CEO and his wife attended his funeral and hosted the family for the repast afterwards.

These actions are not only respectful, they are kind, generous, and human. They inspire loyalty of the highest order and are remembered.

### Respectful actions: Especially for staff

*It's lonely at the top. Show empathy and respect for your leaders.*

Case study: Supreme Court Justice Ruth Bader Ginsburg's funeral took place on September 29, 2020. The social media post featured an unforgettable photo of dozens of her former clerks standing vigil on the steps of the Supreme Court, paying their final respects to their manager. The post had over 39,000 views. Even in death, even in the middle of a pandemic, RBG's staff stood by her to the end.[48]

Here is what I wrote: "Goose bumps. They flew in, they showed up, they stood up, and they stayed and they CARED. They loved her. They wouldn't be anywhere else. Every assistant on the planet understands this photo of Ruth Bader Ginsburg's clerks lining up to show their respect to the woman, the force, the manager who 'treated them like family.' True loyalty like this cannot be faked."

We know that leaders earn more money than staff. Usually a lot

*Doug Mills / The New York Times / Redux*

more money. It may be tempting for staff to be critical of leaders' performance because of this. Sometimes it is hard to feel sorry for a person who makes more in a month than you do in a year. Think again.

It's tough being in charge. There are reasons not everyone wants to be a CEO or an executive. It is hard work, and every day is filled with stress and an avalanche of responsibility. CEOs still only get the same twenty-four hours each day as everyone else, so cut them a break. A big one. This is respectful.

Show empathy. Support your leaders to be better ones by telling them information that would help them. For example, if a leader's flight has been delayed, making him late to the office, the assistant will make sure to have everything ready for his arrival, including food choices. This kind of thinking ahead in context to the situation will make the leader's day easier.

Be supportive. When something good or bad happens, your leaders appreciate feedback. After all, they are human beings, too. Write an email expressing congratulations, condolences, or pride in what has happened. Staff may think these acts don't matter, but they absolutely do.

## Getting schooled on respect

If it is true that respect is the number one most important workplace value, and that the lack of it is the foremost reason why people resign from their jobs, then what is to be done? Interpersonal education and communication training is needed. Education and empathy are key. The dollars that it will cost to train business owners, executives, and managers are far outweighed by the profits to the bottom line generated by an effective and optimally performing staff who feel respected.

The problem is complex and a one-size-fits-all solution does not exist. Working on the issue of respect in the workplace will only produce positive results. The goal is to create a consistently positive environment where respect is the norm. A culture of respect is enthusiastically supported, expected, and promoted by everyone involved in the running of a company. The results may just be magical.

# STAFF MATTERS QUESTIONS

1. What ideas about respect in this chapter would work in your company?
2. What issues around respect matter to you?
3. Who needs to be involved in order to build a more respectful organization?

"You need to learn to level with people without leveling them."

**Foster and Dunlap**

# CHAPTER FIFTEEN

# Disrespect

Disrespect: To show or express contempt, which is viewed as insulting, offensive, outrageous, unfair, wounding, hurtful, discourteous, impertinent, impolite, rude, inconsiderate, impudent, and insolent.

Disrespect destroys people and companies. It is poisonous and toxic. You've heard the Benjamin Franklin quote that one bad apple spoils the bunch? It does.

Disrespect is a root cause for breakups. It was for mine.

Disrespect starts wars. Respect builds bridges.

Love beats hate, but hate sure causes a lot of pain and suffering first.

Disrespect costs big money. Ask any human resources professional about the cost of a revolving door of staff. The price tag in both dollars and morale is staggering, which is why it is critical to understand what happens when a culture of disrespect is permitted to exist.

Disrespect can be slow, traumatizing, demoralizing, transformative, figurative—and sometimes even literal—death. Is this hyperbole? Overly dramatic language? Not even close.

My TEDx talk in February 2022 was called "The Real Reasons People Quit." I point to workplace bullying, sexual harassment, racism, discrimination, and unfair compensation practices as the primary reasons, and all of them are examples of disrespect. They are also not the reasons typically given in letters of resignation and exit interviews, which tend to be less provocative and less truthful.

Response to the TEDx talk was swift and strong. The day after the talk aired, an Italian colleague wrote, "What you said is true. The main reason why people leave their job is lack of respect and/or recognition. You never leave a company but you leave a boss. The company can be [profanity], but if you have a great boss, things look brighter."

There are too many areas of disrespect that are going unsaid and unaddressed. This was my reason for the TEDx talk and, now, for this chapter.

No ultimate new workplace can exist in a climate of sustained disrespect. It is like drinking poison every day and then wondering why you feel so terrible.

There's a distinction between disrespectful words and behaviors and workplace bullying. The topic of sexual harassment—another kind of disrespect—will be covered in a separate section in this chapter. Sometimes there are fine lines and blurry boundaries between all three of these topics, but there are also important differences and distinctions to notice. What all of these behaviors have in common is that they are disrespectful.

The impact of these behaviors is vital to acknowledge if we are serious about building a better workplace for our children, the staff of the future.

This subject is messy and complicated and there are no quick, easy answers. What is disrespectful to one person may be no big deal to another. My goal is to reveal the spectrum of behaviors and reactions that I see all over the world. I leave it to you to decide how much they matter and what price you are willing to pay in your particular situation and workplace.

## Before you read one more word

Thank you for examining this truly tough and serious stuff. To me, there can be no meaningful exploration of the workplace without addressing the disrespect that exists. Period.

Take a moment to think about the people you genuinely care about in your life, whoever they may be—your parents, children, partner, spouse, siblings, friends, etc. As you read this chapter, imagine how you would feel if these people told you that any of these disrespectful behaviors were happening to them? Think about what you would advise them and how you would suggest they respond. It is in that thought process that we will change the world, if we see the value in doing so.

## Disrespect in real life

- Social (media) proof: If you check out the articles about workplace bullying posted on social media, you will see that the more detailed and explicit they are, the more comments and views there are proving what a big problem we have.

- In November 2018, 20,000 Google employees worldwide walked out to protest discrimination, racism, and the treatment of women and minorities at the company. Organizer Claire Stapleton said that the walkout wasn't just about women but also about people of color, contractors, and others at the company who have experienced "feeling diminished or disrespected, have experienced feeling unsafe." The walkout was intended to begin a serious conversation on the issues. Since the walkout, the company has revised its policies for reporting misconduct into one site with live support.[49]

- In November 2007, the Broadway theater stagehands strategically went on strike in the heart of the holiday season. It lasted nineteen days and cost millions of dollars to the theaters and New York City. At one point a few days into the strike, negotiations between the union and the producers stopped cold. Silence, no talking. Why? A union representative commented during this time, "We want respect at the table. The lack of respect is something we are not going to deal with." Millions of dollars

per day were lost, and it was respect that was being de-
manded. Disrespect stopped everything and the price
was very high.

- In 2019, Kaiser Permanente's labor union voted to place
  their 80,000 employees on strike. "We definitely understand the hardship that this may cause, but we're unable
  to take the disrespect," said a customer service representative. The strike was averted.[50]

- The country was stunned on October 30, 2007, by the
  murder of celebrity realtor/former rock band promoter
  Linda Stein, allegedly by her pregnant Personal Assistant
  in New York City. The assistant was sent to jail and had her
  baby there. Ms. Stein was beaten to death with the same
  yoga stick that she used to hit the assistant. The media
  reports that the assistant was provoked to violence after
  allegedly having marijuana smoke blown in her face repeatedly, being "yelled at all the time," and being hit with
  the yoga stick.

  How could this have happened? And more importantly, how could it have been avoided? Is this *The Devil
  Wears Prada* irrational manager from hell coming to life?
  Life imitating art, only worse? This murder is indicative of
  a much bigger workplace issue. It is about abusive behavior, usually verbal and emotional but sometimes physical,
  between employers and staff.

While most employer-assistant relationships don't involve physical violence, most staff can understand and relate to the feelings of
resentment, humiliation, and being disrespected that motivated this
tragic event.

---

**UNIVERSAL TRUTH:** When people are subjected to disrespect, it is impossible to do excellent work because of the mental distraction of resentment and silent rage.

## Fatal disconnect

All of the examples above reflect a serious disconnect between the staff trying to reveal workplace problems and the leaders who were in charge of making the decisions about those problems. I suspect the leaders in the examples above wish they could have turned back time and done some things differently. One need look no further than the daily news to see evidence that desperate people do desperate things.

What I see all over the world are staff being pushed to their limits, to their breaking points. They arrive at a mental place where it is no longer a choice to take action, and they are willing to pay whatever price necessary. That sometimes means staff putting their jobs, and even their lives, in jeopardy, since they can no longer tolerate the disrespect and feel chased away.

Most often, this manifests as staff quitting their jobs or getting fired. That is a lose-lose-lose situation. The staffer has lost a job and in many cases is traumatized by the experience. The managers have lost someone they painstakingly hired, and the company now has to pay to replace that staffer.

We can and should do better.

## Racism and discrimination

"Our lives begin to end the day we stay
silent about things that matter."
**Dr. Martin Luther King Jr.**

In the workplace, racism and discrimination are disrespectful behaviors that feed a toxic work environment. They can lead to attrition, verbal and physical conflicts among staff, and prolonged stress. I do not want to oversimplify this complicated and painful subject. It is important to address it because racism and discrimination are hurting the staff of every color, gender, and religious faith, no matter whether they are the target, the perpetrator, or the bystander.

Our workplaces are paying a high price for racism and discrimination. The economic impact of minorities not having equal opportunity in the United States is costing $5 trillion per year in lost revenue, according to a September 2020 Citi GPS report.[51]

Tim Ryan, Senior Partner and Chairman of PwC US, has not only made diversity, equity, and inclusion (DEI) a high priority, but he decided to make the data around those issues public and transparent. This data includes racial and gender representation in all offices in the United States. In February 2021, he said, "Vulnerability is a necessity if we want to lead effectively. Our people appreciated our candor."[52]

In addition, the data shows that LGBTQIA+ employees are less satisfied than other colleagues at work, and diversity, equity, inclusion, and belonging leaders are turning their attention to these challenges. If issues of racism and disrespect are preoccupying employees, leaders need to make it a priority to figure out ways to openly and honestly address the concerns in an authentic way, just as Tim Ryan chose to do.

## What are examples of disrespectful behaviors?

- Ghosting. Choosing to not reply to emails, texts, or phone messages. Ghosting leaves people worrying and wondering where the breakdown in communication is happening, causing frustration and wasted time.
- Slow response. People have to chase you down for answers, which is another big time waster. The busiest people I know try to respond to communications within twenty-four hours, even if it is with the help of an assistant. They view a timely response as part of their brand, and it would be disrespectful to not respond in a timely way.
- Being late. This sends a message that your time is more important than anyone else's.
- Publicly blaming and throwing people under the bus.
- Taking credit for another staffer's work.
- Gossiping and talking about staffers behind their backs. It

feels a lot like junior high school, and none of this is appropriate in a professional workplace.

- Skipping over feelings. Despite a frantically paced world filled with technology and devices, the workplace is still populated by human beings with feelings who benefit from being dealt with in a personal way.
- Unfair policies. The staff know when rules are not applied equally. Open favoritism is demoralizing to the ones who are not the "favorites."
- Omitting the words "please" and "thank you" from correspondence. Without these words, the communications can come across as demands rather than requests. Example: "Get me that information by the end of the day." I suggest erring on the side of being polite. The time saved is not worth the potential for unintentionally insulting the recipient and being viewed as a disrespectful dictator.

## Case study: Maria

I heard from Maria, a high-level Executive Assistant, who wanted my help to find a new job. She had quit her seemingly great job of three years because her CEO manager had suddenly become unreasonable, moody, and sometimes verbally abusive. I asked Maria if she had discussed the problem with her manager before quitting, and she said no. Weeks later she wrote to say she regretted not talking with him because her former colleagues said that he was going through a divorce, which had been the cause of his foul demeanor. The manager had been so distraught that he had not asked for a discussion, either.

Disrespect and poor communication cost both Maria and her manager dearly. Maria regrets not finding the courage to respectfully say to her manager, "What's going on with you? This is so not like you. How can I help?"

This story highlights the fact that women, in general, will do almost anything, including quitting their jobs, rather than confront negative and disrespectful situations. More about this in chapter 16, "Sex."

## Case study: Kim

An experienced Executive Assistant, Kim supported her CEO executive. Every Monday morning, there was a staff meeting in the conference room attended by about fifteen people. At most every meeting, the CEO verbally humiliated Kim. In front of the team, the CEO would say things like, "Kim, how could you be so stupid?" or "That is a terrible idea. Why would you do that?" Kim felt mortified, paralyzed, and frightened to make more waves. Kim also could not afford to be fired.

After a year of these meetings, Kim had had enough; she no longer cared if she got fired. One Monday morning at the meeting, the CEO called her an idiot. Kim calmly collected her papers, stood up, and left the room without saying a word. The CEO followed her out and said, "Kim, what's wrong?" Kim calmly said, "Every Monday morning you say terrible things to me. Today it was X and last week it was Y. It is wrong and you cannot talk to me like this anymore. Today is the last time." The CEO was genuinely shocked and said, "I had no idea. Please come back into the meeting, and we will talk more about it later today." To Kim's knowledge, no other staffer had ever told the CEO how they felt about her language and intimidating style of managing people.

They talked later that day and Kim finally told the CEO exactly how she felt. The CEO listened, apologized, and claimed that she had been unaware of the impact of her behavior until that day. The CEO improved her communication, but Kim resigned after three more months. Years later, the trauma of that experience is still present in Kim.

## Impact of disrespect

*Backlash on social media*

Consider the story of the Google walkout. In *The Power of Nice: How to Conquer the Business World with Kindness*, authors Lisa Kaplan Thaler and Robin Koval write, "A small misdemeanor can be flashed around the world, and no amount of advertising can help a company un-Google itself from bad behavior."

*Backlash on crowdsourcing sites like Glassdoor*

Staff can use sites like Glassdoor to write anonymous reviews about what it is really like to work at XYZ company. You can view ratings of the executives, the culture, and the compensation. Most people know to take these reviews with a grain of salt. That said, it is difficult to ignore many reviews that are saying essentially the same things.

*Negative word of mouth*

People talk. Especially about bad behaviors. Friends do not encourage friends to work at a company where the staff is disrespected.

## Extreme disrespect

*The Hollywood Reporter* published a story about movie producer Scott Rudin on April 7, 2021, titled "Everyone Just Knows He's an Absolute Monster."[53] The article is an exposé on Rudin's abusive behavior over a period of *decades*. Decades. Rudin was the inspiration for the 1994 revenge film *Swimming with Sharks*, a painfully brutal depiction of abuse inflicted by a Hollywood agent on his young and ambitious assistant.

Rudin was known for throwing epic, profanity-laced tantrums, literally throwing laptop computers, taking revenge, and being vindictive. He chased people out of show business and traumatized untold dozens of human beings through the years, a few of whom I know personally.

Rudin managed people through fear, intimidation, cruelty, and physical violence. The bigger problem is that he was not the only one, not by a long shot.

Why was his behavior permitted for decades? The article cites that his films have earned 151 Oscar nominations and millions of dollars. But at what price? I would say the human price is staggeringly high. I also wonder what stories have still not come to light because of fear.

Until people stand up for respect and hold abusers accountable, the vicious cycle will not stop. There will be no ultimate workplace until we choose humanity over money. Can we envision rewarding respectful and kind behavior over abuse? Can we envision making wildly successful and even more profitable films in a climate of respect rather than one of demoralized terror?

I can envision it, and I will continue working toward it every day.

## Workplace bullying is a global epidemic

> "Too many of us are not living our dreams
> because we are living our fears."
> **Les Brown**

Workplace bullying is a global epidemic that chases good people away. When people resign from companies, they often do not say the truth about why they are leaving. They quit, run out the door, and do not look back. And, more than likely, they searched for their new job on company time without feeling one drop of remorse.

That's what bullying does, and all of this was happening long before the pandemic of 2020. In our workplace, there is far too much leading by intimidation, which causes fear and suffering in silence.

Because of the lack of training for leaders in general and specific training to deal with bullies, this has been an issue shrouded in silence. The targets of bullying sit quietly, hoping that the problems will solve themselves. This complicit silence is destroying companies and gulping profits . . . yet it persists.

Here's the unacceptable reality: leaders either have no idea this is happening or are looking the other way.

If and when exit interviews are conducted, it is easier for staff to say that they "found a better opportunity that fits my current goals" rather than say the real reason, which is that they have had enough of one or more bullying behaviors.

*What behaviors constitute workplace bullying?*

- Yelling
- Using profanity

- Name-calling
- Public humiliation
- Making threats
- Leadership by intimidation
- "Nasty-gram" emails, texts, and/or social posts
- Showing favoritism
- Withholding information
- Ostracizing others
- Sabotaging work
- Physical violence
- Sexual harassment

A few U.S. states have established laws against workplace bullying. At this moment, there are zero federal laws in the United States against workplace bullying. There are several in the works, but none have been enacted yet. One of the reasons is that lawmakers are having difficulty defining workplace bullying and finding language that names exactly what workplace bullying is. That leaves it up to individual company leaders to decide if, when, and how to take action against these destructive behaviors.

The Workplace Bullying Institute reports that 79.3 million Americans have either witnessed or experienced workplace bullying. Current data shows that 35 percent of all offices are affected by some form of workplace bullying. Seven out of ten employees who quit their jobs do so because of bullying.

*Did you ever wonder where the phrase "going postal" comes from?*

In 1986, Felix Nater was the Public Information Officer for the office of the Chief Postal Inspector, Public Affairs Branch of the U.S. Postal Inspection Service in Washington, D.C., when the call came in about the shooting of twenty postal workers inside the post office of Edmond, Oklahoma. After this incident, there were about fifteen more work-related events involving violence in post offices. Hence the media-derived term "going postal" was born. One thing I took away from research on the topic was that the Postal Service believed change and improvement on violence prevention needed to come from the top. Changing the image about the safety of post offices became an internal requirement.

Here are Nater's comments from our conversation.

> "Everyone was in shock when the 1986 shooting occurred. Change was slow-moving in a large organization like the Postal Service. As a huge organization, it was like turning an aircraft carrier on a dime. It took time. The Royal Oak, Michigan, Post Office shooting in 1991 propelled needed policies and procedures in the right direction.
>
> "In that shooting, a letter carrier shot and killed his former manager and four employees, wounded four others, and then committed suicide. Looking back, I think that was the tipping point for change. In 1992, national Workplace Violence Teams were formed, and I was working out of the New York division on a Workplace Violence Prevention Team called the Violence Interdiction Team. My work on the team resulted in the design of my Violence Interdiction Model, which has become the foundation of my consulting model. The goal is to build a RAP philosophy— robust, agile, proactive. *Get everybody involved* was my theme."

Nater is now a Workplace Violence Prevention Consultant who says that workplace violence is highly underreported, mainly attributed to fear of retaliation. This is consistent with SHRM's (Society for Human Resource Management) research from March 2019, which reported that "workplace violence is on the rise" and one out of seven Americans do not feel safe at work. It follows, then, why an overwhelming number of people want to continue working at home in the aftermath of the pandemic. Workers want to feel safe and they feel safest at home.[54]

Nater comments on the current workplace: "A staffer thinks: Why return to a hostile workplace where unfairness is rewarded, and complaints fall on deaf ears? At home I am more efficient and don't have

to deal with the aggravation. When at work, there are caustic personalities to contend with. Spoken and unspoken rules. Supervisors who
test behaviors that transcend legal aspects of work rules. Bullies who
are sanctioned. Approved favoritism. Unfair adjudication of concerns.
Conflict with CDC risk mitigation strategies and poor administration.
Disregard of personal views related to the wearing of masks and medical conditions despite the exception rules. Politics and the workplace.
Race and systemic discrimination in the workplace.

"Staff enjoy the independence and peace of mind at home. They
yearn to be removed from the toxicity, in a safe place where there is
less stress and medical conditions are less apt to be agitated. In short,
dysfunctional workplaces are full of conflict. If that is the case, staff
do not feel safe or secure and believe that no one is protecting them."

*One definition of workplace bullying that lawmakers are deliberating*

> *DEFINITION: Persistent, offensive, abusive, intimidat-*
> *ing, or insulting behavior or unfair action directed at*
> *another individual, causing the recipient to feel threat-*
> *ened, abused, humiliated, or vulnerable.*
> *These health-harming behaviors can include ver-*
> *bal, physical, or sexual abuse and cause work interfer-*
> *ence and undermine the individual's rights to dignity*
> *at work.*

In my work, Executive Assistants report that company leaders are
often "clueless and oblivious" to the rampant bullying going on every
day. Furthermore, staff generally view HR departments as impotent
and unwilling to stand up for employees, especially if bullying is not an
explicit priority of leaders. HR is seen as a protector of management.
Even worse are reports that HR staff and/or the leaders are themselves
the bullies inflicting traumatic pain on the staff.

My students ask, "How do you distinguish between a bully and
someone with a difficult and strong personality?" My answer to them
is "frequency." Everyone understands people having a bad day, but bullies have a track record of continuous and frequent toxic behaviors. As
in years of it.

Managers are bullying staff. Staff are bullying fellow staff. And everyone stays silent. Why?

*Why is everyone so afraid?*

Fear is causing widespread suffering in silence. On a scale of 1 to 10, with 10 being the most, staff reports that their stress level ranges from 7 to way over 10 because of bullying. In addition, staffers feel alone in the problem since they often do not know who they can trust to share this uncomfortable information. There is a general feeling that HR will not be able to do anything to help.

It is important to note that some companies have "anonymous hotlines" for staff to call if they have an issue to report. Many staff report that they do not feel safe calling the hotline for fear of being found out and suffering retaliation.

These very real common fears are of:

- Losing their job
- Making waves
- Stepping on toes
- Backlash, repercussions, and retaliation from being labeled a troublemaker

*The price we are paying*

> "Bullying ruined my life. After eight years at the company, I was on disability and suicide watch for over twelve months. My doctor was desperate for answers and even wanted to perform shock therapy. I have never felt so low."
> **Anonymous 2014 quote from one of my students**

Workplace bullying is costing companies dearly in terms of staff turnover, reduced productivity, increased sick time, and presenteeism where staffers are performing only the bare minimum to keep their jobs.

Targets of and witnesses to bullying are paying the price in the following ways:

- Stress-related illnesses
- Anger issues
- Trouble sleeping
- Preoccupation and a state of constant worry
- Eating disorders
- Headaches
- Excessive smoking
- Excessive drinking
- Excessive drug use
- Depression
- Nervous breakdowns

### "Bullies are like termites"

In my conversation with attorney, business expert, and author Hanna Hasl-Kelchner, we talked about workplace bullying. "I've seen countless examples of abuse of power in the workplace. Bullying is a very serious problem because bullies are like termites. They quietly chew up employees' self-esteem, hollow out employee engagement, and create dysfunctional shells while on the surface things look great. It's only when you dig behind the scenes in confidential conversations with employees that you discover the rot."

### "Forever"

In my classes, I ask, "How many of you have witnessed or experienced workplace bullying in your career?" Typical response: 60–75 percent of people in the room raise their hands. I then ask, "When you experience the feelings of bullying such as anger, sadness, depression, how long does the trauma last? Just for the day it happens, or the week, or the month?" Some of my students shout back and others say it in a whisper, "Forever. The trauma and pain of workplace bullying last forever." Bullying manifests itself physically, and you can perceive its impact with your eyes. Before my audiences say out loud how long the trauma lasts, I see it in their slumped bodies and sad eyes. This. Is. Real.

Is that OK with you? If not, this is one reason out of a thousand why we must act to end workplace bullying in all its forms. Truly, our kids are counting on us.

To build an ultimate new workplace, we must set clearer expectations at the beginning of all staff's employment and stop looking the other way when people break their agreements.

### Stop making excuses for bullies

A January 2021 *Harvard Business Review* article warns of giving bullies a pass when they abuse employees but act nicely afterwards. Leaders end up "reinforcing the cycle of mistreatment that pervades so many companies." The writers of the piece recommend implementing zero-tolerance policies for toxic supervisory behavior and "consistently adhering to those policies."[55]

I can confirm from my work that assistants understand the difference between "making nice" and "faking nice" in order to manipulate the situation and get away with bad behavior. Staff yearn for accountability and for leaders to address this behavior that has no place in the workplace.

Jim Clifton, CEO of Gallup, puts it this way: "Remove abusive managers. No organization should tolerate managers who destroy the lives of people you rely on to get work done. In today's workforce, bad managers are your highest risk."

### Women bullying other women

The hard truth is that women bully other women in the workplace. As a result, we hear the terms "queen bee syndrome" and "mean girls." In mass media, television shows like *Mad Men* and *The Office* and films like *Mean Girls* and *The Devil Wears Prada* are busy perpetuating these stereotypes about women who cannot get along. They turn on one another in order to get ahead without caring who they trample in the process. On one hand, these television shows and films are entertaining and reflect harsh reality. On the other hand, it is no mystery why some men believe this is the way it is with all women and, as a result, believe that women are incapable of real leadership.

When Sheryl Sandberg, former COO of Facebook (now Meta) and author of the groundbreaking book *Lean In*, appeared on the cover of *Time* in 2013, the headline read, "Don't hate her because she's successful." This alludes to one of the points in *Lean In*, which is that the more successful a man is, the *more* he is liked; but the more successful a woman is, the *less* she is liked. This reality is chasing talented women away from powerful positions because they feel ostracized, ridiculed, and alone. Worse, the situation discourages talented women from even trying in the first place, which helps account for the low numbers of female CEOs in America.

Why do women bully other women? The roots of these behaviors begin in childhood with the ways young girls are socialized. From a very early age, girls are taught to view other girls as competition and adversaries. They are taught to compete for the approval of men. They judge themselves and other girls harshly, especially around issues of physical appearance—body, clothes, and possessions. This can give girls a perceived high status, a sense of confidence, and also a boost to fragile self-esteem.

In my classes, I teach that a girl's Achilles' heel is her addiction to the approval of others. That's a deeply rooted socialization that is very difficult to shake without coaching, experience, role models, and aging. I had it, and I admit that I still have it to a degree.

Young girls hear, "Wait until your father gets home" and "You'd better behave or you'll go to the principal's office" and "Make yourself pretty for so-and-so." In general, the strong message girls receive is that a man's opinion is more valuable than a woman's, and a man is smarter and wiser than a woman. Because of this ingrained socialization, women believe it and behave accordingly—even when confronted with strong evidence to the contrary.

These messages travel with women as they become adult professionals and they can manifest as workplace bullying. We see socialized behaviors such as:

- Groups of women will intentionally exclude a colleague by not inviting her to lunch because she is not liked.

- Women are told to "stay in your lane" and "know your place."
- When a personality conflict arises, women will decide to simply not deal with that person ever again. While that goes against logic and professionalism, especially in a place of business, these behaviors exist.
- Women will see colleagues handling something incorrectly and intentionally choose to not intervene. They do this out of fear of retaliation and being viewed as a know-it-all.
- Women will say, "I never want to work for a woman," and they are often not able to say why.

Abused people often abuse others, and it is often unconscious. Therefore, when girls are bullied by other girls, they continue the cycle as they age—unless something or someone intervenes to break the cycle. Awareness can help break these destructive cycles.

The workplace is no place for bullies—male, female, or any gender. The bottom line is that putting others down is not a way to be viewed more positively. Quite the contrary. For women, a better future for themselves and their daughters means choosing to recognize and resist the socialization which does not serve them. It means choosing to like and strongly support women by doing it openly, proudly, generously, and without apology or discomfort.

*The fix: What can you do if you are being bullied?*

Staffers must speak truth to power, as uncomfortable as that is. They can break the silence by uniting to send a well-documented and signed letter to the CEO, the head of HR, and board members. There is great power in having a group of people who agree to be accountable for the data-rich information shared in a factual and unemotional letter sent to the right people.

Using terms such as "hostile work environment" contains the implied threat of possible legal recourse. It is easy to dismiss a single person acting alone but much more difficult to ignore a group of valued and concerned employees. Sweeping the problem under the proverbial rug becomes less likely when there is a group presenting the facts about a bullying situation rather than just one person.

For workplace bullying to be reduced and eliminated, company CEOs and leaders need to put muscle into anti-bullying initiatives. The most powerful way to begin? Make it safe to talk with one another and ask the direct question "Is workplace bullying a problem in our company?" Then get ready to get an earful, especially if candor is rewarded and not punished.

Silence is the enemy of today's workplace, whether working in person or remotely. Until our company leaders recognize the problem and take positive action, the situation is going to get messier. We can make the choice to gather our collective courage to reject these cultures of disrespect that are poisoning staff and companies from the inside out.

### Speak up! The words to say to bullies

My students confirm that it can be excruciatingly difficult to confront disrespectful bullies in the workplace, but it is vitally important to do so. Once confronted, a bully will move on to someone else, which is classic bully behavior. However, most people, especially women, find it almost impossible to confront a bully. In fact, they will do practically anything to not confront one, including quit.

According to Dr. Laura Crawshaw, author of *Taming the Abrasive Manager: How to End Unnecessary Roughness in the Workplace,* most managers who bully (she terms them "abrasive leaders") behave the way they do out of fears of incompetence, inadequacy, and failure. The abrasive leader believes they are solving a problem with their style of leading by intimidation. They justify their behavior with ideas like, "I have to come down hard on them so that the work gets done/we hit the deadline/we don't go over budget."

Dr. Crawshaw also says that many abrasive leaders are oblivious to the suffering they cause. If that is true, then employees have a choice in how to respond. They can flee and move on or they can fight, which she says can be "terribly risky and ineffective." Speaking up to managers who bully requires courage. A lot of it. It also takes support, training, and coaching. Dr. Crawshaw warns, "These strategies are doomed to failure if you show fear or anger."

With preparation and coaching, my students have met with some success by looking their bully leaders in the eye and clearly and calmly stating:

"We need to talk about what just happened in the meeting. I won't be spoken to in that way."

"No one talks to me like that. Today is the last time."

"We need to talk about how we work together. When you said ABC, you may not realize it, but it made me feel XYZ and that is not productive or motivating."

"Have I done something to offend you or hurt your feelings?"

I know from personal experience the strength it takes to speak up to bullies. I also know that addressing the proverbial elephant in the room by confronting the bully results in increased self-esteem and self-respect, as well as respect from others.

Assistants will say to me, "Bonnie, I can't speak up. I'm afraid of losing my job." I respond, "If you keep staying quiet, I'm afraid you are going to lose you." Bullying behavior is soul destroying.

Too many staff are quitting their jobs before even one conversation with the bully. Not every job can be saved like this, but these conversations often buy time and alter the partnership for the better, even if it is fractional.

> **UNIVERSAL TRUTH:** The good news is that when staff muster the courage to speak up to bullies, not only do they not get fired, but the work relationship transforms. Frequently, the relationship gets better, at least temporarily, which is some relief.

*What leaders need to know and do about bullies*

Firing the bully is not the answer. At least, not at first. While it may seem antithetical, the way to manage bullies is to provide support, education, and coaching.

In my conversation with psychologist Dr. Susan Strauss, she said, "The data is clear. I spend a lot of time in courtrooms in America serving as an expert witness on bullying in schools and in the workplace.

I believe that bullying education needs to begin as early as first grade. The data is clear that without training, children who are bullies at school will grow up to be bullies in their companies. And those who are abused tend to abuse others. We cannot look the other way and hope the problem will solve itself. The damage is cumulative. Our company leaders need coaching to give them the courage to take action and break the cycles of bullying and abuse."

My student said, "We are all so relieved that after five years, the bully manager was finally fired." This is seen as good news, but it also means that for the past five years, the bully was permitted to traumatize an unknown number of staff. My goal is to reduce that time to five days or weeks, rather than years. Sadly, the trauma doesn't end there. Data shows that the witnesses to bullying bear almost as much of the pain of it as the targets themselves. In other words, the silent bystanders can be experiencing excruciating discomfort; often, it is enough to make them quit.

Without coaching, the fired bully will move on to another company and most likely bully a whole new group of people. The toxic cycle will begin again unless our leaders see the value of putting a stop to bullying before it even begins. It is one thing to establish zero-tolerance policies for workplace bullying for executives and staff. It is quite another to act on those policies. This requires enforcement, accountability, and clear and fair consequences. This is not easy stuff to take on.

Assistants tell me that sometimes leaders are not taking action because the bully is a rainmaker, someone who brings in a lot of money to the company. What is useful in that circumstance is to look at the employee retention rates to see the cost of replacing the staff whom the bully is chasing away. I ask leaders to decide whether confronting the rainmaker is worth it. Chances are those staffers running for the exit are going to work for the competition in search of a kinder, more respectful culture—even if it means making less money.

For the long-term health of your company, it is worth asking staffers to reveal the real reasons they are leaving. They probably won't even have to say a word. Their eyes and their bodies will tell you everything. Just look.

*What if you are a bully?*

There is a plethora of information about what to do if you work for one of these tyrants, but what if *you* are the workplace bully inflicting all this pain and suffering? One of my students shared that her executive had the nickname of "Dragon Lady," and the executive was proud of it. The rest of the staff viewed this executive as "sick and demented." What reputation do you want?

Answer these six questions to determine if you are a bully:

1.  Have you yelled at someone today and on most days?
2.  Do you slam doors when you are angry?
3.  Have you publicly humiliated and demoralized cowork-ers by calling them morons, idiots, and other disparaging epithets?
4.  Do you throw things, stamp your feet, and pound your fist on the table to make your point?
5.  Do you make fun of coworkers with mean-spirited insults?
6.  Do you enjoy that people are visibly afraid of you?

If any of these answers were "yes," here are five things to do about it right now:

1.  Hire a counselor or coach who specializes in bullying behaviors.
2.  Have one-on-ones with your most valuable coworkers and give them permission to tell you the truth. Take notes.
3.  Apologize to those you have hurt. Sincerity counts. There is never a bad time and it is never too late to say you are sorry.
4.  Speak with your HR department to set realistic and action-able policies regarding bullying. Involve your coworkers in the creation of these policies and then work with HR to post them on your website.
5.  Encourage your coworkers to openly communicate with you as often as needed. Emphasize that they will not receive retribution.

The bad news is that you have been a bully. The good news is that you want to make a change. Help is available.

## Sexual harassment is disrespectful behavior and abuse of power
## #MeToo, #TimesUp, #HandsOffPantsOn

Note: The data shows that women are the primary targets of sexual harassment and that men are the primary harassers. For these reasons, I will be using the pronouns accordingly.

*#NotSurprised*

Women of the world have known about the sexual harassment situation in our workplace for a long, long, long time. Experts point out that sexual harassment is not really about sex at all. Rather, it is more accurately abuse of power exerted by the strong upon the weak.

Sexual harassment has been a taboo and stigmatized subject and the cause of much personal shame and embarrassment. It creates discomfort of the highest order and can cause symptoms of nausea, headaches, and sleepless nights. Sexual harassment can feel like a terrorist attack because you rarely know when or how it is going to happen or what is going to be the trigger.

One surprise, at least for me, is that the subject became front-page news in 2017 and it has stayed there. The silence is broken and there is no putting this genie back in the bottle. I am sincerely happy that I lived to see the day.

True story: A female assistant to a Hollywood director was on the set of a movie. During a break from filming, the director was standing with a group of male studio executives and technicians. The director suddenly grabbed the startled assistant around her waist from behind and lifted her up and down several times in front of everyone. After he let her down, he said, "See? I told you they were real!" The executives all laughed, and the mortified assistant got away as quickly as possible.

That is sexual harassment. It is a form of workplace bullying that is equally, if not more traumatizing, than other forms of bullying for the target.

Eighty-one percent of women have experienced sexual harassment in their life and many have willed themselves to stay quiet out of abject fear and simply not having any road map or role models to help them understand what to do. These behaviors have somehow become their "normal." They sit at their desks, isolated and alone in the problem, often paralyzed, terrified to speak up for fear of retaliation. They avoid and resist conflict at every turn and most would be loath to bring charges.

Until now it has felt far too dangerous to speak up.

The women of our workplace desperately want to feel safe to do the job they were hired to do without having to contend with sexual harassment—from overt demands for sex to more subtle toxic cocktails comprised of demeaning judgments on their clothing and bodies.

*How women are handling harassment*

While speaking with a group of female college students, I was told that when they go to the gym or move around in the world, they intentionally wear baggy clothes, no makeup, their hair in a ponytail, and a hat. All of this is designed to help them avoid unwanted attention. We discussed the wisdom of taking a self-defense class to build confidence in protecting themselves.

An Executive Assistant told our class that she has always been considered voluptuous and has constantly garnered a lot of male attention. Rejecting breast reduction surgery, she intentionally gained weight in order to stop the attention. These events traumatized the assistant for the rest of her career.

Sexual harassment is about power and taking unfair advantage of those whose livelihoods depend on the more powerful. I hear stories of single moms who are the sole financial supporters of their families and their primary worry is job security. When fundamental survival issues are at stake, women will themselves to stay silent and plaster on a fake smile rather than put their children in jeopardy.

Sexual harassment also happens to men in the workplace, and that needs to stop, too. The UCSD Center on Gender Equity and Health released a 2019 national report on sexual harassment—43 percent of men reported experiencing some form of sexual harassment in their lifetime. There has been a rise in legal cases brought by men against women who make unwelcome sexual advances toward them.[56]

## #MeToo, #TimesUp, #HandsOffPantsOn

Sexual harassment was on everyone's minds once it hit the media headlines in a big way in 2017. These hashtags were born as a result of Hollywood producer Harvey Weinstein's sexual harassment court case. As of this writing, at least 100 women, many top Hollywood actresses, have accused him of sexual harassment. It began with one woman coming forward to tell her story, then another, and another. One thing that held women back from coming forward were legal confidentiality agreements, called NDAs—nondisclosure agreements—but others mustered courage, risked legal backlash, and came forward, anyway.[57] The Weinstein case opened the floodgates for dozens more famous and not-so-famous entertainers, politicians, and businessmen to be held accountable for sexual harassment. The targets of harassment have found the courage that comes with knowing so many more were in their shoes. Finally, the targets knew they were not alone and decided enough was enough. Since 2017, over 200 high-profile men have been formally accused of sexual misconduct. Once the men were fired or stepped down, over half of their replacements have been women.

Other high-profile examples from August 2021 include Governor Andrew Cuomo of New York, forced to resign after eleven women accused him of sexual harassment. Mike Richards, Executive Producer of the hit show *Jeopardy*, was named Alex Trebek's replacement as host until numerous examples of harassment, misogynistic sexism, and bigotry were revealed.

The American Olympic female gymnasts are among 156 women who accused the team doctor Larry Nassar of sexual abuse. In 2017, Nassar was sentenced to sixty years in federal prison and up to 175 years in Michigan state prison for criminal sexual misconduct.[58]

The sexual harassment lawsuits continue, and companies have been forced to pay millions of dollars in settlements. The price we are paying as a society is much higher in the form of human pain and suffering.

I am reemphasizing that the trauma from these behaviors is real and lasts forever. It often destroys women's confidence and their ability to enjoy trusting, healthy relationships with men or women. Men are affected, too, as a result, and it is turning many into "manbassadors," supporters of women and willing to stand up on their behalf.

Sexual harassment is not only a "woman's issue." This problem impacts men and children, too, and warrants serious attention in the workplace.

### Nondisclosure agreements (NDAs)

Although I never was asked to sign one, nondisclosure agreements are common in the celebrity assistant world. They are legal agreements designed to control what staff can and cannot say about their employers, during and after employment. In general, they are intended to prevent "tell all" books and articles. For some assistants, they are a mere formality, but for others, these ironclad agreements have been their worst nightmare. They feel silenced and muzzled, prevented from telling the truth about what they experienced for fear of very real and serious financial repercussions.

I recommend that any staffer being asked to sign such an agreement should consult with their lawyer before agreeing to or signing anything.

### What if you're not famous or rich? What are you supposed to do about being harassed?

Most working women are not famous or rich. Most cannot afford high-priced lawyers to file a lawsuit against their executive or company. Most don't want to do this at all.

True story: Carol is in her fifties now and remembers this experience like it was yesterday. She was in her thirties and excited to be working in a large pharma company. Her executive would often stand next to her while she was sitting at her desk. He would rub his groin against her arm to make sure she felt his erection and then he would act like nothing was wrong or unusual. Carol recalls being stunned and paralyzed. She would try to avoid getting in that situation, but often it was unavoidable. She never said a word to him, to HR, or to her husband until after her executive was fired for fraud. Carol regrets not speaking up and she would react differently if she had to live it over again. If it happened again today, what would Carol say to her executive now? Here's what she could say:

- "I don't know what gave you the idea that what you are doing is welcomed by me, but it is not. Don't do it again."
- "How about we call your wife/girlfriend/partner and tell them what just happened?"
- "How would you feel if your daughter [first name here] had that happen to her? What would you tell her to do?"
- "This had better be the last time you do that or my husband/police/security will be here before you know it. That is not a threat. It is a promise and a fact."

Many women wonder if this new spotlight on sexual harassment will make things different now. Do women really have any new clout? Despite the media attention, the fear of speaking up is not going to go away in a minute. It still takes tremendous courage to speak up when something negative is happening, especially about sexual harassment. It took a very long time to get to this place, so it's going to take a while to move us to a brighter, more enlightened culture of respect. I am optimistic about the progress I see happening.

*The price we are paying for sexual harassment*

- More sick time for employees
- Absenteeism
- Low morale
- Lower productivity
- High turnover of staff
- Lower profits
- Suicides

*Backlash to the movements*

- Do some women use sex and their bodies as weapons and for manipulation? Yes. They need to be held accountable, too.
- Do some women lie about being harassed? Yes, but it is rare.

- Are men harassed? Yes. They now have a voice, also.
- Are women the harassers, too? Yes. Their targets are speaking up about them now, also.
- Male executives have said to me, "I don't even know if I can hug a woman anymore." My response is, "Ask her." In the workplace, an even better policy is a no-touching one. Staff will say, "But I'm a hugger. We hug everybody here." Every team needs to decide on the culture around touching in their company.
- Male executives also say, "This has all gone too far. I think the solution is just to not hire women." To that extreme idea I say, "How about you just keep your hands to yourself, and there will be no cause for accusation?"

*Solutions to end sexual harassment in our workplaces*

Leaders need to set the expectation for all staff before they are hired that these behaviors are unacceptable and that there will be very real consequences if they occur. Solutions that work or fail depend on the CEO. It is generally agreed that no real or meaningful change will happen unless leaders at the top of companies are in full support of ending harassment. If they are not, nothing will happen. Their support makes or breaks a safe workplace. Staff are paying close attention. Ways leaders can create a safer workplace include:

- Culture—Make it safe and expected for targets of sexual harassment to expose the problem immediately.
- Training—Have mandatory and regular trainings and education about sexual harassment.
- Incentives—Reward staffers who stand up in support of others.
- Go public—Publicize these ideas on company materials, including the website.

*Sexual harassment training in the workplace*

As of this writing, only six of fifty states require training on sexual harassment: California, Connecticut, Delaware, Illinois, Maine, and New York. The District of Columbia "recommends" training. Everywhere else the training is optional. One key motivation to have training is to reduce costly lawsuits caused by hostile work environments. Also, insurance companies offer reduced pricing if companies offer the training.[59]

Where it exists, the training typically consists of interactive video training, sometimes involving an in-person component for group discussions. Training using virtual reality (VR) is being introduced as well. Video training is less costly than the in-person component. In all cases, staff report that the training is especially effective if the recommended behaviors are strongly endorsed and modeled by senior leadership.

One trend has been an increase in "civility" training, which addresses a broad range of disrespectful behaviors, including sexual harassment. It also includes workplace bullying, racism, social justice, and microaggressions. The training highlights the need for mutual respect, empathy, fairness, and dignity for all staff. Its wide scope, however, makes staff question the effectiveness of this umbrella approach.

All trainings have a price tag, so company leaders have to weigh the cost benefits of training compared to the potential risks of not offering it.

In general, staff have the following attitudes about training:

- Any training about disrespect in the workplace is better than no training at all.
- They question whether the people who really need the training are getting it, especially if the incivility and abuses of power are coming from leadership.
- They observe that training, without clearly communicated policies around accountability and consequences for violations, is pointless and a waste of time and money.

The bottom line is that if company leaders are serious about setting clear expectations about the ways staff behave with one another, education and trainings are necessary and will benefit the company and the staff for the long term.

## Final words about disrespect in the workplace

I share the sage words of psychologist Dr. Maddy Gerrish, "Do not reward bad behavior. Not in children, not in teens, and not in adults. Not at home, not in the workplace, not in life. Just because someone is 'in charge,' does not give them the right to behave disrespectfully and abusively. There is a big difference between someone having a bad day and chronic bad behavior."

We have arrived at a watershed moment in the workplace. We have an opportunity every day to break the silence and to build a transparent ultimate workplace that is fair and holds people accountable for bad behavior. This will most likely become messier before it becomes cleaner and clearer. That's okay. I say bring it. What's the alternative? The silence is hurting us.

The given is that pressures abound in the modern workplace, and supervisors experience stress over workloads and deadlines. This stress often gets passed to the nearest target, the staff. Sometimes managers act out this stress in the form of abuse, which should not be acceptable by anyone's standards. All staff, including leaders, need training in stress management and coping mechanisms.

It seems simple enough—on the surface. If employers treat staff well, they will receive excellent work. Conversely, if employers exhibit varying degrees of abusive behavior, the result will be a revolving door of staff requiring "combat pay" and signing bonuses for candidates to even consider accepting the job.

Education, coaching, and interpersonal communication trainings are needed. The dollars it will cost to train leaders how to manage people well will be far outweighed by the profits generated by an effective and optimally performing team that feels safe, valued, and respected. If we seek to build a workplace where our daughters and sons do not have to fear being disrespected, bullied, or sexually harassed, aren't we willing to do whatever necessary to make that happen? Every member of a business constituency can be a part of the solution. The ball is in each of our courts to be intentional, starting today, about what we do about workplace bullying, sexual harassment, and all disrespectful behaviors.

## STAFF MATTERS QUESTIONS

1. What ideas about disrespect in this chapter are in play in your company?
2. What issues around disrespect matter to you?
3. Who needs to be involved in order to raise awareness about disrespectful behaviors in your organization?

"The 2020s has to be the decade of us sitting down and saying what we are going to do to harness the power of women. I look at the statistics. Seventy percent of high school valedictorians are women. More than 50 percent of college graduates are women. Then I find that only 7 percent of CEOs are women and only 2 percent of VC (venture capital) money is going to women. Talk about emerging markets! One of the biggest emerging market opportunities we have in the US is women."[60]

**Indra Nooyi, former CEO of PepsiCo**


"I want every little girl who's told she's bossy to be told instead that she has leadership skills."

**Sheryl Sandberg, author of _Lean In_**


"Some things just cannot wait. Men must stand up now for women's equality."[61]

**Rick Goings, Chairman Emeritus of Tupperware Brands Corporation**

# CHAPTER SIXTEEN

# Sex

This chapter about gender is going to raise many messy issues and probably provide more questions than answers. I am constantly reminded that we—society, that is—didn't get here in a minute. If we believe change is needed and that equality is our desired result, let us all learn from history and understand that it is going to take some time to get us to a new and better place.

We need to expose the elephants in the room and the deeply embedded stereotypes about the sexes. This cannot, should not, and will not be a women-vs.-men story. If there is any "war" to be fought, it should be the one on ignorance. What you are about to read includes not only hard data, but also generalizations and observations that I stand firmly behind because I have seen them with my own eyes over and over again.

Women and men are different. There, I said it. Different, yes. Equal, yes—or at least they should be. In the workplace, these differences manifest themselves as a variety of needs and priorities that must be uniquely responded to. In other words, women and men often react and behave differently in response to the same workplace situation. Another important difference is that women are still primarily responsible for raising children and doing the majority of the housework, a gender discrepancy that contributes to women being underpaid, some severely.

Real solutions to the problems we face require men being involved in an enthusiastic way, and not only because it is the right thing to do; it just makes sense. It's more than time. Sex in our workplace is a complicated and messy situation that brings up a lot of strong opinions and feelings. And to that I say, "So what?"

## Human issues

To my readers of all genders, ages, and races, I urge you to keep an open mind as you read the data about sex and gender. This is not political. These are not just women's issues. These are human issues and family issues. Gender equality is everyone's business. My intent is to expose all of what I see happening in the world between the sexes in order to inspire change. Much of it is mighty depressing, anger provoking, and in some cases, devastating; but this information can also motivate us to find real and long-lasting solutions to these issues. That will happen only by shining a bright light on all of the ugly truths of our workplace, not by denying that they exist in the first place.

Have women made progress in society? Yes. Have they made enough? Read on so you can decide for yourself.

## LGBTQIA+ communities

LGBTQIA+ stands for:

Lesbian
Gay
Bisexual/Pansexual
Transgender
Questioning or Queer
Intersex
Androgynous/Asexual
+ Other genders & sexual orientations

LGBTQIA+ community members are important staff in our workplace and deserving of the same respect, professionalism, and understanding that other staff receive. More inclusive pronouns are becoming mainstream, and employees are stating their preferred pronouns on social media profiles and in email signatures. You will notice "Pronouns: She/Her" or "He/Him" or "They/Them."

It is a matter of respect to refer to a person by the name they wish to use and by their preferred pronouns. It is important to be sensitive about saying, "Hello, ladies and gentlemen," because there may be people who do not identify as either. When in doubt, simply and respectfully ask, "What pronoun and name shall I use?"[62]

## Women

Because issues about sex are front of mind for women in our workplace, I write articles about sexism, feminism, gender discrimination, and the wage gap. There is an unmistakable and irrefutable connection between power in business and the genders. That connection has much to do with bullying, sexual harassment, and the ability to negotiate for and earn fair compensation. It seems that "whoever has the gold makes the rules" is a dictum that still applies, at least until more women take leadership seats on boards and within companies and have the power to design and enact policies of their own.

## What can leaders do to support women in the workplace?

**GEORGENE HUANG,** *CEO and Cofounder of Fairygodboss*
"The pandemic has wreaked havoc on women's careers, and women's unemployment numbers are skyrocketing. Between disproportionate numbers of women working in industries that were hit hardest by the pandemic, such as tourism and hospitality; essential job functions, such as nurses and other healthcare workers; and women taking on more of the household work, such as family or childcare; there are few factors actually working to help women in the workplace. While there

isn't one solution that will fix every issue women are currently facing, Fairygodboss found four solutions that can help women stay in or return to the workplace.

1.  **Pay and promote them**. Improving compensation is the number one thing an employer can do to make it more likely for a woman to stay at her job (followed by promoting more women into leadership).

2.  **Help them.** While 64 percent of working moms report having colleagues or managers who are helping them with their workload, only 42 percent actually asked for help—meaning nearly a quarter of the working moms struggling felt like they couldn't ask for help.

3.  **Recognize burnout and offer flex work.** The negative effects of burnout are reaching an all-time high, so it's critical to implement a flexible work policy and give employees resources to help them deal with burnout.

4.  **Get serious about D&I (Diversity and Inclusion).** Women, and especially women of color, are more likely than men to take a company's stance on racial and gender equality into consideration during their job search."

**GLORIA FELDT,** *legendary international feminist leader,*
*President of Take the Lead*
Gloria's message to women: *"Be intentional about your life and what you want to accomplish, but understand there's no choice you make that you can't change."*

As a former President of Planned Parenthood, Gloria Feldt has been working tirelessly for fifty years to bring about equality for women. In our conversation, Feldt told me her life's mission still is to help women recognize their own power and get through the barriers. One of the main barriers is the deeply engrained socialization about how women view power and their own relationship to it.

Feldt believes that the future of the workplace will be about women successfully collaborating with men and with one another. Seeing herself as a "deliberate optimist," she views the current landscape as a powerful opportunity to increase gender and racial diversity.

## Progress with diverse women leaders: Slow and happening in fits and starts

**JOHN DONAHOE,** *CEO of Nike*

In 2020, Nike CEO John Donahoe announced a five-year plan to increase the number of women and people of color on the staff. Donahoe also pledged a commitment to maintaining pay equity through 2025. Nike is tying executive compensation to success in hitting these targets. Donahoe said, "Our brand would not be what it is today without the powerful contributions of Black athletes and Black culture."

**ROZ BREWER,** *CEO of Walgreens*

In March 2021, Rosalind "Roz" Brewer took over as the CEO of Walgreens Boots Alliance. At the time, it made her the only Black female CEO of a Fortune 500 company. In 2022, Brewer was joined by Thasunda Brown Duckett, CEO of TIAA, out of a total of forty-four female CEOs.[63]

There is much data to highlight the benefits of adding women to top management teams. Organizations are more open to change and increase their focus on research and development. One important caveat to this study of data over a thirteen-year period is that changes only happen when there is more than one woman on the management team. One is not enough.

The number of women on corporate boards is pretty grim, although with some progress made since 2019. In addition, too few women hold the roles of Senior Vice President, Vice President, Director, and Manager.[64] To turn this around and increase the number of women in the leadership pipeline, it will require intentionality by leaders and rewards for those who make progress.

## Words matter

**AL-HUSEIN MADHANY,** *Vice President of People, Moveworks*

"In and out of the workplace, women are often referred to by men and by other women as desserts: honey, cupcake, muffin, sugar, sweetie, peach, cutie, snickerdoodle, etc. This does not help women, particularly in front of their male colleagues. Contrast this to how male colleagues in the workplace regularly refer to one another in augmentative terms: champ, dude, boss, chief, sport, captain, big guy, etc. What I continue to witness is that men build each other up with their language in the workplace, knowingly or unknowingly. In fact, even in my executive coaching practice, I have heard of male Executive Assistants being referred to as 'boss' or 'captain' by executives in their office, all while their female CEO is regularly referred to as 'honey' by other women in the office.

"This dynamic does not help in elevating our collective respect for women. Indeed, language is an ambassador for our perceptions of each other. And almost everyone has been guilty of this. Although it is difficult to change workplace habits in which we have been acculturated for decades, we can begin by raising awareness and acknowledging the inequity in our language. We can then model different and more equitable language toward one another in the workplace. Change starts with us."

### Relevant workplace data: Sex by the numbers

- 56.1 percent of the American workforce are women aged 16 and over.
- 47 percent of the global workforce are female aged 14 and over.
- 58 percent of the undergraduate college degrees are being earned by women.
- 44 female CEOs are running Fortune 500 companies in America, compared to 456 run by men. There are two women of color who are CEOs of Fortune 500 companies.
- 2 million cases of violence against women and men in the workplace occur annually.[65]
- 8 million days each year are lost to the stress and illnesses due to harassment and violence in the workplace.
- 60 percent of female financial advisors report they have experienced sexual harassment at work.
- The Equal Employment Opportunity Commission (EEOC) received 13,055 complaints of sex-based harassment in 2018, a marked increase from 2017 and the beginning

of the #MeToo movement. In 2021, the number dropped
to 5,581, mainly due to the remote and virtual work
environments.

- Only 13 percent of employees would report sexual harassment if they saw it.
- Only 5 out of every 1,000 rapes result in a felony conviction.[66]

## Women as humans

> **UNIVERSAL TRUTH:** If people are not viewed as human, it
> is much easier to victimize, abuse, demean, and destroy them.
>
> **MORE TRUTH:** The saying goes that power corrupts, and
> indeed, it can. In general, men are in power and have been for
> a long time. Powerful people sometimes take unfair advantage
> of others because they can. Sometimes those in power are
> painfully out of touch with what is really going on in their orga-
> nizations; this is made even worse when they are surrounded
> by people who will not speak the truth out of a combination of
> fear and self-interest.

Mass media has had an enormous impact on the dehumanization
of women. Here are some reasons why:

- The consumption of pornography from a young age—by
both boys and girls—is causing serious and long-lasting
psychological harm. The human brain is not fully formed
until age twenty-five. The unrealistic view of gender roles
depicted in pornography causes uneducated children to believe those extreme images are "how it is supposed to be."
- Social media platforms and apps make it very easy to alter
the physical appearance of people, rendering them car-
toonish or giving them unrealistic attributes, therefore
making it easier to disregard and dismiss them. Deepfake

videos and photos are created by sophisticated software, making computer-generated images that look, move, and sound like an actual person.

- Given the ease of hitting "Send" or "Post" to communicate hurtful and demeaning messages, cyberbullying is more prevalent than ever. The sender does not have to see or feel the impact on the recipient.
- Ultraviolent films, video games, and TV shows perpetuate stereotypes about whole groups of people—women, ethnicities, races, religious believers—as opposed to portraying people as unique individuals.

Data shows that women of all ages, ethnicities, and education levels are under attack. They are suffering violent misogyny on multiple fronts—physically, emotionally, and financially. Women alone cannot stop this dangerous and sometimes fatal trend. Men must participate as strong advocates for change for their wives, mothers, sisters, daughters, friends, etc.

## Women's and men's brains are different. Why does this matter?

Science, chemistry, and brain makeup have much to do with how humans respond to stress. In the workplace, these hormonal factors greatly impact how men and women behave on a daily basis.

Males have more testosterone, which is the hormone related to aggression, competitiveness, physical strength, and lower and louder voices. This hormone is also related to ego, empathy, and the ability to understand what others think and feel.[67]

Females have more estrogen, the hormone related to nurturing, sensitivity to stressful situations, and depression. Estrogen is also essential for sexual reproduction. It is the reason why women tend to have higher-pitched voices than men. Women are generally more concerned with feelings and relationships.

Voices matter: There is data to show that people with lower voices earn more money than people with higher voices, regardless of gender.

It is also generally believed that high-pitched voices are comical and not taken as seriously as low-pitched voices. Just think of your favorite television show characters to see this in practice.

## Socialization: How women and men differ on power and in leadership

> "The most common way people give up power
> is thinking they don't have any."
> **Alice Walker, author of *The Color Purple***

Power comes in many forms. It is often associated with position and money, especially with the ability to negotiate. Studies by social psychologist Adam Galinsky make the case that the desire and pursuit of power and status has everything to do with gender socialization and its resulting psychological impact.[68]

### Men

In general, men are taught from childhood to "be a man." They are socialized to believe that they possess an inherent power and strength and the right to do anything in life they desire.

### Women

In general, women are at their most powerful when they are advocating for others rather than for themselves.

Women are eager to seek consensus and be conciliatory in negotiations with teams.

When women don't self-promote, they are viewed negatively. When women do self-promote, they are also viewed negatively.

**Examples:** Female students in my workshops report that they are accused of being overly aggressive when they try to make their point assertively. They emphasize that men are rarely referred to in this way.

Women the world over report that when they are deeply concentrating on their work, they are asked by men "What's wrong?" and "Are you angry?" "Resting bitch face" (RBF) is a real thing that I have only heard attributed to women. This face often makes men uncomfortable, and as a result, women are told that they should "smile more." To say that this is deeply frustrating for women is an understatement.

## Unconscious bias: The double bind for women

This is the classic "damned if they do and damned if they don't" dilemma. That is, the very same qualities that are praised in males may still be judged negatively in their female colleagues. Some of these judgments are more subtle than others.

As I move around the world in my speaking and teaching career, I inevitably find myself in a room of professionals and often encounter a male and a female standing together. I make it a practice to not assume the male is the executive and that the female is the assistant or somehow subordinate to the man. I will often ask the woman first, "What is your role in the company?" I want men to see that I am respecting the women around them.

For men, I urge you to comment on a female colleague's terrific work, not on how attractive she looks in that dress. When you flip the script and imagine a woman commenting on a man's physical appearance, you can see how far we have to go.

*Examples of unconscious bias*

Awareness is the only way to change the status quo. Here goes:

- Men are called ambitious. Women are called bitchy or bossy.
- Men are viewed positively when they advocate for a raise. Women must be very careful how they ask for a raise, as they run the risk of being viewed as too ambitious, needy, or self-promoting.

- Men are called humble. Women are called too self-effacing.
- Men are called confident. Women are called queen bees.
- When men show feelings or cry, they are called strongly sensitive. When women show feelings or cry, they are called weak, overly emotional, and even hysterical or crazy.
- Men who talk strongly are called tough. Women who talk strongly are called profane and foul-mouthed.
- Men have networking groups and clubs. Women have cliques.
- Men are macho if they enjoy sex. Women are sluts if they enjoy sex.
- Men are considered adorable heroes for taking care of their children, whether they have a job or not. Women are expected to be attentive mothers no matter what their work status is and are quick to be shamed for what may be perceived as favoring work over motherhood.
- A "dad bod" is cute and sexy. A "mom bod" is fat and un-attractive. In fact, a new mom is expected to look like she did pre-baby immediately after giving birth.
- Men's clothes have pockets. Most women's clothes do not.
- Women's breasts are considered too risqué to be seen while breast-feeding in public. Yet check out the mass ad-vertising for well-known lingerie stores.

## The landmines of stereotypes and myths about women

Do women really talk more than men in business meetings? Um, ac-tually, no.

Yoshiro Mori was forced to resign in February 2021 as head of the Tokyo Summer Olympics Committee. In a discussion about bringing more women onto boards, Mori complained that women caused meet-ings to run long by talking too much. When asked about his remarks at a news conference, he said, "I don't listen to women that much lately, so I don't know."[69]

Women know very well the dynamic in meetings when they at-tempt to speak and are interrupted by a man who then "mansplains" her comment. It is referred to as "manterrupting." Other terms gaining popularity in response to male-heavy gatherings are "manels" (all male panels) and "manologues" (a long-winded speech).

Adam Grant, organizational psychologist from the Wharton School, says that "women face the harsh reality that it is better to stay silent and be thought polite than to speak up and jeopardize their careers."

Women experience backlash and criticism if they point out these behaviors. One effective strategy is for other women in the meeting to interject to say, "Joe, excuse me. Julie, I'd love to hear the rest of your idea. Can you finish that thought?"

## W.A.I.T.: Why am I talking?

Top leaders train themselves and their teams to use the W.A.I.T. strategy from David Emerald's book *The Power of TED.*[70] Ask yourself the following questions:

- Am I talking for approval and to be overly helpful? (Rescuer)
- Am I talking to control and take charge of the situation? (Persecutor)
- Am I talking to complain and whine about all I don't like? (Victim)
- What is my intention behind what I am about to say?
- Is there a question I could ask that would help me better understand what the other person is saying and perceiving?
- How might I simply listen and let go of my urge to talk at this moment?

## The glass cliff

The term "glass cliff" was coined in 2004 by Professor Michelle Ryan and her colleague Alex Haslam of the University of Exeter.[71] It refers to the idea that women leaders are brought into a company at a particularly challenged time. These women have broken the glass ceiling; but if a woman in that situation fails, she falls off the cliff and becomes the person to blame. Two women who have broken the ceiling are Mary

Barra, the CEO of General Motors since 2014, and Jacinda Ardern, the Prime Minister of New Zealand since 2017. Other examples are Marissa Mayer, former CEO of Yahoo, who was brought in to compete with Google, and Theresa May, the UK's Prime Minister from 2016 to 2019 who had to address the Brexit controversy.

A study by Zenger Folkman found that women are rated by their teams as better leaders during a crisis.[72] Women were rated positively on thirteen out of nineteen competencies on the 360-degree reviews. Why? The reason has to do with engagement and the ability to communicate, collaborate, motivate, and inspire.

## The virtual world and sexual harassment

One might think that sexual harassment is reduced with more staff working from home and communicating remotely via videoconferencing software. Unfortunately, harassment still exists in the virtual world, but it looks a bit different. As you read the following examples, consider whether you can envision these things being said to a man:

- Before the videoconference begins, a male executive says, "Heather, you should wear your hair down like you used to at the office. You look better like that."
- "Lindsay, you look better when you smile."

Cleo Stiller, the author of the book *Modern Manhood*, told me, "My advice for men in the workplace is to not comment on the physical appearance of women—period. Err on the side of not going there because you cannot predict how a woman will respond to these comments. If a man wants to pay a woman a compliment, choose to highlight a work accomplishment. Stay away from physical appearance."[73]

## Webcams

Some women are uncomfortable being on camera because of their home workspace environment. For example, some women have no choice but to take calls from their bedroom, which can make them feel vulnerable and set up for inappropriate comments. The "blur background" feature on video software has helped this situation immensely.

Nonetheless, the work-from-home (WFH) reality is causing leaders and HR professionals to create policies around the use of webcams. The ability to create virtual and blurred backgrounds reduces the possibility of embarrassing comments about one's personal home office space that could cause discomfort and lead to conflict. After all, the pandemic forced many in our workforce to create a home office with very little notice and this meant having to improvise in a space that was not intended for work, such as a bedroom. Perhaps for the first time, staff were seeing inside their colleagues' homes and, in many cases, meeting their family and pets.

One other trend is to give staff at least twenty-four hours' notice about whether webcams are required, requested, or optional. Webcams are being viewed as an important way for staff to stay connected and develop rapport.

## Double standards

*Money*

One of the biggest differences between women and men is how much money they earn. This is known as the gender wage gap, which is covered in chapter 13.

It bears reiterating that if no action is taken to change the status quo, it is estimated it will take 136.5 years to reach gender wage equity. The United Nations predicts it may take up to 257 years.

Too many women feel stuck and paralyzed in jobs they want to leave because they do not have any financial cushion on which to rely. Often they are so frightened to lose their paycheck that they stay silent about the serious problems they see in the workplace. They resist asking for more money out of fear of being rejected or fired. Their concern about providing for their children is overwhelming and takes top priority.

The fact that many women are struggling to make ends meet is not only a female problem. It affects everyone in a family and society as a whole. This is also crucial information for leaders of companies to know and to pay serious attention to. In general, women will go to great lengths to not attract negative attention. They go into survival mode. The most effective leaders work to connect with their staff regularly and make it safe for their team to honestly answer the question, "How are you doing?" "Fine" often does not really mean fine.

### The "pink tax"

The money situation gets worse for women. Not only are women not making the money they deserve, but they are also being charged more for essential toiletries and services. It is called the "pink tax" because many of these items are pink and designed to be attractive to females. The data shows that the price of dry-cleaning a woman's shirt is more than that of a man's. The same is true with shaving cream, deodorant, skin creams, and cosmetics. The short-term fix? Women can buy the items marketed to men. The long-term fix? Women need to let companies know they are onto their tactics.

### The "mommy penalty" and the "mommy tax"

Being a working mother is costing women more money. Family leave policies and benefits for parents in the American workplace are slowly improving, but we have a long way to go. Working mothers often feel grateful to have a job and therefore trapped into accepting lower wages and less responsibility in exchange for schedule flexibility. Mothers are often penalized financially when they need to take time off to care for a sick child. The same is true for those taking care of aging and sick relatives, a responsibility that often falls to women.

## Case study: Rebeka Adamson

Rebeka Adamson is an Executive Assistant in New Zealand. When we met in 2007, Adamson was seven months pregnant with her second child. In a coaching session, she told me she wanted to leave her current job, and she had been contacted by a company to see if she was interested. She was concerned the new company would not be interested in her because of her pregnancy. I urged Adamson to go to the interview and to be up front about her plans for maternity leave, etc. She decided to approach the interview with the intent to get an offer.

To Adamson's happy surprise, she was extended an offer and was even able to negotiate a salary 10 percent higher than her current compensation. For her family, this was life-changing money that was much needed. The company was happy to wait for her through her maternity leave, and when she did start, Adamson would not only work as an EA but would also have the increased responsibility of eight direct reports because of her experience and stellar leadership skills.

Pregnant women often feel extra vulnerable while applying for jobs, and for good reasons. As a result, Adamson almost did not go for the interview; she was anticipating a rejection. She also worried she would need to take less money because the company was going to have to make compromises because of the pregnancy. What she learned from the hiring manager was that her skills, talents, and reputation overrode those compromises and that her value was evident. The bottom line is that the skills to fulfill any given job description equal money, even if you are pregnant and if you have children. You don't get if you don't ask.

## More hard truths about women in the workplace

- **Working moms feel guilt.** I felt tremendous guilt both at home and at work. When I was home, I felt guilty about what I had not been able to finish at work. When I was at work, I felt guilty about not being a good wife and mother, not to mention daughter, sister, and friend. I often felt not good enough at anything.
- **A woman has to prove herself repeatedly, especially in tech companies, in order to justify a promotion or more responsibility.**[74] It is a demoralizing experience that chases talented women away from potentially successful careers.
- **"Himpathy."** When women are sexually harassed and/or raped, the default behavior by society too often is to blame

the victim rather than the harasser or rapist. Women are told that they dressed too provocatively, that they led their attacker on, or that they must be mistaken. For this reason, far fewer women bring charges against their attackers. They have the very real fear of not being believed by the people in power.

- **Gaslighting.** In general, women know who the harassers are and find themselves in an "avoidance" mode. They are vigilant and alert to danger in the effort to stay safe. When confronted by a man telling her that she is "imagining" or "fabricating" the problem, she may work to avoid him even more. To speak up may put her in more danger. Sometimes she believes she is the problem or is imagining the problem. That is called gaslighting, and the result can be profoundly traumatizing and psychologically damaging.

## (Dis)belief and denial

Psychologist Dr. Rayna Cooney commented, "Denial is the strongest human protective mechanism, and explains why, when faced with indisputable evidence, a person can deny its existence."

As I travel, one of the most painful experiences women share with me is a time when they have not been believed. As young girls, women are socialized to be "good girls," to "follow the rules," and to "tell the truth." As adult women, when they act according to this training and are not believed, they become disillusioned and paralyzed into silent rage.

While it is true that some women lie about being victims of harassment or bullying to take advantage of the system, the data reveals that very few women lie, in part because of the excruciating pain of speaking up and the financial expense associated with it. The feelings of shame and embarrassment usually prevent women from coming forward. In fact, most men underestimate how big a problem bullying and harassment actually is. In 2021, 81 percent of all women reported having experienced some form of harassment.[75]

According to Dr. Cooney, denial can be about anything—bullying, harassment, or the wage gap. Even murder.

Dear readers, the denial is real. We have a very serious problem on our hands. How can we solve problems some people don't even believe exist?

## Wait, there's more: Sexist bias in browser searches

If you doubt that sexism, gender inequality, double standards, and discrimination exist, look no further than an online search to see the images that show up for each gender. You will see that many follow sexualized stereotypes.[76]

Examples:

- School girl | School boy
- Woman | Man
- Female secretary | Male secretary
- Female actor | Male actor
- Best writers of all time
- Best singers of all time

## Clothes matter

There has been much talk about Mark Zuckerberg's hoodies and Steve Jobs's black turtlenecks. Women simply cannot dress as casually as men do without being scrutinized under a critical microscope. Can you imagine any female CEO or high-level executive showing up on stage in a hoodie and being taken seriously? You may be thinking of a few exceptions, but in general, this is a real double standard.

In general, if a woman changes her hairstyle, gets new eyeglasses, or loses/gains weight, it is noticed and commented upon by both women and men. This is generally not true for men. There is the famous example from 2014 of the Australian male newscaster who wore the same suit for a year, and no one noticed. In contrast, female newscasters receive constant feedback about their clothing and appearance. This is sexism. One news report on the story aptly read, "Women apparently can't win when it comes to what they wear at work."[77]

## *Feminist* and *feminism* are not dirty words

Negative stereotypes abound for the words feminist and feminism, resulting in rejection and contempt for these terms. At their extreme, the words have come to refer to radical, shrill, and bitter women who hate anything to do with men. The truth is that if you do an online image search of the word "feminist," you will see many pictures of men along with women.

Feminism is about everyone having an equal voice. It is not about a battle between women and men. It's not about women gaining power over men. It's about women valuing men and men valuing women.

As a female leader, I say thank you to female and male feminist activists Sojourner Truth, Elizabeth Cady Stanton, Susan B. Anthony, Gloria Steinem, Barbara Jordan, Shirley Chisholm, Betty Friedan, Ruth Bader Ginsburg, Oprah Winfrey, Parker Pillsbury, Gloria Feldt, Karen Nussbaum, Ellen Cassedy, Jane Fonda, Dolly Parton, Lily Tomlin, Tarana Burke, John Stuart Mill, the Dalai Lama, Alan Alda, Serena Williams, Michelle Obama, and so many more who have stood up and spoken out for equal rights.

Human beings in a free society should have the right to have a say in their governments, laws, cultures, and values. Everyone should be able to define themselves and assert their value, independent of other sexes' opinions, and to claim the same rights and freedoms as anyone else. This is what equality would look like and this is what feminism is about. Feminism aims to give an equal and uninterrupted voice to females.

However, women currently do not enjoy the same rights and freedoms as men. It will take men joining the effort toward gender equality for it to happen. When women gained the right to vote in 1920, it was won by men fighting for it, too. Just as ending slavery in America in 1865 took the efforts of non-slaves, so it will be with achieving true equality for women.

Feminist and feminism are not dirty words. They are important words, right up there with freedom, humanism, equality, and justice.

The bottom line: If you want your daughters, granddaughters, and any females you care about to be paid fairly and treated respectfully in the workplace and in life, you are a feminist.

## How women behave with other women— deeply rooted "default" socialization

Years ago, I was speaking with Nancy Fox, who is a business coach, speaker, and author. I was talking about how badly some women treat other women and how poisonous it can be. Fox listened to me, paused, and said, "Bonnie, I used to be one of those women until I almost got fired." To this day, I am moved by her honesty in admitting that she had behaved like a backstabbing bully.

Fox explained, "I was a merchandising executive for a leading lingerie company. I was highly motivated by career promotion and money and I felt I needed to do whatever it took to get ahead. I didn't think much about who I was hurting in the process. Apparently, I pissed off lots of my colleagues and one day, my boss called me out on my behavior. She told me that I was great at my job, but they would let me go if I didn't turn things around with my colleagues. She told me the hard-to-hear truth that my performance wasn't more important than my ability to work well with people. Wow, what a powerful lesson. That was the wake-up call I needed."

In my classes, I ask my students to imagine a workplace where women enthusiastically and happily support each other—a workplace without manipulation and victimization, without passive-aggressive behaviors, where bullying between women is practically nonexistent. Sound good? If yes, why then is it so hard to make it happen?

Changing ingrained socialization will require an awareness of the invisible default button that is deep inside all women. It will depend on our commitment to *shut it off.*

The messages women received loud and clear when we were young girls are steady and strong, and they stay. As in forever. These messages can become ingrained as autopilot behaviors and unconscious bias, an internal default button of a sort.

These are some of the socialized messages young girls receive from families and society alike:

- Know your place and don't veer too far from it.
- Don't step on toes. Don't make waves or trouble.
- Be seen, not heard. And, sometimes, be invisible.

- Be pretty, be quiet, and be perfect—at least in how you look. Women are trained to compete with one another for the approval of men. These messages have exploded with conflict in light of the issues with sexual harassment and the #MeToo and #TimesUp movements.
- Approval from men is the most important thing.
- Be loyal to men, even if you believe they are wrong.
- Don't come across as too smart or a know-it-all. Don't brag or toot your own horn—you might be viewed as conceited or full of yourself.
- Be critical and "judgy" of other women. Compare and be envious.
- Smooth everything over at all costs—even if it means apologizing for things that are not your fault.
- When receiving feedback from another woman, the default behavior is to be defensive and suspicious of motivation.
- Be grateful for any job, and don't question the money you are being paid.

*Other examples of the default behaviors*

Women judge ourselves harshly for pretty much everything, often feeling we don't deserve the raise or the attention or the promotion. We feel badly about taking credit for something great that we did. We judge our female colleagues harshly when we see their success and we feel envious and say things like, "I did a better job than her last year and nobody noticed me." We allow our male executive's bullying behavior to slide and excuse it with statements like, "Well, that's just the way Andrew is." If we're honest, we would say that we would never allow "Andrea" to get away with a fraction of what we allow "Andrew" to get away with.

I see that women are deeply conflicted by all these mixed messages. They instinctively know that they have a responsibility and obligation to speak up, yet many stay silent. Fear wins. And here's the scary truth: because the socialization is so deeply rooted and normalized, *women often don't even realize why they feel the way they do.* For example, a woman who is commenting on a successful woman may say something like, "I just don't like her. I don't know why. I just have a feeling."

That's the default at work, and it takes introspection and coaching to get to the bottom of what is really happening here.

Women tolerate bullying and sometimes don't even know that's what it is because it has become so normalized and part of their daily experience. Many students have said to me, "I didn't realize that I was being bullied until you explained what it was. I thought my situation was just how it is for everybody." That's the default in full swing.[78]

I am shocked by the number of stories of "queen bee" and "mean girl" junior high school–type behaviors in billion-dollar workplaces. One example is a female staffer putting together a business lunch and intentionally leaving out a colleague because "we don't like her." Women need awareness and we need leadership to show us another way.

Data shows that women apologize much more than men, and for things that are not anything to apologize for. However, women don't forgive as easily, and we never forget a misstep, especially with other women. We forgive men much more easily. The hard truth is that when women don't get what we want from men, we often take it out on other women.

Our default button tells women to take things personally, to take offense. If that's true for you, I urge you to resist and reject that first impulse, that automatic behavior that tells you to be suspicious of the motivations of other women.

Given the complexity of our global workplace, women need to become clear about what is going on and to speak up about what they know. We can now understand how we get trapped in the default. Old habits are hard to break. What I see all over the world is that these behaviors are slowing us down and stopping some of us dead in our tracks, preventing us from fulfilling our goals and dreams. Too many are quitting their jobs over it or even landing in the hospital from stress. Furthermore, our children are watching closely and modeling these behaviors. Unless we turn off the default and break the toxic patterns, the cycle begins again.

*What's the long-term fix?*

- Women need to shine a light on this invisible default button buried deep inside. Then it becomes a conscious decision about how to move forward with possible new choices.

- To raise awareness with one another, women and men can have conversations about what the default looks like.
- Women and men can create a new normal, a new default together. They can design new policies that work for everyone and can be sustained.
- Women can choose to cut themselves a break and to cut other women breaks. They can choose to be more understanding when women make mistakes.
- Women can take a fresh look at their relationships and partnerships with men—whoever and wherever they are—to see how the default is in play.

The impact on the community is profound when women reject the default and choose to see other women as collaborators, allies, and partners.

We know that women make excellent leaders, but there are too few in leadership positions. When women feel sincerely supported by other women, they lose the fear of being ambitious and seeking leadership positions. However, as Sheryl Sandberg points out in her book *Lean In*, many female leaders leave before they have to because of the loneliness at the top—or even partway to the top. It is because of default socialization.

Women everywhere can generously support other women to achieve leadership positions and to remain in them even when they make mistakes or when they fail. There is a serious double standard in the world about how women view women leaders and how women view male leaders. Women generally hold one another to a higher standard than men. When women stop tearing one another down and choose to build one another up, families and companies benefit.

What I know is that women can create a new normal for ourselves that is based on respect and the freedom to give feedback without fear of retaliation. Women need to do a better job at setting expectations with one another—to set a standard that makes it safe to speak more directly and honestly and to elevate one another.

I fight hard every day to shut off my own default button and to make sure it stays off. We can't underestimate the pull of the social-ization; but if we really work on it, we can break vicious cycles and patterns, and our lives will change for the better.

## How men behave: Deeply rooted default socialization

Just as women receive powerful messages when they are little girls, men receive equally powerful default socialization as little boys. Here are some examples:

- "Be a man." "Man up." Boys are trained to hide, disregard, and lie about their feelings. They are taught that crying is weak and bad. Boys get the message early that to be a man means to be strong and to deny having feelings. The mes-sages are mixed, though. Sometimes a man will be seen crying and it will be viewed as "sensitive and moving." It is understandably confusing.
- Boys are taught to deny not only their own feelings but the feelings of others as well. Sensitivity, compassion, and vul-nerability are viewed as weaknesses. This causes sadness and depression.
- To talk about being sad or afraid is viewed as negative. This would explain the popularity of the TV show *Mr. Rogers' Neighborhood*. Fred Rogers was determined to give chil-dren a safe place to express themselves.
- Boys are made to prove their masculinity throughout their lives through sports, physical strength, and sexual prowess. They are rewarded with approval by other boys and men.
- Boys are taught to win at all costs.
- Boys are taught to honor a code of silence to protect other boys and to not be a "snitch."
- Boys are taught that womanizing is accepted and often ex-pected behavior.
- Boys are taught to use violence to solve problems.
- Boys are taught to highly value and to pursue power, money, and sexual conquests.

- Boys watch pornography from early ages and are taught to not see the humanity in girls. In pornography, boys see girls as sexual objects who enjoy being degraded and dehumanized. Boys come to believe that that is the kind of sex girls enjoy, which explains why boys are genuinely shocked when girls do not respond positively.
- Boys are taught to make fun of girls and these behaviors can turn misogynistic and even violent. An example that starts in grade school is about a girl's period and the term PMS, which stands for premenstrual syndrome. Adult men come up with dozens of disparaging alternative meanings, such as Psychotic Men Slayerz, Pissy Mood Syndrome, and Pardon My Stupidity.

## Relevant data about boys

Awareness can result in change. Here goes:

- 1 in 4 boys are bullied in school.
- According to the U.S. Department of Health and Human Services, approximately 1 in 6 boys will be sexually abused by the age of 18, and most of them aren't saying a thing about it out of shame and confusion.[79] Boys use alcohol, nicotine, and drugs as a way of dealing with their feelings.
- Boys turn to gangs and cults as places for friendship, a sense of belonging, and outlets for aggression.
- Boys become depressed and turn to suicide because they are taught they cannot ask for help.
- In 2017, the *Journal of the American Medical Association* (JAMA) reported that suicides for boys between the ages of 15 and 24 are at an all-time high.

It is not difficult to see a connection between the dangerous default messages to young boys and eventual behaviors in the workplace when these boys grow up to be adult men. How do we undo these powerful default messages? Awareness, education, and coaching are the keys to reconnecting the head to the heart for boys and men alike.

## What men can do: Be a manbassador

Manbassador is a term that was coined in 2013 by Harvard Business School. It was part of a program designed to bring male students into the serious conversation about gender disparity and gender inequality. A manbassador is a man who believes in the empowerment and advancement of women.

Manbassadors are not afraid of the hard facts around these issues and take positive action on behalf of women. These men know there may be some strong backlash, including name-calling such as pussy, wimp, and whipped. Despite this reality, manbassadors will call out bullying and harassment and they do not tolerate abusive behaviors toward women or men.

Manbassadors do the following:

- Set plans and goals for getting more women into management and leadership. Involve women in the process.
- Speak up and stand up for women in public settings.
- Establish clear and transparent evaluation criteria for roles.
- Require diversity in hiring.
- Implement unconscious bias training for all staff and especially anyone involved in the hiring process.
- Don't penalize women for promoting other women. Reward them.
- Avoid tokenism and having only one woman in any given group. This onliness is very isolating and chases women away. Work toward fifty-fifty representation and be transparent about it.

## What women can do

I heard Sheryl Sandberg, author of *Lean In*, speak in New York City in

2013. She said, "Women must talk to and support one another to succeed. Talking can transform minds, which can transform behaviors, which can transform institutions. When increased numbers of women hold positions of power, that will become the new normal and we will all stop being so surprised by it."[80]

- Apply for more jobs, even if you are not totally qualified.
- Understand the power of the default behaviors that come from socialization and work to identify them before you get sucked into the cycle.
- Go out of your way to help other women. Work hard to not be the "only" one. "Onliness" leads to "loneliness," which leads to isolation and quitting.
- Apologize less and do not apologize for things that are not your fault. Women apologize ten times more than men. I urge my students to cut the "I'm sorry's" by a third.
- Train others to not interrupt you. Women are interrupted three times more than men. Politely say, "Excuse me, I wasn't quite finished," then go on to finish your thought.
- Don't allow others to take credit for your work. Politely say, "I'm happy that you liked my idea. Shall we get together to go over my research in more detail?" Better yet, another colleague at the meeting can say, "Yes, isn't Beth's idea terrific? She presented it last week and I particularly like how she is planning XYZ. Great job, Beth."

## What did Iceland get right? The road to equality

In 1980, the women of Iceland went on strike for one day. Ninety percent of the women refused to cook, work, or take care of their children. Classical theater fans will be reminded of the ancient Greek play from 411 BC by Aristophanes called *Lysistrata*, in which the women deny sex to men until they end the Peloponnesian War. The name of this day in Iceland was called "Women's Day Off" and it was considered a watershed moment for equal pay and reducing sex discrimination in Iceland. The country was paralyzed.

Iceland President Vigdis Finnbogadottir commented, "Things went back to normal the next day, but with the knowledge that women are as well as men the pillars of society. So many companies and institutions came to a halt, and it showed the force and necessity of women. It completely changed the way of thinking."

Men were generally supportive of the action. Finnbogadottir, a divorced mother, was elected the first female President of Iceland in the summer of 1980. She remained the president for sixteen years.

In 2022, Iceland is considered the most gender equal country in the world, followed by Finland, Norway, New Zealand, and Sweden.[81]

In Iceland, women earn ninety cents to every dollar a man earns. Of the elected officials in Iceland, 47.6 percent are women, and they are all led by a female Prime Minister. Iceland leads the world in family leave policies, day care benefits, and closing the wage gap. The United States is the only industrialized nation that does not guarantee workers paid maternity leave, and it has the worst maternal death rate in the developed world. The message is clear that women and families benefit from having more women in power in government and in companies. The U.S. Congress is 27 percent female.

## How do we progress toward equality between women and men?

Publicly held companies based in California (there are about 600) worked to meet the requirements of a new state law that requires that they have at least one woman on their boards of directors by December 31, 2019, or face a $100,000 fine. Illinois passed a 2019 law requiring businesses to report data of female and minority board membership, but the law was struck down in 2022.

The road to change is through supporting the pipeline. The data makes clear that women are excellent leaders when given mentorship, training, and a supported career path. A strong pipeline of executive talent truly can begin in grade school and be supported through high school and college with leadership training.

Whether made of glass or cement, the ceiling and the barriers for women need to come down. Women need strong career ladders built of rungs that go not only up and down but side to side—even when women are mothers and caregivers. The benefits are clear. Gender diversity on a team results in stronger, more innovative, more productive, and more profitable organizations. When companies proactively nurture female leaders, it is good for the bottom line; it is even better for engagement, productivity, morale, employee retention, and staff recruitment. Gender diversity gives companies a competitive advantage when women are represented at every level.

My hope is that this chapter enables leaders to better understand what is happening for both women and men in our workplace. That is how we make change for our children and theirs.

## STAFF MATTERS QUESTIONS

1. What were the most surprising things you learned about sex and gender in this chapter?
2. What challenges about sex and gender need to be immediately addressed in your workplace?
3. What resources do you have to address these challenges?

"Bonnie, I may not always agree with you and I may not always do what you say, but I always want to know what you think."

**Olympia Dukakis**

# CHAPTER SEVENTEEN

# Confidence

Olympia Dukakis really meant it when she told me she always wanted to know what I thought. Almost forty years later, I realize how much these words helped build my confidence. She trusted me, and as a result, I felt confident and free to speak my mind. It is a powerful feeling and one I share with those with whom I work. In my personal experience as well as global observations, I see that confidence is serious business and the single most important differentiator in the workplace. In general, it will be the person with high confidence and lower abilities who will get the job over the person with low confidence and higher abilities.

To have low self-esteem and low self-confidence can be self-fulfilling prophecies in the workplace, a setup for low advancement. After all, if you are not confident in your abilities, why should others have confidence in you?

Confidence and self-esteem are often elusive for women. They are difficult to secure and even harder to hold onto once you have them. In the previous chapters about secrets and sex, it is clear that adverse life events can destroy confidence in mere minutes.

People with low confidence are often told to "fake it until you make it." That is easy to say but hard to do because confidence—and the lack thereof—is visible in our bodies and on our faces. It can be perceived in the way we talk and the way we walk.

This subject is vital in a book about building an ultimate new workplace because confidence can be the difference between success and failure. For example, can you imagine the test of confidence for Scott Rudin's young assistants, none older than twenty-five, who I reference in chapter 15? It does not surprise me that Rudin's verbal abuse demolished the confidence of those around him, making them feel powerless to fight back. Again and again, I have observed examples of staffers who quit their jobs because their lack of confidence made it easier to resign than to stand up to the bully.

These events can destroy confidence *for years*. Typically, the more extreme the situation, the more the staffer needs the support of mentors, family, peers, and therapists.

## How to build confidence

Confidence is cumulative. Successes build on one another, and we use what we learned from former experiences in our current situation. It is true that experience is a great teacher. However, when we experience setbacks, it is important to have trusted mentors and a support team around us to give us realistic, truthful perspectives.

Here are actionable ways to build your confidence.

- Solicit feedback. Confidence does not happen in a vacuum. It is a group activity. We gain confidence through responses from the people in our orbit.
- Seek mentorship from people you trust to have objective and honest feedback on how you are proceeding.
- Discuss what things are in your control and in your power and what things are out of your hands.
- Schedule a postmortem following a project or a group event. Commit to reviewing what went well and what did not in order to improve the next time. Real-time feedback is invaluable to building confidence.
- Seek additional education and certifications, and read books to enhance your knowledge of the subject at hand. No education is wasted.

- Achieve goals to build confidence. The process of deciding to do something, such as to study for and gain a certification or a degree, is a quantifiable achievement that no one can dispute or take away.
- Be courageous about criticism. It's very important to consider the source of criticism, but if it is from someone you trust, know they would not be investing the time if you were not onto something. Work to really take in the critical feedback and think, "What can I learn from this?"
- Slow it down, lower the pitch of your voice, and turn up the volume. To speak quickly and too softly at a high pitch sends a message of low confidence. It may communicate that you just want to get a conversation over with and your message is not worth hearing anyway. Be intentional about slowing down your delivery, lowering the pitch of your voice, and adjusting its volume to be certain you are being heard. You will be taken more seriously. Try it.
- Stop apologizing unnecessarily. Women apologize far too often, and when we do, it indicates low self-confidence. Replace "I'm sorry" with "Thank you." Rather than, "I'm sorry we need to reschedule the appointment," say "Thank you for working with my schedule to make the change."
- Disagree assertively without being aggressive. Say, "I totally understand your point, but I am concerned about another factor that may be the deal-breaker. Let me tell you what I mean."

## What destroys confidence

In my work, I meet many people who tell me they have something to prove. They are trying to manage the fear of not being good enough or worthy of their position due to scarring experiences such as being bullied in school or told that they do not qualify for a job because they lack a degree.

*Factors that eat away at confidence*

- Being judged negatively for something you have no control over, such as age, race, religion, or physical ability or appearance.
- Socialized messages from childhood, such as that you are not smart, capable, or trustworthy.
- After mustering the courage to negotiate for a salary raise by presenting a professional and well-documented business case, being told, "We want you, but we can't pay you. Take it or leave it."
- Leaders and/or peers who go radio silent with no explanation.

## Case study: "Rock of Insignificance"

*Victoria N., Executive Assistant in Washington State*

"I got my start in the administrative field in the 1970s, when we were called Secretaries. It was a common opinion in those times that Secretaries were a dime a dozen, a nameless cog in the corporate machine, and dumb. The belief was that our work was mindless, but we best look good while we're doing it. I dealt with many instances of sexual harassment in the form of inappropriate remarks and touching. I felt I was viewed as a faceless sex object who just typed and answered the phone. As a hardwired introvert, I chose to deal with these instances by being the one who left the company.

"Despite being a highly effective professional, I began to buy into the idea that I had little value and it ate at my confidence. It was like a heavy rock that I picked up and put in an invisible backpack and carried around for my entire forty-year career—my Rock of Insignificance. At the Be the Ultimate Assistant conference in 2019, what grabbed my attention the most was when Bonnie Low-Kramen said, 'You are the CEO of You, Inc.' This was a revelatory moment for me. In that moment I took back my power and dropped that backpack with the heavy rock. I chose not to be insignificant ever again."

## Imposter syndrome

Imposter syndrome is defined as doubting your abilities and feeling like a fraud. It disproportionately affects high-achieving people, who find it difficult to accept and own their accomplishments as genuine.

I will never forget when Olympia Dukakis was told that she had received an Oscar nomination for her role as Cher's mother in the 1987 film *Moonstruck*. Early on, director Norman Jewison had predicted it, and as the weeks got closer to the Academy Awards, Olympia became the odds-on favorite in Las Vegas. The oddsmakers were right. She won the Oscar for Best Supporting Actress.

Right up until the ceremony, Olympia had a genuinely hard time wrapping her head around all the attention for her work in the film. At age fifty-six, she had already enjoyed a long career playing classic roles like Mother Courage, Hecuba, and Mary Tyrone in *Long Day's Journey into Night*. About *Moonstruck*, she would matter-of-factly say, "This part just wasn't that hard. I don't deserve an award for that." She felt like an imposter.

Olympia finally understood the reason for the award when her close friend and fellow actor explained to her, "Olympia, every role you've ever done shows up in Rose in *Moonstruck*. You bring all of that experience to the character. That's why you will win." That explanation made sense to Olympia and, frankly, it has helped me put aside my own imposter syndrome when it has raised its head. I hope this revelation will do the same for you.

Some of the most high-achieving people have admitted that they have had imposter syndrome. I remember being very surprised when this admission came out of James Corden a few days before he was to host the Tony Awards. I think of Corden as oozing with confidence, not to mention extraordinary talent. When I heard the interview, my thought was, "Wow, if James Corden feels like an imposter, what hope is there for the rest of us?" It is important to note that you just never know what is happening with people on the inside. Looks can be very deceiving. We don't know what might be a trigger to something that happened long ago.

Ann Hiatt, leadership strategist and the former Chief of Staff for Jeff Bezos at Amazon for three years, has written about her own imposter syndrome and strategies she has put in place to ensure that crippling fear and anxiety about her own abilities have never held her back. She comments, "During my twelve years at Google, I started labeling emails that included praise and positive feedback which I could pull up anytime I needed motivation and reassurance. By seeking out and savoring this feedback you will build a network of trusted peers and mentors."[82]

Finally, one way to build confidence is to fight back the fear that eats away at it. This was Olympia's advice to me, which I call upon quite often and share with my audiences.

"Don't waste time on fear, Bons. Fear is boring."
**Olympia Dukakis**

## STAFF MATTERS QUESTIONS

1. When you think back on your career, what were turning-point events that helped build your confidence?
2. What events eroded your confidence and how did you find it again?
3. What are three ways to build your staff's confidence at your company?

"Nearly all men can stand adversity, but if you want to test a man's character, give him power."

**attributed to Abraham Lincoln**

"If your actions inspire others to dream more, learn more, and become more, you are a leader."

**John Quincy Adams**

# CHAPTER EIGHTEEN

# Leadership, Power, and Sitting in the Rain

Power: Possession of control, authority, or influence over others

**CATHLEEN SCHREINER GATES,** *CEO of SimpleNexus*

"Power means the ability and authority to influence outcomes. Therefore, it can be applied to situations to drive outcomes that do not serve any good. In my career I have absolutely seen abuse of power, which can be both subtle and obvious. In my workplace experiences, I most often saw the abuse of 'position power.' That is someone using their position authority to intimidate, stifle creativity, push people out of a company, discriminate, create toxicity in a team, etc. I have seen it all. Companies must have a zero-tolerance policy for this and must create and nurture a culture where it is safe to bring these abuses to the attention of the right people who have the power to do something about it."

*Memorial service for Olympia Dukakis, New York City, 2021*

*Photo © Bonnie Low-Kramen*

As I have already written, Olympia Dukakis, my employer for twenty-five years, passed away on May 1, 2021. The memorial event was held on Sunday, August 8, at the Delacorte Theater in Central Park, New York City. The photo above is from the event.

Picture this. The Delacorte is a completely outdoor venue. The event was scheduled between 6:00 and 8:30 p.m. and it poured rain from 6:00 to 8:30 p.m. We knew we were taking a chance with the weather, and as a precaution, we urged guests to bring umbrellas. People flew in from all over for this event, and there was no alternate date in case of rain.

Two hundred and fifty of Olympia's family, friends, fellow actors, directors, playwrights, screenwriters, set designers, lighting technicians, hair stylists, makeup artists, wardrobe supervisors, casting directors, and doctors showed up. Most people had umbrellas, but many did not and got drenched. We sat there in the steady rain to honor the legend named Olympia Dukakis. We all bore witness to the life and work of the woman, the artist, the larger-than-life human who changed all of us just by knowing her.

What a lesson in leadership, love, and respect. I sat there thinking that there was nowhere else I would rather be. I also wondered who would sit in the rain for me. Who would sit in the rain for you? An interesting question to ponder.

I wrote the following article for *Executive Support Magazine* about what I learned about leadership, power, and partnership from my work with Olympia Dukakis. It seems fitting to include it in this chapter as we think about the future of leaders exerting power.

---

## A True Partnership: Olympia Dukakis and Bonnie Low-Kramen
## August 11, 2021

*On movie set for* Over the Hill, *Sydney, Australia, 1990*

"I just want to be a good plumber." This is how Olympia Dukakis approached her craft of acting. Her job was to put all the parts of a character together and to make it solid and strong. And it wasn't enough to give just one or two great performances a week. A "good plumber" delivers a great performance eight shows a week for the run of a show. That's what good plumbers do. Her commitment to excellence in all details mattered. No leaks. Olympia thought of all professions like this.

As an assistant, I became a good plumber too. I worked to be as great an assistant as Olympia was an actress, and I wanted to do it not just on some days but every day. I realized that that's what "ultimate assistants" do.

For 25 years, I had a front-row seat supporting an extraordinary woman who powerfully touched millions of hearts and minds. Olympia Dukakis went from working as a respected New York City theatre actress, whose name her agents advised her to change because it was too ethnic (she refused), to an internationally known and adored movie star who became an easily pronounced household name. Olympia catapulted to fame in a matter of months. I was by her side for all of it. Speaking of names, she was "Oly" and I was "Bons."

Olympia's life was changed forever by her Academy Award for the film *Moonstruck*, and so was mine. What a ride. It is everything you think it would be and a whole lot more. And I learned. Wow, did I learn about show business, about being a working woman, about making hard choices, and about life. I wouldn't have traded it for the world.

When I started working with Olympia at the Whole Theatre in January 1986, I was hired as the PR Director. No one got hired without Olympia's approval, so my interview was on a snowy night since that was the only time she had. We liked each other right away and she hired me on the spot. I was impressed by her obvious authority as Producing Artistic Director. She wore her power without apology, which was a lesson right there. There was no question that she was in charge, and I thought it was very cool to be a woman running a theatre. I had no idea what would happen after she asked, "When can you start?"

My job was to write press releases about the plays we were presenting, which included classics by Chekhov, Shakespeare, and Williams and musicals by Kander and Ebb. As an English and Theatre major at Rutgers University, this job was perfect for me. This job also meant that I had to spend a lot of time with Olympia and the whole creative team. Perfect.

We began. Neither of us dared to think our work together would last for 25 years, which leads me to one of the first lessons I learned.

1. **Be present.** Be here now. In a world filled with distractions, pay close attention to the person and the situation right in front of you. Olympia had a gift of making you feel as if you were the most important person in the room. Her eyes were laser-focused, her smile was electric, and her curiosity was endless. She asked probing questions that made you know she did not miss a thing.

2. **Do your job.** It would make Olympia frustrated and not a little angry when a limo driver would turn around and ask, "So, how do I get there?" She would ask me, "Isn't that his job to know?" No matter what your job, do it with pride and excellence every day. If you need to ask someone else how to do it, either learn it or do something else.

3. **Respect everyone.** No exceptions. Olympia would often return to New York after working in Hollywood and half-kiddingly say, "Bons, you are so lucky that you work for me. People treat assistants like crap." What I got to see with my own eyes again and again and again were the benefits of respecting everyone. I watched the lighting people be extra careful with Olympia's angles. I saw the special care that the hair, makeup, and costume people took with how Olympia looked in a scene. They did it because Olympia respected their craft. In a movie, Olympia wanted to get it right in a minimum of takes, and she knew that any one of those people could make or break a scene. I learned that respecting everyone is not only the right thing to do, it is also the smartest thing to do.

4. **Enjoy the mess.** Theatre is a collaborative art, and I learned that also goes for any workplace. Any group of people coming together to make something is exciting and messy. Olympia would embrace and enjoy the messiness of any process—the discussions, the rehearsals, and the renovations on the apartment—because that is what it takes to get the end results.

5. **Speak up and say the hard thing.** Time after time I got to watch what happened to a group of people when Olympia said the thing that was on everyone's mind. When she did, they visibly relaxed and were relieved. Whether it was the actor who needed to be fired or the budget that needed to be cut or the scene that just wasn't working, Olympia was usually the one who spoke the words that needed to be said but could also hurt people's feelings. She had a way of getting to the heart of the matter with honesty and compassion, which breeds respect. I can think of dozens of people to whom she had to say hard things, and they stayed loyal and loving friends forever. One of those people is me.

6. **"No one will go to theater jail over this."** I made my share of mistakes over the years and I was grateful and relieved when she said this to me. This was Olympia's way of keeping things in perspective and allowing for the mistakes that inevitably happen. Olympia knew that the price she paid for delegating to me and anyone else is that she gives up control and needs to expect occasional mistakes. I made very sure that the doozies only happened once, and Olympia depended on that.

7. **Stand up for what and who you believe in.** Even if it is controversial. Olympia practiced non-traditional casting and played one of the first transgender characters in the *Tales of the City* miniseries. She was an outspoken and fierce advocate for the LGBTQIA+ communities. Because she grew up facing discrimination as a Greek American, she fought inequity every chance she got. When Olympia accepted the Academy Award, she ended

her speech by raising her arm with the statue and proclaimed, "OK, Michael, let's GO!" She was supporting her cousin Michael Dukakis, who was running as the Democratic nominee for President of the United States.

Olympia showed up for her family, her friends, her students, her fans, and for me. In 2004, I gave Olympia the final draft of my book *Be the Ultimate Assistant* to review and offered her free rein to take out anything she did not like. She called me two days later and said, "Bons, you really have something here. Don't change a word. Oh, and I'll write the foreword." She did.

8. **Everything is negotiable. Everything.** This includes salary but also having the contents of a hotel minibar removed and some of the excess furniture too. You don't get if you don't ask. I learned to say what I needed because other people were not mind-readers. I watched Olympia ask for what she needed to do her work and most of the time, she got it. She was able to quasi-patiently tolerate the negotiating process and "let it cook."

9. **Don't read reviews.** Olympia was very focused on today and the future. She made it a practice to not read reviews, and she didn't want the rest of us to tell her about them—even when they were raves. She did not want her performances to be colored by these words no matter what they were. Her attitude for all of the reviews was to say, "See that newspaper? It is going to be wrapping up someone's fish tomorrow." How's that for a way to handle the haters? Don't get sucked in by anyone else's opinion of you. Seriously consider the source.

10. **Fear is boring.** I am grateful that I now know that most of the things we worry about turn out to be okay. So much time is wasted on worry and fear. It might be easier said than done, but I hold onto Olympia's words. "Don't waste time on fear, Bons. Fear is boring." It was her way of telling me to take big, giant bites of life and to not be afraid to fall on my face. What a role model for that!

Olympia Dukakis may be gone, but she's not really. Not for me and not for so many others. How do I know?

In the hundreds of emails I received after Olympia's passing away on the morning of May 1, 2021, many of the messages said, "You and Olympia had something so special. You were very lucky." The thing is, I don't want our partnership to be a unicorn. We were tested many times along the way and we worked very hard to address the challenges and move on stronger.

If you are reading this, I hope you have a partnership that is mutually respectful and that you both feel truly supported. If you don't, I hope some of these lessons will help you get there.

---

When I posted the article on my blog, it was viewed over 27,000 times.

In today's world, we see a tremendous shift in power in the global workplace as leaders navigate work-from-home realities and talent shortages. What is clear is that the most successful leaders are the ones who are trusted by their teams because they collaborate and cooperate with them rather than dictate to them.

## STAFF MATTERS QUESTIONS

1. How do leaders exert their power in your organization?
2. What ideas about leadership and power from this chapter would work in your company?
3. How would your company leaders benefit from training to improve their understanding of power?

"Never underestimate the power of a small group of committed people to change the world. In fact, it is the only thing that ever has."

**Margaret Mead, anthropologist**

"One of the core values of our company culture is caring. As a part of my job, I get to volunteer and have had the pleasure of planning philanthropic events, coordinating fundraisers, and making money donations to charitable organizations I truly care about. We host group activities that genuinely help our community, and I couldn't be happier. My company supports me to learn, grow, try new things, and be rewarded for volunteering."

**Kristen Olmstead, Executive Assistant, Denver**

# CHAPTER NINETEEN

# Incentives

The number one most important thing leaders can do to understand what motivates and incentivizes the staff to achieve stellar results is . . . *ask them*. Incentives are not one-size-fits-all.

Happy employees stay twice as long at companies as unhappy ones. The questions to answer are:

- Are happy employees also productive ones?
- Is employee retention always the goal?
- If leaders want not only to attract talented staff but also to inspire staff to stay, what are the most effective ways to do that?

Leaders who understand incentives know that what makes their people tick and what drives them will be different for each person. It is a mistake to automatically assume the answer is money. Money is a driver for many staff and certainly part of the picture, but only a part. The smartest leaders never lose sight of the staff's need for respect and belonging. They will be the ones with the most loyal teams.

This chapter is meant to give you other ideas of incentives for staff.

## Guilt-free incentives

All incentives for staff need to be wholly endorsed and supported by the CEO and management. This point is critical to offering incentives that will be treasured, embraced, and sought after. For example, staff may receive an extra day off as a prize of some kind. However, the only way that staff will actually take that day off is if they will not receive backlash or have to pay some other price for doing it. These ideas apply to perks like "unlimited PTO (paid time off)." Leaders need to be keenly aware of this very real guilt factor that comes when staff see strings attached to incentives.

In the new workplace, the ability to have guilt-free flexibility in a work schedule is seen as one of the biggest incentives for staff.

Amy Weinblum, former Chief of Staff to Oprah Winfrey, shared her way of maintaining a strong and happy team who worked in a busy and pressured environment. She made it her practice to prioritize taking vacations. One way she did this was to call a special staff meeting during which the team would plot out their vacations for the year ahead. The team got the message that it was not if but when they would take time off. This transparent system enabled the team to know when everyone else was taking their vacations, and this supported planning backup and solving any conflicts. Weinblum said, "I made sure they knew that making (and keeping!) doctor's appointments was important, and I really wanted them to take good care of their health. The team usually responded with a combination of surprise and relief. This kind of consideration is absolutely vital for a busy team."

## Monetary incentives

The pandemic hit the restaurant business very hard, including the family-owned Whataburger fast-food chain based in San Antonio. In March 2021, CEO Ed Nelson and Senior VP of HR and Brand Culture Pam Nemec announced giving employees "extra-mile bonuses" as a thank-you for all their hard work through the pandemic. The 46,000 employees are called "family members" and received bonuses totaling

$90 million. The company leaders have also doubled 401(k) retirement contributions.

The company is strong and planning to build thirty-five new restaurants. The right incentives are a win-win for the company and a recipe for long term success.[83]

Compensating your staff fairly in a transparent and logical way should be a given in the ultimate new workplace. What follows are ways to reward staff monetarily for their continued good work.

### Cash bonuses

Cash bonuses are wonderful incentives, especially for staff who are already happy in their work. Some companies have formal review processes that are tied to bonus structures. Leaders found that when bonuses are distributed at the end of the year, staff wait to resign until the first quarter of the following year, when there would be a mass exodus. In response, companies are now doing quarterly reviews and bonus payouts to stagger resignations.

Another point about performance bonuses: in many companies, only some groups of employees are eligible for performance bonuses. This automatically sets up an us-vs.-them dynamic. The administrative staff is often one group that is not eligible, no matter how well they perform. If a sense of belonging is as important as I am painting it to be, then you can see how this would be demotivating. I urge leaders to reconsider their policies about performance bonuses and design a fairer system that is more inclusive. The ROI will be evident.

### Discretionary or spot bonuses

These bonuses could be in money, paid time off, gift cards, or other prizes. They are typically given as acknowledgment for going above and beyond.

### Tuition reimbursement

In a workplace changing by the minute, professional development has never been more important. Reimbursement plans vary widely in companies. I urge leaders to create good plans, make these benefits well known to staffers, make the rules for applying fair, and encourage staff to take advantage of the opportunities to keep learning.

### Company discounts and perks

Whether they are discounts on food, clothing, travel, pet supplies, or entertainment, staff love saving money whenever they can. Popular perks include:

- Free or low-cost workouts
- Free or low-cost healthy food
- Free or low-cost massages
- Free or low-cost nutritional counseling

### Childcare support and tutoring assistance for children of staff

Childcare has emerged as a burning and urgent challenge for many staff, and the high costs are a big burden to shoulder. Companies are offering financial assistance for the children of staff, and it is a welcome incentive.

### Hilton's way

As a "Best Place to Work," the Hilton Hotels leadership shows their commitment to the employees and their families. They offer an adoption benefit of $10,000 per child to be adopted, travel discounts, and parental leave to support the family during the transition. The website's careers material uses the phrases "thrive at Hilton" and "for all."

## Nonmonetary incentives

As I have emphasized, money is not the only way to incentivize staffers. The following examples are ways companies can demonstrate respect, belonging, and support.

## Feedback and reviews

All humans yearn for feedback. Staff need frequent feedback, not only at annual review time. The importance of feedback in the workplace is minimized and overlooked in many companies, mainly because leaders are uncomfortable giving verbal feedback. The discomfort is exacerbated by the lack of training for providing feedback. Feedback is an important incentive for staff and a key to employee retention. Essentially, staff wants to know how they are doing more frequently than at an annual review. These interactions are a form of stay interviews. (See chapter 8.)

## Mental health and wellness programs

The pandemic highlighted the mental health and wellness challenges faced by the staffs of the world. Stress, anxiety, and loneliness have been running rampant since March 2020. Removing the stigma associated with mental health provides a huge incentive for staff and shows them that their leaders are compassionate and empathetic.

## Trophy or award

Public acknowledgment with a physical trophy or award can be tied to the company culture, the mission/vision statement, and/or a monthly or annual event.

## Off-site appreciation events

Staff attend a sporting event, tour, barbecue, concert, or play as a group and sometimes staffers families are included in these events. Some companies offer elaborate experiences that require extensive travel arrangements.

## Put down the phone

Believe it or not, it is an incentive for staff to know that leaders will put down their phones during a conversation to give them undivided attention. Try it.

*Opportunities to volunteer and make*
*contributions to causes that matter*

Julie Kavanaugh, Executive Director of Administration/Chair of Philanthropy at Vectrus, Inc., said that volunteerism is a core value at the company. She assisted in coordination of the leadership team at Vectrus to assemble bicycles for the children of military support. The staff have fun together while feeling fulfilled by helping others in need. Sometimes staffers' families can get involved with the activities, too.

*Kudos boards: Virtual and in person*

This board can be physical or virtual. It is a way for teams to express gratitude and give shout-outs to one another. These messages are especially meaningful and important when some of the staff are working at home and others are in the office.

*Say thank you—in detail*

Say it in a handwritten card. Say it in a one-on-one meeting. Say it in front of everyone at a staff meeting. Say it in a company email communication. Whatever you do and however you say it, include some details. I urge leaders to say thank you to staff and staff to say thank you to leaders. Gratitude works as an incentive in every way.

*No-meeting days*

This leadership-sanctioned initiative helps teams that are burned out on meetings by video, in person, or both. Caveat: since assistants are usually the ones scheduling the meetings, it is important for leaders to help assistants prioritize the meetings that can be pushed into future weeks.

*Expensify's way*

Staffers at Expensify are invited to work from a different country for three weeks each year, and their families can come, too.

*Extra vacation time, unlimited PTO, and sabbaticals*

Again, time off is only a great incentive if staff do not feel guilt for taking the time. It is essential to have an excellent backup plan in place for when staff take vacation.

## STAFF MATTERS QUESTIONS

1. What incentives does your company offer?
2. What ideas from this chapter could work at your company?
3. In your career, what have been your favorite incentives?
4. Ask someone significantly older or younger than yourself: What are your favorite incentives?

# CHAPTER TWENTY

# Workplace Hacks: Assistants' Tricks of the Trade

As a former assistant and current employer of one, I admit to wearing two hats as I write this chapter. I hope these hacks support you to do your work better, faster, easier, and happier—no matter what role you perform.

1. **People say things to assistants that they would never say to leaders. It's just human nature.** Given their position on staff and the high emotional intelligence the job requires, assistants get to see and hear everything. These are universal truths no matter what part of the planet you are on. This makes assistants even more valuable as a resource for leaders and HR.

2. **Do you want people to trust you? The fastest way to make that happen is to keep your word and do what you say you will do.** If you want people to feel like they can completely trust you and take your word to the bank, prove it. Assistants know that people remember everything about your behavior, especially if you are the leader. People also love to talk about leaders who do not keep their word.

   **Example:** A popular business newsletter includes the

statement, "If you have any comments about this newsletter or ideas for future topics, we would love to know them. Send an email to XYZ." I did exactly that. I received no response, not even a generic "Thanks for your email." That experience colors my opinion of the editor, the publication, and the umbrella organization. It says their system is flawed, and a top assistant would be calling this issue to the leader's attention. Essentially, don't write it if you don't have a mechanism in place to handle what is being requested. Will I stop reading the newsletter? No. But this experience is duly noted for the future.

3. **Follow-up. The devilish details.** Part of the DNA of top assistants is managing the most minute details, the things that give other people headaches. If crossing the t's and dotting the i's matters to you, let your assistant handle it. Assistants devise systems to flag deadlines to know what, when, and how people need further information. If, for example, a team member is expecting information by the end of the day on Wednesday, an assistant will review the schedule to check whether it can actually happen. If they see the information will not be ready until Thursday morning, the team member will receive an email (or message via their preferred method of communication) giving the update. This thorough communication and close attention to detail minimizes stress and confusion. It also builds rapport and respect. The unwritten words are, "You can depend on me. I haven't forgotten you. You are important." Yes, all that happens in one short update.

4. **Radio silence. The three-strikes rule.** Assistants know that technology is not 100 percent reliable. Anyone who has had an email go into their spam folder or has never received a voicemail or has had a computer crash knows that it is best to give others the benefit of the doubt about tech—at least three times. Most of us do not have enough hours in the day and receive more emails and text messages than we can handle. If assistants do not receive a response to an email, they do not assume negative intent. Rather,

they may try another method to reach the other person. Once there have been three attempts at communication with no answer, then another tack is needed. Pick up the phone? Send a text or IM? Talk with their best friend? The bottom line is that radio silence is a time waster, can be annoying, and can be read as disrespectful. If it happens often, the result is a decrease in people wanting to go out of their way for you. Avoidance has lots of cons and very few pros. Assistants work to respond to every message within twenty-four hours, if only to say that they will reply by X day. And then they follow up.

5. **Honey really is better than vinegar.** Kill 'em with kindness. The top assistants to the most powerful leaders on the planet are nice people and will go above and beyond for others. These assistants know the influence and power they have, but the best among them don't abuse it. The first strategy to get cooperation from others is to be kind—until that doesn't get the result. Then they do what they must to accomplish the task, but kindness is the go-to because it works.

6. **Your network is your net worth.** The most high-profile and powerful assistants in the world attend trainings and meetings in large part because of the networking. You just never know when you will need assistance from a particular person, and it is so much better if you have actually met them. Respect everyone. Don't dismiss or underestimate anyone. These principles are an assistant's secret sauce.

   **Example:** Do you remember the 2010 volcano eruption in Iceland that disrupted air travel for seven days between Europe and North America and grounded 95,000 commercial flights? An assistant in New York City needed to call on her network of assistants in Europe to organize a small private plane to take her executive from London to Spain to lead an urgent meeting. The assistant knew to explore her options for other means of transportation. What she learned from her network is that smaller private planes could fly at higher altitudes *over the ash*. Problem solved.

The assistant was a rock star problem-solver thanks to her network.

7. **Color codes at work!** Color is helpful in providing visual cues in calendars and email, which saves precious time. Top assistants use agreed-upon colors on calendars to easily distinguish between leaders. A color key is also used to differentiate between various kinds of meetings—blue means personal, green means leadership team, red means the board, etc.

   Color is also used inside the body of email threads. For example, one easy way for a leader to see newly added information is to look for the blue text. The assistant can see new information from the leader in green text. Urgent information from either of them might be in red. Again, this is all about saving valuable time by using an agreed-upon coding plan.

8. **More shorthand: Subject line codes and folders.** How can a busy leader easily and quickly communicate the level of urgency of a forwarded email to the assistant? The subject line can begin with the letters A, B, C, or D. The letters communicate the level of priority: A = handle this today, B = important but not urgent, C = get to this when you can, or D = make this go away. Obviously, the leader can add more information, but an easy and mutually agreed-upon code can save loads of time.

   Depending on the partnership, most assistants have access to their executive's inbox, and it can be useful to decide which kinds of emails are automatically filtered and handled by the assistant. Along these same lines, the executive and assistant can agree on a customized system of email folders which can be categorized as: Discuss, Assistant Handled, Thinking About, etc.

9. **Email signatures.** Leaders are adding a line to their email signatures that names their assistant and provides contact information. The unspoken message is, "Call my assistant to ask your question and you might get your answer even faster." That is very often true.

10. **Help others understand the why, the context.** At every turn, avoid any temptation to say, "Do it because I said so." The more information people have about why you need something done, the better they will help you accomplish it. It is possible that by giving context, you may get an idea that is even better than what you started with. People need to mentally grasp the urgency of a situation through clear context, and once they do, just get out of the way and let the assistant get it done.

## STAFF MATTERS QUESTIONS

1. What assistant hacks can you use immediately?
2. How can assistants be more fully leveraged at your company?
3. What surprised you about the ideas in this chapter?

"We all have two choices: We can make a living or we can design a life"

**Jim Rohn, personal development expert**

# CHAPTER TWENTY-ONE

# Next

What's next? As I worked to finish this book, the workplace continued to morph. It remains to be seen whether the four-day workweek will become a "thing." Is "work from anywhere" here to stay? The fallout from the pandemic on where we work, when we work, and how we work will take years to settle and recalibration is messy, given how humans resist change. The only way to build a system that is resilient is for leaders to collaborate with their staff to arrive at solutions that are realistic, viable, and sustainable.

If this book has made any point, it is that all the answers to future workplace problems can be found by collaborating with the people who are already employed by companies—the staff.

## Are we ready for the next crisis?

As we look to the future, one of the biggest questions is "Are we ready for the next crisis?" One can easily understand how this question is keeping leaders up at night, and the staff, too. None of us know what tomorrow will bring, and none of us can say that we won't be touched by what comes next. It may be the next health crisis, cyberattack, mass shooting, war, social/racial crisis, terrorist attack, or natural disaster.

Or? The hackers are getting smarter, as are the drones and robots. How do we keep our data and our people safe?

The future must include leading-edge training for staff on how to more deftly prepare for whatever challenges come their way. The enormity of the stress and anxiety caused by the changes in the world cannot be overstated, and the staff of our workplaces need our leaders to engage with them in unprecedented ways. It seems that we have all been tested economically, physically, emotionally, and spiritually. The HR professional who described 2020 as a "grim day-to-day torture filled with death and destruction" is not alone. He represents thousands of frontline office workers who were shaken to their core. He represents all staff who need leaders who will face each day's uncertainties with optimism, hope, and truth, while also admitting that they don't have all the answers.

## Ideas about the future from business experts

Jim Clifton, CEO of Gallup, and Jim Harter have cowritten *Wellbeing at Work*. They believe that weekly and detailed feedback from managers to remote workers can result in higher performance than in-person teams. The issue is "poorly skilled managers" who either don't know how or who have never learned how to give feedback. The future will be about upskilling our managers to become coaches who commit to giving ongoing meaningful and useful feedback and to being held accountable for "engagement and performance."[84]

Leadership expert Jeff Haden states: "Start managing by outcomes, not hours. Because to make it work, your employees will definitely have to increase per-hour productivity. Consistently manage by outcomes and your employees will then have a genuine incentive to be more efficient and effective while working. If I know I get Mondays off as long as I work hard every Tuesday through Friday, I'm a lot more likely to kick ass."[85]

## Be alert to the signs of burnout

Humans have paid a psychic price for the events ever since 2001, and to build an ultimate new workplace, we need new strategies and new skills to meet the challenges presented by having to tackle these solutions, often via webcam. Leaders and staff need training to notice the signs of burnout and know the words to say in response, such as, "You seemed to be frustrated at the meeting today. If there is a problem, can we talk about it and see how we can sort it out?" Then listen.

*Forbes* writer Mark Murphy has issued a blunt prediction about the kinds of new skills leaders will need in a postpandemic world. "Make no mistake, if leaders don't learn how to build their employees' resilience, optimism, etc., companies can expect a workforce suffering from extreme burnout and a mass exodus of their star employees as soon as the labor market recovers." I agree wholeheartedly, and I also think that leaders need additional support. After all, no one prepared them for this, either.[86]

Signs of burnout:

- Detachment
- Isolation
- Heightened stress
- Headaches and other physical ailments
- Distraction
- Mistakes
- Frustration
- Agitation
- Personality changes
- Depression

When staff is burned-out and frustrated, they quit. They will quit sooner if other well-paying jobs are readily available. If there is a shortage of talent, it is vital for company leaders and HR professionals to directly address the root causes of that shortage and identify what is preventing candidates from coming forward.

Incentives for staff to stay at a company include:

- Flexibility about working from home and flexibility in their work schedule. One policy most definitely does not fit all.
- Culture that genuinely supports work-life balance and is not merely lip service

- Addressing physical safety issues and mental health issues with compassion
- Culture that rewards treating people with respect and dignity
- Investment in professional development/training/growth/career advancement
- Culture where regular one-to-one and team feedback is the norm
- Commitment to and investment in diversity, equity, inclusion, and belonging initiatives
- Transparent and equitable policies around compensation
- Company culture that supports recognizing and rewarding top performers
- Commitment to an ongoing and truthful dialogue between leaders and staff in the form of surveys, town hall meetings, and one-on-one meetings to openly discuss issues that arise

## Advice from CEOs for young professionals and new graduates

**JEFF JONES,** *CEO of H&R Block*
"The keys to long-term relevance are curiosity, learning, and patience. A first job is highly unlikely to be the last, so learn as much as possible, raise your hand for the hardest problems, and start building your reputation as an indispensable member of the team."

**ARVIND KRISHNA,** *CEO of IBM*
"First, be curious. Be insatiably curious. Second, be persistent. Remember that many of the world's brightest innovators and boldest leaders succeeded not necessarily because they were the first to conceive an idea, but because they were the only ones who worked hard enough to turn those ideas into a practical reality. Curiosity and grit."

**BOB SEGERT,** *CEO of Athenahealth*
"Taking action is only half of the equation. The other half is accountability. Sometimes people define accountability as 'being able to take

the heat when things go wrong,' but I think of accountability as 'doing whatever it takes to make something a success.' An account-able worker is one who drives forward with a true ownership mind-set and is able to look around corners, anticipate potential problems, and align the right resources against a task."

**HEIDI ZAK,** *CEO of ThirdLove*
"Earlier in my career, I didn't think about my network or building it, and I wish I would have valued it more. Keep in mind that your net-work is every single person you meet, every person you interact with. Always be your best self, as you never know when your paths may cross again. You'll find that you lean on different people at different points in time."

## Ultimately . . .

What I know for sure about the future workplace is that the old hier-archical models for work are no longer serving the new world. In con-cert, collaboration, and cooperation with the leaders, it will be the staff who are capable of designing a future workplace that serves the people in it. With support and encouragement, the minds and hearts of the staff will provide a bottomless supply of ideas to build our ultimate new workplace. We need to talk with each other.

It's time.

## STAFF MATTERS QUESTIONS

1. What advice would you give to a young professional or new graduate entering the workforce?
2. What ideas from this chapter could work at your company?
3. What are the top three ways to break down silos between leaders, assistants, HR, and recruiters in your organization?

# ACKNOWLEDGMENTS
# & GRATITUDE

*Staff Matters* is nothing if not a group effort. It simply would not exist without the support and strong belief in the project by so many people. I am endlessly grateful for the willingness of people to open up and share honestly about their work experiences, as well as their unfiltered stories about how things really are. Your stories live inside me and I am indebted to every one of you.

Thank you to my life partner, Robert Sanders. Your unconditional love, belief, and candid feedback every step of the way have been essential.

Thank you to my family for your love, patience, and support—Adam, Linsey, and Madison Kramen, Jason, Rachel, Zachary, Stephanie, Matthew Weisenthal, Kate, Jacek, and Grace Janzcewski and Kristen Sanders and Eric Thornburgh and Mike Sanders.

Thank you . . .

Vickie Sokol Evans for having my back in more ways than I can name. I cannot imagine any of this without you.

Laura Schreiner for your love, support, and always showing up when it matters most.

Angelica Canales for your bottomless well of wise counsel, your amazing editor's eye, and friendship for over twenty years.

Jennifer Wilner—my assistant and friend, without whom I could not do what I do.

Melba J. Duncan for writing the foreword and for being one of my earliest role models for workplace excellence. Thank you for always answering my calls.

Jack Zenger for revealing such a big piece of the workplace puzzle.

Shelly Berman Rubera who saw what this project could mean and supported me every step of the way with astute editing and expert coaching.

The eagle-eyed editors, astute readers, word nerds, and believers—Devon Frederickson, Laura Schreiner, Robert Arciniega, Sharon Summerfield, Linda Niederman Silver, and Jennifer Kasius.

My forever friends Adrienne and Bruce Rogove, Kathryn Eaker and Ray Potter, Gail and Michael Scaramella, and Toby and Bob Mack.

A heartfelt thank-you to everyone I interviewed for *Staff Matters*. Every conversation informed these pages. These people include every Be the Ultimate Assistant student since 2011. Though many of you go unnamed here, you are my treasure of insight. Thank you for trusting me with your stories. Special thanks to Dr. Rayna Cooney, Doug Meyer, Cathleen Schreiner Gates, Ike Saunders, Julie Kavanaugh, Leslie Ayvazian, Patrick Healy, Leni Miller, and Nancy Fox.

There are those who may not be here anymore, but they are very much alive and present in *Staff Matters*. These include my parents, Ruth and Sol Low. Olympia Dukakis and Louis Zorich were extraordinary role models for what it means to be a working professional and a good human and they gave me the ride of my life. Thank you to the wise Dr. Maddy Gerrish, who helped me know myself in order to know others. I would not be the person I am without these people.

Thank you to the Dukakis/Zorich family for treating me like one of you—Stefan, Elda, Peter, Elvy, and Christina Zorich, Apollo and Maggie Dukakis, Michael and Kitty Dukakis, and Patty and Arthur Dukakis.

I am grateful to my speaking and writing colleagues and friends from New York Celebrity Assistants, *Executive Support Magazine*, Private Service Alliance, IAAP, SHRM, and all the professional business associations around the world. Special thanks to Johnny C. Taylor Jr., Lucy Brazier, Douglas Conant, Gloria Feldt, Monique Helstrom, Ann Hiatt, Helen Monument, and Felix Nater.

Thank you for the extraordinary care, commitment, talents, and skills of the teams at Smith Publicity led by Marissa Eigenbrood, Girl Friday Books led by Mari Kesselring, Target Marketing led by Ken Gillette and Gina Onativia, and CycleHere Media led by Donald and

Janice Jones. Thank you for going on this journey with me and working so hard to get it right.

Finally, thank you to the readers of this book. Long after I'm gone, I want to thank you for finding authentic ways to move closer to the ultimate workplace for your children and grandchildren.

I know that I stand on all your shoulders. Thank you from the bottom of my heart.

**Bonnie Low-Kramen**

# JOB DESCRIPTIONS

If you have ever wondered what it takes to perform the duties of a CEO, Executive Assistant, Human Resources professional, Recruiter, or business school professional, here are examples of job descriptions.

---

# CHIEF EXECUTIVE OFFICER, CEO (SOURCE: SHRM)

The Chief Executive Officer provides leadership for all aspects of the company's operations with an emphasis on long-term goals, growth, profit, and return on investment.
Supervisory Responsibilities

- Oversees the ongoing operations of all divisions in the company.
- Manages and directs the company toward its primary goals and objectives.
- Oversees employment decisions at the executive level of the company.
- Leads a team of executives to consider major decisions including acquisitions, mergers, joint ventures, or large-scale expansion.
- Promotes communication and cooperation among divisions to create a spirit of unity in the organization.

## Duties/Responsibilities

- Works with the board of directors and other executives to establish short-term objectives and long-range goals, as well as related plans and policies.
- Presents regular reports on the status of the company's operations to the board of directors and to company staff.
- Oversees the organization's financial structure, ensuring adequate and sound funding for the mission and goals of the company.
- Reviews the financial results of all operations, comparing them with the company's objectives and taking appropriate measures to correct unsatisfactory performance and results.
- Ensures the company's compliance with all applicable laws, rules, regulations, and standards.
- Negotiates with other companies regarding actions such as mergers, acquisitions, or joint ventures.
- Serves as the company's representative to the board of directors, shareholders, employees, customers, the government, and the public.
- Performs other related duties to benefit the mission of the organization.

## Required Skills/Abilities

- Excellent managerial and financial skills and the ability to take leadership over any business operations area.
- Superlative communication skills, particularly the ability to communicate as a leader.
- Thorough understanding of management and financial practices in all areas and phases of business operations.

## Education and Experience

- Extensive professional experience in leadership roles.
- Education may vary; an advanced degree in business administration, finance, or law is preferred, but not required.

*Physical Requirements*

- Prolonged periods sitting at a desk and working on a computer.
- Must be able to lift up to fifteen pounds at times.
- Must be able to navigate various departments of the organization's physical premises.

---

# C-SUITE EXECUTIVE ASSISTANT/ ADMINISTRATIVE BUSINESS PARTNER (SOURCE: THE DUNCAN GROUP)

*Scope of Position*

This role is not routine; it encourages strategy and productivity.

Learn and adapt to culture. Understand and uphold company's mission, values, and purpose, and support executive in philanthropic endeavors and commitments. Represent executive in all aspects of the business with a cooperative and helpful attitude.

Improve the executive's workplace experience by adjusting to personal style, while creatively channeling priorities to achieve objectives. *Key competency: Management expertise.*

Responsible for working as a contributing member of the executive office team within the operating framework necessary to successfully implement the executive's directives. Attend meetings. Coordinate activities as directed. Anticipate needs in order to ensure that all required information is confirmed and at hand. *Key competency: Anticipate.*

Provide extensive administrative support, including the management and coordination of projects, with detail accuracy. Offer acute sensitivity for the importance of time urgency, exceptional anticipation skills, and an enviable personal touch. Demonstrate consistent follow-up to ensure task completion. Consistently operate with a sense of urgency while not losing sight of the details. *Key competency: Focus and precise techniques.*

The challenge is to develop a relationship that enables a response to the executive's needs and to work as a member of the team, jointly discerning common objectives and resolving issues. The pace of activities and the work itself will be highly challenging. Must have appropriate potential to provide service orientation and logistical management. *Key competency: Relationship management.*

Monitor trends in business, technology, office administration, and business systems; recommend appropriate changes. *Key competency: Manage through complexity.*

Ease decision-making. Serve as liaison for matters of importance on behalf of the executive. *Key competency: Sense of timing.*

Aid integration: ensure that projects get completed in a timely manner. *Key competency: Planning and organization.*

Coordinate activities and functions with internal and external constituents. *Key competency: Social intuition.*

All actions taken on behalf of the executive should reflect the intrinsic desire to employ the most cost-effective methods. *Key competency: Financial acumen.*

## Qualifications: Important and Relevant Factors

- College degree preferred but not required.
- Impressive style, manner, communication, and collaboration skills to represent the executive's office.
- Experience in managing large or complex projects; comfort with ambiguity.
- Confidence to ask questions for clarification before taking action. Confirm priorities.
- Sense of humor.
- Vested interest in the integrity of the job. Appreciate the value of executive lifestyle management.
- Good judgment, common sense, discretion, confidential matters management.
- Essential traits: decisiveness, sensitivity, credibility, political/current events–savvy, meticulous, energetic.

- Ability to organize, coordinate, and manage complex details. Own and acknowledge errors without blame.
- Creative in managing priorities, handling more than one task at a time, exercising distraction control with judgment and common sense.

*The Profile*

Smart. Knows who's who in the world of business, nonprofits, and international politics and development. Well read. Strong presence and style; refined; poised under pressure; unflappable; evident enthusiasm for the role; highly organized. Exercises initiative. Superb coordination and time-management expertise, with the interpersonal talent to instill confidence in others in order to meet agreed-upon assignments. Flexible and forward-thinking. Extremely trustworthy, with the ability to handle confidential matters and sensitive information or situations with discretion. Highly credible, strategic, diplomatic, empathetic and proactive. 24/7 availability; flexibility to be "on call" (phone, text) as needed. Committed to new learning to manage in the global workplace.

---

# HUMAN RESOURCE MANAGER (SOURCE: INDEED)

An HR manager is the go-to person for all employee-related issues. This means that your HR manager duties will involve managing activities such as job design, recruitment, employee relations, performance management, training and development, and talent management. The job of HR manager is important to business success. People are our most important asset, and you'll be the one to ensure we have a happy and productive workplace where everyone can realize our established mission and objectives. Promoting corporate values and shaping a positive culture is a vital aspect of a complete HR manager job description and specification.

*Responsibilities*

- Develop and implement HR strategies and initiatives aligned with the overall business strategy.
- Bridge management and employee relations by addressing demands, grievances, or other issues including the development and implementation of policies that address workplace bullying and sexual harassment.
- Assume responsibility for biweekly and monthly payrolls.
- Manage the recruitment and selection process.
- Support current and future business needs through the development, engagement, motivation, and preservation of human capital.
- Develop and monitor overall HR strategies, systems, tactics, and procedures across the organization.
- Collaborate on and develop programs including: crisis/disaster/active shooter plans, onboarding plan for in-person and remote workers, and floor plan design for worker health and safety.
- Nurture a positive working environment.
- Oversee and manage a performance appraisal system that drives high performance.
- Maintain pay plan and benefits program.
- Assess training needs to apply and monitor training programs.
- Report to management and provide decision support through HR metrics.
- Ensure legal compliance throughout human resource management.

*Skills*

- Proven working experience as HR manager or other HR executive.
- People oriented and results driven.
- Demonstrable experience with HR metrics.
- Knowledge of HR systems and databases.

- Ability to design strategy along with building leadership skills.
- Excellent active listening, negotiation, and presentation skills.
- Competence to build and effectively manage interpersonal relationships at all levels of the company.
- In-depth knowledge of labor law and HR best practices.
- Degree in Human Resources or related field.

---

# TALENT RECRUITER (SOURCE: GLASSDOOR)

- Source candidates using a variety of search methods to build a robust candidate pipeline.
- Screen candidates by reviewing resumes and job applications, and performing phone screenings.
- Take ownership of candidate experience by designing and managing it.
- Develop job postings, job descriptions, and position requirements.
- Perform reference checks as needed.
- Facilitate the offer process by extending the offer and negotiating employment terms.
- Manage onboarding and new hire processes.
- Stay abreast of recruiting trends and best practices.
- Manage the overall interview, selection, and closing process.
- Ensure all screening, hiring, and selection is done in accordance with employment laws and regulations.

*Qualifications for Recruiter*

- Bachelor's degree in Human Resources, Business Administration, or related field.

- 2 years of recruiting experience preferred.
- Ability to communicate effectively, both orally and in writing.
- Demonstrated ability to establish effective and cooperative working relationships built on trust.
- Excellent organizational and time-management skills.
- Comfort making decisions independently.
- Working knowledge of applicant tracking and HRIS systems.
- Ability to manage a wide range of relationships with a variety of stakeholders.
- Proficient in Microsoft Office.
- Working knowledge of interview techniques and applicant screening methods.
- Deep understanding of employment laws and regulations.
- Familiar with a wide variety of sourcing avenues.

---

# UNIVERSITY BUSINESS SCHOOL PROFESSOR (SOURCE: INDEED)

*Duties & Responsibilities*

- Facilitating classroom and distance/distributed learning.
- Course and syllabus preparation.
- Class curriculum coordination and planning.
- Assessment and evaluation of learners.
- Mentoring and advising of students.
- Holding office hours and meeting with students.
- Research/scholarship mentoring and supervision, particularly of MA theses, PsyD projects, and PhD, EdD, DBA dissertations.

*Skills*

- Proficient computer skills, including with Microsoft Office programs.
- The ability to work independently and be self-motivated.
- High level of accuracy and attention to detail and the ability to problem-solve.
- The ability to explain complex requirements in clear and concise terms.
- The ability to be flexible with workflow to meet the needs of the department and students and to manage multiple tasks per required deadlines.
- The drive to encourage, direct, hold accountable, and guide candidates toward task completion.
- Must demonstrate the ability to work as an effective team member and develop trusting relationships with students and university employees, as well as the Registrar's Office and various academic departments.
- Culturally competent and able to communicate and interact effectively with diverse people.
- Highly motivated and focused, results oriented.
- Ability to exercise discretion and tact in all interpersonal interactions, and to maintain confidentiality.
- Ability to collaborate and partner with other university stakeholders to support candidate success.
- Ability to make administrative/procedural decisions and judgments.

*Minimum Requirements*

- **Education:** Master's, doctoral, or other terminal degree from an accredited college or university, depending upon the needs of the course being taught.
- **Experience:** Appropriate experience in the areas(s) of specialization and expertise.
- **Certifications, Licenses, etc.:** As required by program.

# NOTES

## Introduction

1  Jack Zenger, "We wait too long to train our leaders," *Harvard Business Review*, December 2012, https://hbr.org/2012/12/why-do-we-wait-so-long-to-trai

## Chapter One

2  Business Roundtable.com, https://opportunity.businessroundtable.org/ourcommitment/

3  Bonnie Low-Kramen, "Shining a light on Black assistants: It's not black and white," Bonnie Low-Kramen's Blog, February 2021, https://www.bonnielowkramen.com/2021/02/01/shining-a-light-on-black-assistants-its-not-black-white/#

4  Robin Madell, "95% of Stanford MBA students take a nonrequired course nicknamed 'Touchy Feely.' Here's why alumni say it's been voted the most popular elective for 45 years." *Business Insider*, September 2019, https://www.businessinsider.in/95-of-stanford-mba-students-take-a-nonrequired-course-nicknamed-touchy-feely-heres-why-alumni-say-its-been-voted-the-most-popular-elective-for-45-years-/articleshow/71298258.cms

## Chapter Two

5  "Resident population in the United States in 2021, by generation," statista website, https://www.statista.com/statistics/797321/us-population-by-generation/

## Chapter Three

6   "Hilton and American Express to donate up to 1 million rooms
    to frontline medical professionals during COVID-19 crisis," Hilton
    website, April 2020, https://stories.hilton.com/releases/hilton
    -american-express-team-up-to-donate-rooms

7   "Nearly 2 Million Fewer Women in Labor Force," SHRM.org,
    February 2022, https://www.shrm.org/resourcesandtools/hr-topics
    /behavioral-competencies/global-and-cultural-effectiveness
    /pages/over-1-million-fewer-women-in-labor-force.aspx

8   Maria Aspan, "Could 'returnships' for moms who've left the work-
    force help solve women's economic crisis?" *Fortune*, February 2021,
    https://fortune.com/2021/02/17/returnships-working-moms
    -women-at-work-unemployment-covid/

9   S. Mitra Kalita, "How the best leaders can acknowledge the other
    pandemic: Loneliness," *Fortune*, March 2021, https://fortune.com
    /2021/03/17/how-the-best-leaders-can-acknowledge-the-other
    -pandemic-loneliness/

10  Maria Aspan and Emma Hinchcliffe, "The pandemic has de-
    railed women's careers and livelihoods. Is America giving up on
    them?" *Fortune*, January 2021, https://fortune.com/2021/01/29/us
    -unemployment-rate-women-job-losses-december-2020
    -numbers-workforce-covid-19-pandemic-impact/

11  PwC Survey, "Reimagining the outcomes that matter," PwC web-
    site, January 2022, https://www.pwc.com/ceosurvey

12  "With workplace violence on the rise, 1 out of 7 people don't feel
    safe at work," SHRM website, (March 2019): https://www.shrm.org
    /about-shrm/press-room/press-releases/pages/2019-workplace
    -violence-research-report.aspx

13  Shana Lebowitz, "Here are the best ways to convince your boss to let
    you work from home forever," *Business Insider*, April 2021, https://
    www.businessinsider.com/how-to-ask-your-boss-to-let-you
    -work-from-home-advice?

14  "The future of work after COVID-19," McKinsey & Company web-
    site, February 2021, https://www.mckinsey.com/featured-insights
    /future-of-work/the-future-of-work-after-covid-19

*Chapter Five*

15 Nelson Mandela, *The Prison Letters of Nelson Mandela*, Liveright, 2018.

16 Robert Reiss, The CEO Forum Group website: https://theceoforumgroup.com/

17 Amardeep Parmar, "Bumble founder to become the youngest woman to take a tech unicorn public," *Entrepreneur's Handbook*, January 2021, https://entrepreneurshandbook.co/bumble-founder-to-become-the-youngest-woman-to-take-a-tech-unicorn-public-b6c9fbc76e0b

18 Adam Bryant and Kevin Sharer, *The CEO Test*, Harvard Business Review Press, 2021.

19 Rachel Lobdell, "How Marc Benioff is helping out during the coronavirus pandemic," *Fortune*, May 2020, https://fortune.com/2020/05/05/marc-benioff-leadership-next-podcast-philanthropy-coronavirus/

20 Lauren Thomas, "Read Nike CEO John Donahoe's note to employees on racism: We must 'get our own house in order,'" CNBC website, June 2020, https://www.cnbc.com/2020/06/05/nike-ceo-note-to-workers-on-racism-must-get-our-own-house-in-order.html

21 Robin Madell, "5 business schools offering the best programs and curricula to prepare students for a post-pandemic world," *Business Insider*, April 2021, https://www.businessinsider.com/business-schools-best-mba-program-success-post-pandemic-2021-4

22 Bonnie Low-Kramen, "What would YOU do if you were CEO for one day?" Bonnie Low-Kramen Blog, July 2018, https://www.bonnielowkramen.com/2018/07/06/what-would-you-do-if-you-were-ceo-for-one-day/

23 "A Report on Administrative Professionals and Executive Assistants in North America," ASAP website, September 2022, https://www.asaporg.com/a-report-on-administrative-professionals-and-executive-assistants-in-north-america-2022

24 "9to5, National Association of Working Women," Wikipedia, https://en.wikipedia.org/wiki/9to5

25  Melba J. Duncan, "The Case for Executive Assistants," *Harvard Business Review*, May 2011, https://hbr.org/2011/05/the-case-for -executive-assistants

26  Doug Conant, ConantLeadership Webinar, "Ultimate Workplace, Leveraging Your Assistant in the New World," Facebook, March 2021, https://www.facebook.com/ConantLeadership/videos/ 1182668425539174

27  Gary Rabine, Ditch Digger CEO with Gary Rabine Podcast #37, "Maximizing the value of a CEO with exceptional mentoring with Bonnie Low-Kramen," April 2020, https://anchor.fm/ditch-digger -ceo/episodes/37-Maximizing-the-Value-of-a-CEO-With-Exceptional -Mentoring-w-Bonnie-Low-Kramen-Founder-and-CEO-of-Ultimate -Assistant-Training-echueo

28  World Administrators Alliance, Global Skills Matrix, May 2022, https://globalskillsmatrix.com/

29  "100 Best Companies to Work For," *Fortune*, 2021, https://fortune .com/best-companies/2021/

30  Caroline Hroncich and Ebony Flake, "Cisco says they've cracked the code on curbing the Great Resignation—and it starts with listening," *Business Insider*, 2021, https://www.businessinsider .com/management-strategy-cisco-pandemic-burnout-2021-5

31  Kathy Caprino, "The gap between what C-suite leaders think and what HR executives and employees know about their workplaces," *Forbes*, November 2020, https://www.forbes.com/sites/kathycaprino/2022 /11/03/the-gap-between-what-c-suite-leaders-think-and-what -hr-executives-and-employees-know-about-their-workplaces /?sh=c75cff97adfc

32  Shana Lebowitz and Caroline Hroncich, "The 20 most inspiring HR leaders who are changing how America treats its workers and the exact plans they're using to remake company cultures," *Business Insider*, (March 2020): https://www.businessinsider.com/hr -innovators-who-are-transforming-company-culture-2020-3# maya-marcus-vice-president-of-people-at-palo-alto-networks-12

33  Fedex Employment Pathways, Fedexcares website, March 2019, https://fedexcares.com/sites/default/files/2019-10/2019%20 FedEx%20Employment%20Pathways%20Brochure_FINAL _March%202219.pdf

## Chapter Six

34 The Holmes-Rahe Stress Inventory, stress.org website, https://www.stress.org/holmes-rahe-stress-inventory

35 Oren Liebermann, "Defense secretary to recommend prosecution of sexual assaults in the military to be taken out of commanders' hands," CNN website, June 2021, https://www.cnn.com/2021/07/02/politics/military-sex-assault-commission-report/index.html

## Chapter Seven

36 Novartis, "People and culture, building an inspired, curious, unbossed culture," Novartis website, https://www.novartis.com/our-company/people-and-culture/we-are-inspiring-our-people

37 Chelsea Greenwood, "Managers are starting to make personal 'user manuals' that explain to their coworkers what makes them tick," *Business Insider*, April 2019, https://www.businessinsider.com/personal-user-manuals-work-2019-4

## Chapter Eight

38 Christina Pazzanese, "Women less inclined to self-promote than men, even for a job," *The Harvard Gazette*, February 2020, https://news.harvard.edu/gazette/story/2020/02/men-better-than-women-at-self-promotion-on-job-leading-to-inequities/

39 Roy Mauer, "Employers open to ditching degree requirements when hiring," SHRM website, July 2018, https://www.shrm.org/resourcesandtools/hr-topics/talent-acquisition/pages/eliminating-degree-requirements-hiring-ibm-penguin.aspx

## Chapter Nine

40 Bonnie Low-Kramen, "The real reasons people quit," TEDx Conferences, February 2022, https://www.ted.com/talks/bonnie_low_kramen_the_real_reasons_people_quit

## Chapter Ten

41  Josette Weinstein, "Healthcare's hierarchy of location needs,"
    Resource Center blog, Centrak, 2022, https://centrak.com/blog
    -healthcares-hierarchy-of-location-needs/

## Chapter Thirteen

42  Leslie Stahl, "Leading by example to close the gender pay gap," CBS
    News, April 2018, https://www.cbsnews.com/news/salesforce-ceo
    -marc-benioff-leading-by-example-to-close-the-gender-pay-gap/
43  "2022 State of the Gender Pay Gap Resort," www.payscale.com, (2022)
    https://www.payscale.com/research-and-insights/gender-pay-gap/
44  "States with salary history bans," Paycor, September 2022, https://
    www.paycor.com/resource-center/articles/states-with-salary
    -history-bans/
45  Suyin Haynes, "The global gender gap will take an extra 36 years
    to close after the COVID-19 pandemic, report finds," Time.com,
    March 2021, https://time.com/5951101/global-gender-gap-135
    -years/#
46  Stacy Perman, "Hollywood assistants are in open revolt. Here's
    why," *Los Angeles Times*, November 2019, https://www.latimes
    .com/entertainment-arts/business/story/2019-11-02/la-et-ct
    -hollywood-assistants-revolt
47  "Fact Sheet #17C: Exemption for administrative employees under
    the fair labor standards act (FLSA)," U.S. Department of Labor,
    September 2019, https://www.dol.gov/agencies/whd/fact-sheets
    /17c-overtime-administrative

## Chapter Fourteen

48  Hailey Fuchs, "Ginsburg clerks remember her as a mentor who
    treated them like family," *New York Times*, September 23, 2020,
    https://www.today.com/news/ruth-bader-ginsburg-s-former
    -law-clerks-honor-her-supreme-t192341

Chapter Fifteen

49  Janelle Griffith, "Google changes sexual harassment policies after employee walkout," NBC News, November 2018, https://www .nbcnews.com/tech/tech-news/google-changes-sexual-harassment -policies-after-employee-walkout-n934046

50  Natalia V. Navarro, "'We're unable to take the disrespect': A Kaiser strike could limit patient care, workers say it's necessary," CPR News, September 2019, https://www.cpr.org/2019/09/17/were -unable-to-take-the-disrespect-a-kaiser-strike-could-limit-patient -care-workers-say-its-necessary/

51  Dana M Peterson, Catherine L Mann, Raymond J McGuire, "Closing the racial inequality gaps: The economic cost of Black inequality in the U.S," *Citi GPS: Global Perspectives & Solutions*, September 2020, https://www.citivelocity.com/citigps/closing-the -racial-inequality-gaps/

52  Tim Ryan, "Diversity and the case for transparency," PwC website, February 2021, https://www.pwc.com/fortunetakeontomorrow

53  Tatiana Siegel, "Everyone just knows he's an absolute monster: Scott Rudin's ex-staffers speak out on abusive behavior," *Hollywood Reporter*, April 2021, https://www.hollywoodreporter.com/features /everyone-just-knows-hes-an-absolute-monster-scott-rudins-ex -staffers-speak-out-on-abusive-behavior

54  "With workplace violence on the rise, 1 out of 7 people don't feel safe at work," SHRM.org, March 2019, https://www.shrm.org /about-shrm/press-room/press-releases/pages/2019-workplace -violence-research-report.aspx

55  Shawn McClean, Stephen H. Courtright, Troy A. Smith, and Junhyok Yim, "Stop making excuses for toxic bosses," *Harvard Business Review*, January 2021, https://hbr.org/2021/01/stop -making-excuses-for-toxic-bosses

56  "Report finds California above national average for sexual harassment rates," UC San Diego Health, May 2019, https://health.ucsd .edu/news/releases/Pages/2019-05-23-california-above-national -average-sexual-harassment-rates.aspx

57  Amelia Schonbek, "The complete list of allegations against Harvey Weinstein," *The Cut*, January 2020, https://www.thecut .com/2020/01/harvey-weinstein-complete-list-allegations.html

58  Christina Carrega and Amir Vera, "Larry Nassar has thousands of dollars in his prison account, but he's only making minimum payments to his victims, court documents show," CNN.com, July 2021, https://www.cnn.com/2021/07/29/us/larry-nassar-court -payments-motion/index.html

59  "2021 state-specific sexual harassment training requirements (United States)," Open Sesame.com, https://www.opensesame .com/site/blog/2021-state-specific-sexual-harassment-training -requirements-united-states/#

*Chapter Sixteen*

60  Jessica Mathews, "Indra Nooyi: Women are 'one of the biggest emerging-market opportunities' for corporate America," Fortune.com, June 2021, https://fortune.com/2021/06/23/indra -nooyi-women-c-suite-corporate-america/

61  Pat Wechsler, "Tupperware's CEO on why his company is joining UN's HeForShe to fight for gender equality," Fortune.com, May 2015, https://fortune.com/2015/05/05/rick-goings-tupperware-heforshe/

62  "Pronouns," Gay Center.org, New York City, 2022, https://gaycenter .org/pronouns/

63  Marguerite Ward, "There are now more women CEOs of Fortune 500 companies than ever before—but the numbers are still distressingly low," *Business Insider*, November 2020, https://www .businessinsider.in/international/news/there-are-now-more -women-ceos-of-fortune-500-companies-than-ever-before-but-the -numbers-are-still-distressingly-low/articleshow/79496820.cms Chauncey Alcorn, "The Fortune 500 now has two Black women CEOs. That's actually an improvement," CNN Business, May 2021, https://www.cnn.com/2021/05/01/business/thasunda-duckett -tiaa-black-women-ceo

64  Corinne Post, Boris Lokshin, and Christophe Boone, "Research: Adding women to the C-suite changes how companies think," *Harvard*

*Business Review*, April 2021, https://hbr.org/2021/04/research -adding-women-to-the-c-suite-changes-how-companies-think

65  Terri Mock, "The latest on workplace violence statistics," Ravemobilesafety.com, February 2021, https://www.ravemobilesafety .com/blog/latest-workplace-violence-statistics

66  Lili Loofbourow, "Why society goes easy on rapists," Slate.com, May 2019, https://slate.com/news-and-politics/2019/05/sexual -assault-rape-sympathy-no-prison.html

67  Rob Pascale and Lou Primavera, Ph.D., reviewed by Devon Frye, "Male and female brains: Are they wired differently?" *Psychology Today*, April 2019, https://www.psychologytoday.com/us/blog /so-happy-together/201904/male-and-female-brains

68  Adam Galinsky, "Are gender differences just power differences in disguise?" Columbia.edu, March 2018, https://www8.gsb .columbia.edu/articles/ideas-work/are-gender-differences-just -power-differences-disguise

69  Adam Grant, "Who won't shut up in meetings? Men say it's women. It's not," *Washington Post*, February 2021, https://www .washingtonpost.com/outlook/2021/02/18/men-interrupt-women -tokyo-olympics/

70  Adam Bryant, "Before you speak, remember the W.A.I.T. acronym: 'Why am I talking?'" PR Council, January 2019, https://prcouncil .net/blog/speak-remember-w-t-acronym-talking/

71  Kathleen Davis, "Why women are still falling off the glass cliff," Linkedin.com, March 2021, https://www.linkedin.com/pulse /why-women-still-falling-off-glass-cliff-kathleen-davis

72  Jack Zenger and Joseph Folkman, "Research: Women are better leaders during a crisis," *Harvard Business Review*, December 2020, https://hbr.org/2020/12/research-women-are-better-leaders -during-a-crisis

73  Cleo Stiller, *Modern manhood: Conversations about the complicated world of being a good man today*, S&S/Simon, 2019.

74  Tracey Lien, "Why are women leaving the tech industry in droves?" *Los Angeles Times*, February 2015, https://www.latimes.com /business/la-fi-women-tech-20150222-story.html

75  Jennifer Koza, "Five disturbing sexual harassment statistics we

can't afford to ignore," Fairygodboss.com, May 2021, https://fairygodboss.com/articles/sexual-harassment-statistics

76 James Temperton, "Google's image search has a massive celebrity sexism problem," *Wired*, May 2019, https://www.wired.co.uk/article/google-image-search-sexist-suggestions

77 Jolie Lee, "Male TV host wears same suit for year; no one notices," *USA Today*, November 2014, https://www.usatoday.com/story/news/nation-now/2014/11/17/tv-host-same-suit-sexism/19161031/

78 Bonnie Low-Kramen, "Women: Turning off the default," Bonnie Low-Kramen Blog, September 2018, https://www.bonnielowkramen.com/2018/10/03/women-turning-off-the-default/#

79 "The 1 in 6 Statistic," 1in6.org, https://1in6.org/get-information/the-1-in-6-statistic/

80 Sheryl Sandberg, *Lean in: Women, work, and the will to lead*, Knopf, 2013.

81 "Gender equality by country 2022," worldpopulationreview.com, https://worldpopulationreview.com/country-rankings/gender-equality-by-country

*Chapter Seventeen*

82 Bonnie Low-Kramen and Vickie Sokol Evans, "Webinar with guest Ann Hiatt, former EA to Jeff Bezos," YouTube, April 2020, https://www.youtube.com/watch?v=1HQQ5mp0YX4; www.annhiatt.co

*Chapter Nineteen*

83 Anusha J, "Whataburger thanks employees for 'extraordinary service' by giving them $90 million in bonuses," Upworthy.com, April 2021, https://scoop.upworthy.com/whataburger-thanks-employees-for-extraordinary-service-by-awarding-them-90-million-in-bonuses

*Chapter Twenty-One*

84 Jim Clifton, Jim Harter, Ph.D., "Fully remote teams can outperform

in-person teams with this one factor," Bluezones.com, May 2021, https://www.bluezones.com/2021/05/fully-remote-teams-can-outperform-in-person-teams-with-this-one-factor/

85  Jeff Haden, "Here's the only way a four-day workweek schedule will actually work," *Inc. Magazine*, April 2021, https://www.inc.com/jeff-haden/the-only-way-4-day-work-schedules-actually-work.html

86  Mark Murphy, "In 2021, the smartest companies will be teaching leaders these skills they've never learned before," *Forbes*, March 2021, https://www.forbes.com/sites/markmurphy/2021/03/02/in-2021-the-smartest-companies-will-be-teaching-leaders-these-skills-theyve-never-learned-before/

# RECOMMENDED READING & RESOURCES

## Books

*Apollo's Arrow*, Nicholas Christakis
*The Art of Work*, Jeff Goins
*Be the Ultimate Assistant*, Bonnie Low-Kramen
*Behind the Cloud*, Marc Benioff
*Bet on Yourself*, Ann Hiatt
*The Blueprint*, Doug Conant
*The Boys in the Boat*, Daniel James Brown
*The CEO Challenge*, Patrick J. Below and Jim Moore
*The CEO Test*, Adam Bryant & Kevin W. Sharer
*Connect*, David Bradford and Carole Robin
*Crucial Conversations*, Kerry Patterson and Joseph Grenny
*The Culture Code*, Daniel Coyle
*Dare to Lead*, Brené Brown
*Daring Greatly*, Brené Brown
*Delivering Happiness*, Tony Hsieh
*Drive*, Daniel H. Pink
*Eat, Drink, and Succeed*, Laura Schwartz
*Emotional Intelligence*, Daniel Goleman
*Extreme Ownership*, Jocko Willink and Leif Babin
*Finding Right Work*, Leni Miller
*Good to Great*, Jim Collins
*Go with Your Talent*, Luk Dewulf
*A Great Place to Work For All*, Michael C. Bush
*The Heart of Business*, Hubert Joly
*How Successful People Lead*, John C. Maxwell
*How to Be Exceptional*, John Zenger

*How to Win Friends and Influence People*, Dale Carnegie
*HR from the Outside In*, Dave Ulrich
*Insight*, Tasha Eurich
*Leading at a Distance*, Spencer Stuart
*Lean In*, Sheryl Sandberg
*Making Work Human*, Derek Irvine and Eric Mosley
*Man Enough*, Justin Baldoni
*Man's Search for Meaning*, Viktor Frankl
*Managing Up*, Mary Abbajay
*Measure What Matters*, John Doerr
*Mindset*, Carol S. Dweck
*Modern Manhood*, Cleo Stiller
*The Motivation Myth*, Jeff Haden
*The Networksage*, Glenna Crooks
*Never Split the Difference*, Chris Voss
*The New Extraordinary Leader*, John H. Zenger and Joseph R. Folkman
*Power Moms*, Joann Lublin
*The Power of Respect*, Deborah Norville
*The Power of TED*, David Emerald
*Powerful*, Patty McCord
*Presence*, Amy Cuddy
*Quiet*, Susan Cain
*Reprogramming the American Dream*, Kevin Scott
*The 7 Habits of Highly Effective People*, Stephen Covey
*The Southwest Airlines Way*, Jody Hoffer Gittell
*StandOut 2.0*, Marcus Buckingham
*Start with Why*, Simon Sinek
*The 21 Indispensable Qualities of a Leader*, John C. Maxwell
*Taming the Abrasive Manager*, Dr. Laura Crawshaw
*Team of Rivals*, Doris Kearns Goodwin
*Think Again*, Adam Grant
*Time to Think*, Nancy Kline
*True North*, Bill George
*The Truth about Leadership*, James M. Kouzes
*Value(s)*, Mark Carney

## Newsletters/Blogs/Magazines

*Broadsheet*, Emma Hinchcliffe
*Business Insider*, Dan DeFrancesco
*CEO Daily*, Alan Murray (*Fortune*)
*Executive Support Magazine*, http://www.executivesupportmagazine.com
*Farnam Street: Brain Food*, Shane Parrish
*Leadership Freak*, Dan Rockwell
*Lioness Magazine*, https://lionessmagazine.com/
*OfficePro Magazine*, https://edge.iaap-hq.org/category/officepro
   -magazine/
*McKinsey Daily Read*
*The Riveter—Working Motherhood*
*Work It Daily*, J. T. O'Donnell

## Podcasts

*Bet on Yourself*, Ann Hiatt
*Discover Your Talent*, Dorie Clark
*Diversity Matters*, Oscar Holmes IV
*Forward Thinking*, McKinsey
*Leadership Next*, Alan Murray
*WorkLife*, Adam Grant

## Websites

http://www.bloomfieldco.com
http://www.bosswhispering.com
http://www.ceoforumgroup.com
http://www.christopherbakerstaffing.com
http://www.conantleadership.com
http://www.csa.org
http://www.duncangroupinc.com
http://www.entrepreneur.com
http://www.fortune.com

http://www.freemomhugs.org
http://www.greatplacetowork.com
http://www.hrc.org/resources/employers
http://www.leanin.org
http://www.mckinsey.com
http://www.shrm.org
http://www.stopbullying.gov
http://www.themomproject.com
http://www.talentthinkinnovations.com
http://www.theundercoverrecruiter.com
http://www.workplacebullying.org
http://www.zengerfolkman.com

## Movies/Documentary Films/TEDx Talks/YouTube Videos

*9to5: The Story of a Movement*
*Bombshell*
*Miss Representation*
*The Mask You Live In*
Amy Cuddy, "Your Body Language May Shape Who You Are," TED Talk
Joe Ehrmann, "Be a Man," TEDx Talk
Sheryl Sandberg, Harvard 2012 Commencement Address, YouTube
Steve Jobs, Stanford 2005 Commencement Address, YouTube

# ABOUT THE AUTHOR

Bonnie Low-Kramen is a workplace expert and an international speaker, trainer, writer, and consultant. For twenty-five years she worked as the Personal Assistant to acting couple Olympia Dukakis and Louis Zorich. Her work as a celebrity assistant led her to write the bestselling book *Be the Ultimate Assistant*, design a groundbreaking workshop by the same name, and speak in thirteen countries.

Bonnie is now a CEO who employs an assistant and is globally recognized as one of the most respected leaders in the administrative profession. She is a sought-after speaker on building strong, respectful, and sustainable partnerships between executives and their staff.

In 2022, Bonnie made her TEDx debut with "The Real Reasons People Quit." Her writing has appeared in the *Harvard Business Review*, and her Be the Ultimate Assistant workshop was featured in *Forbes*. She has worked with the Wharton School, Harvard University, Starbucks, Amazon, Rutgers Business School, Campbell Soup Company, and the British Parliament.

Bonnie is known for her fearless advocacy on the issues of workplace bullying, sexual harassment, discrimination, and closing the wage gap. She is a proud cofounder of NYCA (New York Celebrity Assistants), a professional networking organization that began in 1996.

She earned a BA from Rutgers University and is from New Jersey. Bonnie now lives in Florida with her partner and high school sweetheart, Robert Sanders. They share three children and six grandchildren, also known as Bonnie's "why."

Bonnie Low-Kramen wants you to know that she has navigated life through the words of her mother, Ruth Low: *Just try to leave the world a little better than the way you found it.*

She also knows that she most definitely did not get here alone.

Bonnie welcomes your thoughts at www.bonnielowkramen.com.

Made in the USA
Coppell, TX
20 March 2024